DIACHRONIC VARIATION IN THE OMANI ARABIC VERNACULAR OF THE AL-ʿAWĀBĪ DISTRICT

Diachronic Variation in the Omani Arabic Vernacular of the Al-ʿAwābī District

From Carl Reinhardt (1894) to the Present Day

Roberta Morano

UNIVERSITY OF CAMBRIDGE
Faculty of Asian and Middle Eastern Studies

OpenBook Publishers

https://www.openbookpublishers.com

Semitic Languages and Cultures 14.

ISSN (print): 2632-6906
ISSN (digital): 2632-6914

ISBN Paperback: 9781800647220
ISBN Hardback: 9781800647237
ISBN Digital (PDF): 9781800647244
DOI: 10.11647/OBP.0298

Cover images: Wādī Banī Kharūṣ (2018) by Roberta Morano

Cover design: Anna Gatti

TABLE OF CONTENTS

Table of Contents v

Acknowledgements vii

Introduction 1

1.0. Transcription 6

2.0. Glossing System 7

3.0. Abbreviations 8

Chapter 1: Oman, Cornerstone of Arabia 11

1.0. A Brief History of the Sultanate 14

2.0. The Path to the Seventies: The Omani *nahḍa* and the Building of a New Nation 18

3.0. Tribalism, Language, and Identity in Modern Oman 24

4.0. Linguistic Landscape of Oman and the Arabian Peninsula 28

5.0. Bibliographical Sources on Omani Arabic 33

6.0. Carl Reinhardt (1894): Strengths and Weaknesses 39

7.0. The al-ʿAwābī District: In Geographical and Historical Perspective 44

8.0. Participants, Metadata, and Methodology 47

Chapter 2: Phonology 59
1.0. Consonants 60
2.0. Vowels 65
3.0. Syllable Inventory 74
4.0. CCC Cluster 75
5.0. Stress 76
Chapter 3: Morphology 81
1.0. Nominal Morphology 82
2.0. Verbal Morphology 127
Chapter 4: Syntax 159
1.0. Phrases 161
2.0. Clauses 218
3.0. Negation 241
Conclusion 253
References 259
Appendix 271
Sample Text 1 271
Sample Text 2 275
Proverbs 279
A Traditional Song 283
Index 285

ACKNOWLEDGEMENTS

Special thanks to my PhD supervisor and mentor, Janet Watson, whose support over the past few years inspired this work and my future as a researcher.

I am thankful to the University of Leeds and the School of Languages, Cultures and Societies for funding this research with the '110 Anniversary Scholarship.' I also acknowledge the support in publication of the book by the *Cambridge Semitic Languages and Cultures* series and Open Book Publishers.

Thank you to my family in Oman, to Ikhlas, Shihha, Zalkha, Mama Sharifa, Rabʿa, Amal, Manal, Iman, Maymuna, and all the amazing women I have worked with during my PhD fieldwork and to whom this study is dedicated. Thanks to Rashid, Ikhlas's father, who agreed to record the traditional song reported in the Appendix of this work and who sadly passed away a couple of years ago.

This work is entirely dedicated to Oman and the beautiful Omani people.

INTRODUCTION

This study—based on a partial re-elaboration of my doctoral thesis—examines one of the foundational works in the field of Omani Arabic dialectology, i.e., Carl Reinhardt's *Ein arabischer Dialekt gesprochen in 'Oman und Zanzibar* (1894). The pivotal role played by the German author in shaping our knowledge of Omani Arabic over the last century is undeniable. However, due to a set of reasons that this work intends to highlight, a thorough re-analysis and comparison of the old and new data is now essential.

Due to unfavourable political and social conditions, access to the Arabian Peninsula has always been difficult for dialectologists, resulting in reduced attention being given to the Arabic spoken in this area compared to regions such as North Africa and the Levant. Admittedly, researching in the Arabian Peninsula has never been easy, especially for foreigners. This situation is mirrored in the lack of extensive linguistic and lexical studies in the region in general and Oman in particular.

As far as Oman is concerned, the most prominent dialectological and linguistic works date back to the end of the nineteenth and the beginning of the twentieth century (e.g., Jayakar 1889; Reinhardt 1894). More recent works tend, instead, to focus on specific isoglosses or geographical areas, leaving fields like lexicon and syntax almost completely unexplored. Therefore, to date, it is very difficult to trace a homogeneous picture of Omani dialects and to be able to compare grammatical fea-

 https://doi.org/10.11647/OBP.0298.07

tures not only within Oman, but also with neighbouring Arabic varieties.

Some fields are, indeed, more neglected than others in the literature: lexicon and syntax *in primis*.

The lexicon found in various areas of Oman is a rich source of archaisms, classicisms, and foreign loanwords that, when combined together, create a unique system that absolutely deserves attention. It must not be forgotten that this country is characterised by linguistic diversity not comparable to any other country in the Gulf region.[1] In the field of syntax, the latest study by Bettega (2019a) is a huge step forward and we can only hope that more analysis of this kind will take place in the future.

The present study aims to be a first step in this direction. Born of the urgency of expanding our knowledge of Omani Arabic, this study has two main aims: firstly, providing a linguistic analysis and description of the Omani vernacular spoken in the al-ʿAwābī district (northern Oman), based on the speech of 15 informants recruited throughout the area; and secondly, comparing these new data with the set provided by Reinhardt (1894). This comparison is deemed even more urgent in light of tracing the diachronic change the dialects of this area are currently undergoing. The process of the 'gulfinisation' of these dialects—i.e., their tendency to adapt to Gulf Arabic features—

[1] Twelve languages are spoken as main languages in the Sultanate: Arabic, Baluchi, Lawati, Zadjali, Gujarati, Swahili, Qarawi (or *Shehret* or *Jibbali*), Mahri, Hobyot, Bathari, Hikmani, and Harsusi (cf. Peterson 2004, 34).

has sped up in the last few decades, due to both the perception of this Arabic variety as more prestigious and its use in the fields of television and radio broadcasting, education, and business.

In a paper published in 2011, Clive Holes details three worrying phenomena that pose threats to the Arabic dialects of Arabia: (a) the recession of communal dialects in the Gulf region in favour of a linguistic homogenisation; (b) the tendency among younger speakers to code-switch between English and Arabic; and, finally, (c) the pidginisation of Gulf Arabic by the Pakistani and Indian communities living and working in the region. Suffice it to say that in approaching the analysis, Holes (2011b, 130) uncovered a 'kaleidoscope of linguistic variation, which is moving in several directions: partly towards regional homogenisation, but partly also towards new forms of generation-based difference. And the rate at which these changes are occurring is fast.' The Arabic dialects of Oman are not an exception in this sense. By the end of this study, the reader will appreciate the pace of linguistic change in the dialect of the al-ʿAwābī district, whose peculiar syntactic features are slowly disappearing.

Despite the clear flaws presented by Reinhardt's work, which are generally acknowledged by scholars, the German work continues to be a benchmark in the field of Omani dialectology—mainly because of the lack of more recent studies in this vein. The weaknesses of his work, such as its pedagogical intent, the lack of transcription *in situ*, the small number of consultants, and the lack of a syntactic analysis of the vernacular, make the comparison crucial at this stage.

When it came to the structure of this study, I faced the decision of whether to organise it according to similar works that deal with language documentation, or to organise it in a way that would facilitate comparison and visibility of diachronic changes for the reader. Therefore, the study is structured in four chapters and one Appendix, providing both analysis and comparison of the phonology, morphology, and syntax of the vernacular spoken in the al-ʿAwābī district. This structure intentionally resembles Reinhardt's.

The first chapter lays the sociolinguistic and historical foundations on which the documentation and the analysis are subsequently built. This chapter provides the reader with some background information on the history and society of the Sultanate of Oman, the bibliographical sources on Omani dialectology available to date, and the linguistic geography of the Arabian Peninsula as a whole, narrowing it down to Oman and to the al-ʿAwābī district. This section is especially important for those Arabists and dialectologists unfamiliar with the sociolinguistic situation in Oman, but it also serves as a justification for the description of this vernacular in its geographical context.

The chapters from two to four consist of the description and analysis proper of the primary data I have collected in the field during the course of my PhD. Each chapter also presents a detailed comparison with Reinhardt's material, tracing the extent of diachronic change this vernacular has undergone throughout the last century.

The second chapter analyses the phonology of the vernacular spoken by the consultants in the district of al-ʿAwābī: in many instances during the discussion, Reinhardt's notes are given and commented upon on the basis of new research findings.

The third chapter is devoted to morphology, divided into nominal and verbal. Nominal morphology analyses the noun in all its forms, the pronouns in use, the noun modifiers, and the form and use of prepositions. This is, perhaps, the chapter where comparison with Reinhardt's material is most conspicuous. The lexical core provided by the German author is abundant and Reinhardt is very scrupulous in providing the various patterns in use.

Verbal morphology includes the conjugations of the verbs as performed by the informants, followed by remarks on the morphology of participles and the passive voice.

The fourth chapter deals with the analysis of the syntax, i.e., the construction of phrases and clauses. This chapter is particularly important if we consider that Reinhardt's description of the same dialect lacks any proper structured analysis of syntax. He provides us only with a few notes and numerous examples on clauses, without going any further into the discussion. Thus, chapter four provides examples from my own data, extrapolated from the recordings of spontaneous speech and elicitation notes. The chapter includes notes on TAM categories in the dialect under investigation as well as remarks on negation.

In addition to these four chapters, this work includes an Appendix consisting of a list of proverbs spontaneously given by the informants, two sample texts exemplifying some of the grammatical features reported in the work, and a traditional song collected in Wādī Banī Kharūṣ.

This study is intended primarily for Arabic dialectologists with a broader interest in the Peninsular dialects. In the course of the work, I will refer to other vernaculars of the Arabian Peninsula, such as Najdi, Bahraini, Kuwaiti, and Yemeni Arabic (albeit acknowledging that this nomenclature is not exhaustive, since the latter category includes many different varieties). Linguists may also find some arguments interesting, especially the remarks on TAM categories and the use of participial forms.

1.0. Transcription

In the following tables, the reader can find the symbols used throughout this study for the transcription of Arabic phonemes. Toponyms are given in their most common anglicised form, although when first mentioned, they are reported in Arabic script.

Consonants

Arabic	Symbol	Arabic	Symbol	Arabic	Symbol	Arabic	Symbol
ء	ʾ	ذ	ḏ	ظ	ẓ	ن	n
ب	b	ر	r	ع	ʿ	ه	h
ت	t	ز	z	غ	ġ	و	w
ث	ṯ	س	s	ف	f	ي	y
ج	ǧ/g	ش	š	ق	q	ن	n
ح	ḥ	ص	ṣ	ك	k	ة	a ~ e ~ t
خ	ḫ	ض	ḍ	ل	l		
د	d	ط	ṭ	م	m		

Vowels

Short vowel	Allophones	Long vowel	Allophones
/a/	[e]	/ā/	
/i/		/ī/	
/u/	[o]	/ū/	[ō]
		/ē/	
		/ō/	

Other symbols

Symbol	Meaning	Symbol	Meaning
C	consonant	ˈ	stress
V	vowel	<	derived from
$_{1234}$	consonantal root	~	alternative form

2.0. Glossing System

The examples within this study are glossed in accordance with the Leipzig Glossing rules. Here are some basic guidelines:

- For nouns and adjectives, the English translation is given, followed by gender and number, e.g., girl.FSG or girl.FPL, small.FSG or small.MPL.
- Verbs present the English translation according to their tense, followed by the person, e.g., said.1SG or work.2MPL.
- Personal and possessive pronouns are represented by only the grammatical person to which they refer, e.g., sister.FSG-PRON.1SG for 'my sister' or book.MPL-PRON.3FSG for 'her books'; PRON.1SG for 'I' or PRON.3FPL for 'they (F)'.
- Demonstrative pronouns are given considering their deixis (i.e., proximity or distance) and gender, e.g., DEM.PROX.MSG for 'this (M)' or DEM.PROX.FPL for 'those (F)'.

For a clearer display of diachronic variation in the vernacular described in this study, each example is accompanied by the indication of the speaker who uttered it. This is glossed in accordance with the following system: [S (speaker) + number (as reported in the Table 1.1): e.g., [S2].

3.0. Abbreviations

AP	Active Participle
AS	Adult Speakers (age group)
AW	al-ʿAwābī
BA	Bahraini Arabic
CA	Classical Arabic
CONJ	Conjunction
DEF	Definite article
DEM	Demonstrative
DL	Dual
EXIST	Existential
F	Feminine
FUT	Future tense
GA	Gulf Arabic
GEN	Genitive marker
IN	Infix
M	Masculine
MSA	Modern Standard Arabic
MSAL	Modern South Arabian Languages
NA	Najdi Arabic
NEG	Negation marker
OA	Old Arabic

OS	Old Speakers (age group)
PP	Passive participle
PL	Plural
PREP	Preposition
PRON	Pronoun
QA	Qatari Arabic
R.	Reinhardt (1894)
REL	Relativiser
SG	Singular
so.	someone
sth.	something
VN	Verbal noun
WBK	Wādī Banī Kharūṣ
YA	Yemeni Arabic
YS	Young Speakers (age group)

CHAPTER 1: OMAN, CORNERSTONE OF ARABIA

The Sultanate of Oman lies at the south-easternmost corner of the Arabian Peninsula, at the entrance of the Arabian Gulf. With a coastline slightly exceeding 3,000 kilometres in length, the Sultanate's historical, linguistic, and cultural landscapes have been profoundly forged by its geography.

The country is surrounded by the Indian Ocean and the Gulf of Oman on three sides, whilst the interior is isolated from the rest of the Arabian Peninsula by the vast sand desert of al-Rubᶜ al-Khālī (الربع الخالي), also known as the Empty Quarter.[1]

Essentially, the geographical structure of the country makes Oman almost an island (cf. Landen 1967; Wilkinson

[1] This is the largest sand desert in the world, extending into four countries (i.e., Oman, Yemen, Saudi Arabia, and the UAE). The northern border of the Empty Quarter is the mountain range of Jebel Ṭuwayq (جبل طويق in the Najd region, Saudi Arabia); its characteristic linear dunes can reach up to 400 metres in height. The name al-Rubᶜ al-Khālī was unknown to the locals, who generally used the term *ar-Rimāl* 'the sands' (cf. Thesiger 2007, 116–54). A term found in Arabic sources referring to al-Rubᶜ al-Khālī is *al-Aḥqāf* (e.g., al-Hamdānī uses it to indicate a valley between the Ḥaḍramawt and al-Mahrah; al-Bakrī associates it specifically with Ḥaḍramawt; and Yāqūt describes it as a district of Arabia, between Yemen and Oman). Almost nothing is known about the inner portion of this huge desert area; some of the tribes living on the borders of the Empty Quarter include al-Murra to the north-east; Banū Yās, Manāṣir, Rāšid, and ᶜAwāmir to the east; Saᶜar and Bayt Kaṯīr to the south; and Yām to the west (cf. King 2012).

 https://doi.org/10.11647/OBP.0298.01

1987). The northern core of this island is the chain of the al-Hajar Mountains (جبال الحجر), which extends for 650 kilometres from Ras Musandam (راس مسندم), in the Musandam Peninsula enclave, to Ras al-Hadd (راس الحد), the easternmost point in the Arabian Peninsula. The peak of this chain is Jabal Akhdar (جبل أخضر, the 'green mountain'), so called for the luxurious and brightly green landscapes.

Politically, the Sultanate is divided into eleven administrative governorates (*muḥāfaẓāt*), each one being further subdivided into provinces (*wilāyāt*).[2] However, the most significant social, linguistic, and geographical divide within Oman is between north and south.

Northern Oman includes the fertile coastal strip of al-Batinah, with its major cities, shipbuilding towns, and ports; the capital city Muscat; and the al-Hajar range. In this part of the country, near the Persian Gulf, the mountains, and the coast, the major cities of the Sultanate are located, i.e., Sohar (صحار), Rustaq (رستاق), Khabura (خبورة), Sur (صور), Nizwa (نزوى), and ʿIbrī (عبري).

Southern Oman, on the other hand, consists of three main areas: the coast, with fishing and farming settlements; the mountain range of Jabal al-Qamar (جبل القمر), which benefits

---

[2] These are Dakhiliyyah (الداخلية), Sharqiyyah (الشرقية, further divided in 2011 into North and South Sharqiyyah), al-Ẓāhira (الظاهرة), al-Batinah (الباطنة, further divided in 2011 into North and South al-Batinah), al-Buraymi (البريمي), al-Wusta (الوسطى), Musandam (مسندم), Muscat (مسقط) and Dhofar (ظفار).

from the monsoon weather;[3] and the inner part, the vast desert of al-Rubᶜ al-Khālī.

Linguistically, the southern region of Oman (i.e., Dhofar)—together with parts of Yemen and Saudi Arabia—is home to the group of Semitic languages known as the Modern South Arabian Languages (hereby, MSAL), which includes Mehri, Ḥarsūsi, Baṭḥari, Hobyot, Ṣ́herɛ̄t (aka Jibbali), and Soqoṭri. Inhabitants of Dhofar often speak Arabic only as a second language, having one of the MSAL as their mother tongue. The north of the country also hosts a great variety of linguistic diversity: for example, the numerous languages spoken by the various ethnolinguistic communities populating this area as well as the abundant Arabic dialects that showcase interesting syntactical, lexical, and morphological features and are yet to be thoroughly investigated.

This linguistic diversity is the result of historical and political processes that Oman has witnessed over the centuries, but also of the waves of external and internal migration that impacted the Sultanate in the last century.

In the next few sections, I will briefly outline the historical phases of Oman, with some remarks on how the social structure of the Sultanate changed before and after the 1970s. No di-

---

[3] The monsoon season in Dhofar is known as *ḫarīf* 'autumn', but effectively 'monsoon period', and occurs during the months of late June, July, August, and early September. During this period, the whole regions of Dhofar and eastern Yemen are covered in luxurious green and water flows from mountains and wadis. Moreover, the fog produced by the rapid movement of currents creates a unique ecosystem in this part of the Arabian Peninsula.

achronic analysis of linguistic features of the Omani dialect spoken in the district of al-ʿAwābī (العوابي) can disregard the national events of the twentieth century, whether historical or political. As will be demonstrated in the course of this work, Omani society, politics, and language are tightly linked in their essence, especially after the 1970s and the urgently felt need of building a new national identity.

1.0. A Brief History of the Sultanate

Oman's presence in history dates back to the third millennium BCE, when the name *Magan* appeared on Sumerian cuneiform tablets,[4] although human activities were already attested in the Stone Age (ca. 30,000 BCE). There is no doubt that the kingdom of Magan consisted, at least in part, of the territory of present-day Oman (Al-Maamiry 1982).

Cut off from the rest of the Arabian Peninsula by the Empty Quarter, ancient Oman could look only to the sea for its commercial and imperialistic needs. And, indeed, its vocations towards sea trades and explorations go back farther into history: it is well known that Omanis were masters of navigation, being especially able to control the monsoon winds to steer the sails.

The seventh century, coinciding with the rise of Islam, saw the flourishing of maritime trade for Oman and a resultant increase in naval constructions. Thanks to its strategic position at the centre of the Arabian Sea and between the major trade

[4] Tablets of Sargon, king of the Akkadians (2371–2316 BCE), as reported by Ghubash (2006, 16).

routes in the Indian Ocean, it was inevitable that Oman would become a significant hub in the area.

At this point in time, the country also became an asylum for Kharijites and Ibadis, strong opponents of the Umayyad Caliphate (644–750 CE). This split led to a coalition that soon transformed into an Imamate. The first ever experience of an Imamate in Oman was with the election of Julanda bin Masᶜūd, soon killed in 752 CE by the Abbasid caliph, who could not tolerate an independent state so close to his borders.

The history of the Imamate in Oman is well researched in Wilkinson (1987) and marks an important stage for the future of the country. The Imamate tradition—which is nothing more than a dynastic institution—would, indeed, survive until the 1950s. More than on history, this tradition had a strong impact on the Omani sense of identity and belonging, as will be explained later in this chapter, in §2.0. To trace the importance of the Banū Kharūṣ tribe—the main subject of this study—it must be mentioned that the Imamate had only five long-lasting tribal dynasties which played a prominent role: the Julanda, the Yahmad-Kharūṣ, the Nabahina, the Yaᶜrūbī, and the Al Bū Saᶜīd (Wilkinson 1987, 9).

The country was *de facto* starting to develop its double character: on the one hand, the Imamate tradition in the interior, with Nizwa as capital, mainly isolated and tribal; on the other hand, Muscat and the coastal plateau, its maritime power, the great ship-building cities, and trade centres (Wilkinson 1987; Owtram 2004). This duality had significant historical and social impact, among them the linguistic change that this study details.

In the tenth century, one of the major ports in Oman was Sohar. The main goods traded by Omanis were aloes, wood, bamboo, camphor, sandalwood, ivory, tin, spices, and frankincense. By this point in time, Omanis were among the first to reach the shores of eastern African and China, importing linen, cotton, wool, and metal works (al-Maamiry 1982, 3).

Oman's strategic position, as one might expect, attracted the expansionist aims of various foreign populations over the centuries. The sixteenth century marks the beginning of the golden age for Portugal, after Vasco da Gama managed to round the Cape of Good Hope and sail up the coast of east Africa towards the Indian Ocean. The interests of the Portuguese in that area were, though, mainly economic. They had no colonial aims and did not interfere in the local affairs of the countries they were in contact with. The Portuguese presence in Oman lasted for about a century. Alfonso de Albuquerque, who had been Viceroy of India since 1506, conquered the cities of Muscat and Qalhat in 1507 to better control the area between the Persian Gulf and the Indian Ocean. The Portuguese remained there to dominate the area until ca. 1650, when the Yaʿrūbī dynasty came to power and defeated the foreign invaders.

The election of Imam Nāṣīr bin Muršid al-Yaʿrūbī marks the start of a very important historical phase for Oman: under his dynasty, the country rebuilt its prominence in the Indian Ocean and started to expand westward towards the eastern African coast and eastward towards the Persian shores. During this time, Muscat became the most important port in the Indian Ocean. The Omanis could count on the largest merchant fleet in the region, and managed to establish an Omani authority on Zanzibar, Kilwa,[5] and Pemba that lasted for about 250 years.

In 1775, the Yaʿrūbī dynasty was replaced by a new one, the Āl Bū Saʿīd. With the Āl Bū Saʿīd—the current ruling family of Oman—the country saw incredible growth, but also strong British influence in internal and foreign affairs and the first real political division: this was the era of the *imāma* and the *sayyid* (cf. Ghubash 2006).

The British presence in Oman—initiated in 1645 after the expulsion of the Portuguese and the Omani interests in the English East India Company—became increasingly prominent over the centuries, until the whole area of Muscat and the coastal plateau became *de facto* a British Protectorate in 1871 (Owtram 2004), with the British controlling most of the Sultan's foreign relations.[6]

At this point, it is important to understand the historical, political, and social path that made Oman the country we know today, by highlighting the events at the turn of the twentieth century.

Until the 1970s, the official name of the country was the 'Sultanate of Oman and Muscat', which once again emphasises the inherent dichotomy of Oman: the interior versus the coast,

---

[5] This refers to the coastal strip that now belongs to Tanzania.

[6] Owtram (2004, 48) reports that the first use of the term 'Sultan' to indicate the Muscat ruler was by the British, the term being "an anathema to Ibadhis with its negative association with secular tyranny".

the Imamate versus the Sultanate, tradition versus maritime power.

The Imamate of the interior had its headquarters in the cities of Nizwa and Rustaq, perpetuating a ruling policy based on Ibadhi precepts, which essentially reject both Sunni and Shi'a Islam conceptions of leadership of the Islamic community (Owtram 2004, 42). The main characteristic of the Imamate was its autonomy, which was officially established with the Sib Agreement on 25 September 1920. If, on the one hand, the Agreement—sought by the British—did not officially recognise the Imamate as a separate political entity, on the other hand, it left it *de facto* isolated in the interior of Oman (Joyce 1995, 28).

2.0. The Path to the Seventies: The Omani *nahḍa* and the Building of a New Nation

The decades between the Sib Agreement and the ascension to the throne of Sultan Qaboos (i.e., 1970) are pivotal for understanding the state of Omani society today, and especially the extent to which the linguistic landscape of Oman has changed.

Saʿīd bin Taymūr became Sultan of Muscat and Oman in 1932, after his father's abdication. His reign was characterised by strict closure to the outside world, which was deemed even more urgent after western interest in the area due to the discovery of oil in 1930s.

Saʿīd bin Taymūr's main concern was that western influence and interference might undermine his reign, bringing "foreign and modern ideas" which, in turn, would compromise the traditional values and social structures of Oman (Valeri 2017, 62).

Nonetheless, the British presence in Oman was still strong, such that the Sultan needed their intervention to placate the Jabal Akhdar revolt in the late 1950s. The famous British explorer Wilfred Thesiger, who spent several months touring Oman, reported that "the tribes in both the southwest and the northwest of the Jabal Akhdar had no loyalty to the sultan: they followed their imam, whose territory likely contained oil" (Joyce 1995, 53). The discovery of oil and concessions to western countries for oil exploration probably fuelled the long-standing rivalry between the Imamate and the Sultanate.

The Imamate was a strong opponent of western powers and could also count on the support of the Saudis, with whom, however, the Americans and British were in negotiations for oil exploration.[7] Moreover, the interior regions of Oman suffered from even more significant isolation due to the lack of infrastructure, which severely limited the mobility of the mountain populations. The rebellion of the Jabal Akhdar was, therefore, just a matter of time.

The uprising was resolved by the British, who decided to intervene in 1959 on condition that the Sultan reform his kingdom. They occupied the mountains in a surprise operation, find-

[7] The Saudis granted a concession to the American company Aramco in 1933, which was of particular concern for the British in Oman, given the proximity to the Buraimi Oasis. The question of borders was then posed for the first time, with the Saudis stating that they would negotiate them only with the Imamate and not with the Sultanate (Joyce 1995, 54).

ing a way through Wādī Banī Kharūṣ (وادي بني خروص). No longer able to compete, the Imam fled to Saudi Arabia, leaving the country to the Sultan. Soon after, Saʿīd bin Taymūr retired to Salalah, never to return to Muscat.

Valeri (2017, 60) calls the 1960s "the decade of remoteness," and for good reason. The promise made by Saʿīd bin Taymūr to the British went unfulfilled. In fact, when the Sultan moved to Dhofar, he lost any interest in administering the country, leaving this duty to a subordinate with the support of British advisers.

At this point in time, the social and political picture of Oman was as follows: no infrastructure, no form of education, primitive health care, numerous expatriates working for private oil companies, no diplomatic relations, and no international network.

As one can imagine, the only possible outcome of such a situation was economic, political, and social stagnation, which was exacerbated by the country's extreme isolation. Wealthy Omanis moved abroad, starting one of the largest displacements in the modern history of Oman. In the 1960s,

> owning a car or projecting a film, importing newspapers, books or even medicine […] had to be submitted strictly to the Sultan's agreement. […]. Similarly, entry permits for the country, even for journalists or diplomatic missions, were stopped after 1965. (Valeri 2017, 62)

Education was a particularly sore subject. For example, Sultan Saʿīd bin Taymūr considered a western-style education the main cause that led to India's independence in 1947:

> The teachers would come from Cairo and spread Nasser's seditious ideas among other pupils. And what is there for a young man with education? He would go to university in Cairo or to the London School of Economics, finish in Moscow and come back here to foment trouble (Joyce 1995, 58).

As a result of this policy, in 1961, the country counted only three western schools, but about fifty Quranic schools. Omanis who had the means to support their children sent them to schools abroad, to Kuwait, Bahrain, and Qatar.

Health was another big issue. In the 1960s, there were only five hospitals and about forty rudimentary health centres scattered around the country. The population's health conditions were dreadful: "malaria, trachoma, leprosy were common diseases, as well as malnutrition and anaemia" (Valeri 2017, 63).

Moreover, there was no infrastructure. Communications between regions in Oman were very difficult, there were no paved roads, cars belonged only to British and Americans who worked for private oil companies, and Omanis had to travel long distances on donkeys and camels, often through mountains and deserts.

All this was due to end in 1970, when Qaboos bin Saʿīd overthrew his father in a coup on 23 July.

Since the very beginning, Sultan Qaboos's aim was to build a modern nation, positioning it within the international context of the Peninsula and beyond, using revenues derived from the oil industry to give Omanis the welfare they deserved.

As Joyce (1995, 103) puts it, "the task was formidable, the obstacles numerous."

The era of Sultan Qaboos is renowned as the Omani *nahḍa* 'renaissance' (cf. Owtram 2004; Valeri 2017): a country and a people reborn to a new nation, with a new shared identity, and a new name, i.e., 'Sultanate of Oman'.

One of the first pledges of the newly established Sultan was the modernisation of the education, health, and infrastructure fields, deemed vital for the construction of a unified and solid state. In order to do so, the Sultan recalled Omanis who had fled abroad during his father's reign and encouraged them to participate in the efforts in building a new, strong, and independent nation.

In education, a massive literacy campaign was initiated: numerous teaching staff were recruited from Jordan, Egypt, Sudan, and, at a later stage, from Tunisia and Algeria. Between 1970 and 1976, at least 200 new schools were built (Valeri 2017, 78–79) all over the country; in 1986 the Sultan Qaboos University was opened in Muscat, with no fees and free housing for female students. The illiteracy levels of the Omani population went from 41.2 percent in 1993, to 21.9 percent in 2003, to 14 percent in 2010, with females constituting 60 percent of the overall number, the vast majority being over forty years old (Valeri 2017, 79).[8]

[8] These statistics are deemed appropriate, as they give a clear picture of the overall Omani situation in terms of literacy and illiteracy in the last few decades and have been used as one of the criteria for the recruitment of informants in this study (see §8.1 in the present chapter).

In the health sector, twelve hospitals and thirty-two clinics were already up and running by 1975 and by the end of the 2010s, Valeri (2017, 80) reports sixty-six hospitals and 195 health centres scattered all over the Sultanate, in addition to about a thousand others in the private sector. These advances brought an end to many endemic diseases and led to an increase in life expectancy.

In terms of infrastructure and facilitation of mobility for the Omani population, the new government pledged to improve the almost non-existent networks of paved roads,[9] especially to connect those inner parts of Oman that were isolated and accessible only by donkey or camel. Soon after taking his position, the Sultan decreed that "every Omani inhabitant must be reachable by a road suitable for motor vehicles" (Valeri 2017, 77). The first asphalted road was built to connect Muscat and Sohar; by the end of the decade, cities like Nizwa, Rustaq and Sur were also accessible by car.

Sultan Qaboos also launched radio and TV channels, as well as national and international newspapers. In the span of a few decades, Oman had become a strong presence in the Arabian Peninsula and at a global level.

---

[9] Before the 1970s, only ten kilometres of paved roads in the entire Sultanate were available (Joyce 1995, 113).

3.0. Tribalism, Language, and Identity in Modern Oman

A fundamental consequence of this process of modernisation and unification of the country is the posing of questions regarding national identity.

As already mentioned, modern Oman is the result of great bio-cultural diversity developed over centuries of internal and external displacement, maritime trade, and foreign incursions, but also very deep indigenous dichotomy, i.e., Imamate versus Sultanate, tribal versus settled communities, tradition versus modernity.

Sultan Qaboos was well aware of this split and of the newly born state's need of a strong and enduring national ideology to overcome the local solidarities of tribes and ethnolinguistic communities scattered over the country.

The idea of a people paying allegiance to a nation-state unity is very European and was unknown to the Arabs of Arabia, whose loyalty was often based on tribal and blood affiliation (Riphenburg 1998). Oman, like many other polities in the Arabian Peninsula, has been a country fragmented into numerous tribal groups, individually governed by local sheiks or *tamimah.* These tribes were connected by "a group feeling, a solidarity," known as *ʿasabiyya*. Originally introduced by Ibn Khaldun in the *Muqaddimah* (ca. fourteenth century), the concept of *ʿasabiyya* has long been debated in the literature.[10] Valeri (2017,

[10] For more details on this, the reader is referred to Ibn Khaldun (1980), Wilkinson (1987), and Kayapinar (2008).

15) defines it as "a solidarity based on personal relations (genealogical, matrimonial, nepotistic, etc.) and acts as a group or thinks of itself as such." It translates as a sort of tribal vigour that can only be channelled by a sheikh. Sultan Qaboos's strategy was to give a new shape to the *ʿasabiyya* in Oman, integrating it into his own national ideology discourse and political legitimisation. In the new Sultan's socio-political vision, the tribe as a political entity did not receive any official recognition or role to play. Acknowledging any position for the tribe would mean accepting a past where Oman was not united, but torn by antagonistic factions.

Nevertheless, tribal affiliation still plays a role in Omanis' sense of belonging and cultural identity. The numerous ethnolinguistic communities in the territory often find a distinctiveness in the cultural heritage and traditional values that result from these affiliations. This is the reason why heritage held a key position not only in Sultan Qaboos's politics, but also in the discourse on national identity. A "timeless Omani national identity" (Valeri 2017, 109) became the purpose of Sultan Qaboos's process of legitimisation and was built on the individual solidarities among the Omani population.

As far as linguistic diachrony—the focus of this work—is concerned, it is pivotal to understand the role played by language in the construction of this new rhetoric of national identity and the impact that the opening and modernisation of the country had on local vernaculars.

Sultan Qaboos's language policy defined Standard Omani Arabic (i.e., the one spoken in Muscat) as the official language of the Sultanate, because "if all Omanis were able to speak Arabic, they were more likely to be reached by the regime's ideology" (Valeri 2017, 110). This variety of Omani Arabic soon became the one employed by the government for official communications, by the media (e.g., radio, TV, newspapers), and, most importantly, as the main language for primary and secondary education. At university level, most of the instruction is conducted in English, whereas teachers vary widely in terms of linguistic background. As mentioned earlier, in the initial stages of the literacy programme, the governments had to recruit teachers from abroad, since Omanis lacked the skills required.

In more recent years, the Gulf countries have witnessed a process of linguistic 'homogeneisation' towards a koineised form of Arabic, which includes various Gulf traits at the expense of more characteristic regional traits (cf. Holes 2011b).

Despite the linguistic switch, a process of 'Omanisation' of various professions, including teachers, has started. In 1970, foreigners represented 7 percent of the total workforce (in both the public and private sectors), and ten years later this number jumped to 65 percent (Valeri 2017, 178). This process—initiated by Sultan Qaboos and continuing now under Sultan Haitham bin Tariq (who succeeded Qaboos following his death in January 2020)—was part of a more extensive plan that sought to push Omanis into the labour market. From 1987 to this day, a series of official decrees—the last one dating to July

2021—have forbidden the hiring of foreigners in specific job categories.[11]

The linguistic landscape of Oman has consequently been shaped by these policies over the years, as well as by its geography, history, and population displacement. Local vernaculars—especially those spoken in the inner part of the country—are slowly being replaced by Muscat Arabic or other Arabic varieties perceived as more prestigious,[12] e.g., Gulf Arabic. The influence of Levantine and North-African varieties of Arabic also impacted on these vernaculars, because of the employment of foreign teachers in education. Crucial in this context is also the influence generated on the indigenous vernaculars by Omanis who returned to the country after the 1970s after spending many years in countries like Egypt, Tanzania, Yemen, and Zanzibar. In more recent times, Indian and Pakistani workers employed in the *mazrʿa* 'palm gardens' around the Sultanate have also played a part in reshaping the linguistic landscape. Finally, social networks and global communications have contributed to the widening of Omanis' linguistic borders.

As language is the reflection of what we are and how we are perceived by others, it is undeniable that these changes have impacted Omani identity. A great effort has been made to record and preserve, for example, indigenous plant names, especially thanks to the creation of the Oman Botanic Gardens in

---

[11] Accessible online at https://www.omanobserver.om/article/201103106/oman/labour/omanisation-of-several-professions-from-july-20.

[12] I use here the term 'prestige' as employed in sociolinguistic studies, i.e., the level of regard attributed by a speech community to other languages or dialects.

Al Khawd (الخوض, Muscat). Holes (2011b) reports some of these changes in other Peninsular countries as well as in Oman, and the speed of variation and change is striking.

4.0. Linguistic Landscape of Oman and the Arabian Peninsula

The 1967 work of T. M. Johnstone, *Eastern Arabian Dialect Studies,* is one of the pioneering attempts to describe the linguistic situation in the Arabian Peninsula and an unparalleled account of the "eastern Arabian dialects" spoken in Kuwait, Bahrain, Qatar, and the Trucial Coast (i.e., Dubai). In this work, Johnstone (1967) classifies Omani Arabic as a variety separate from all the others. His sources, at that time, were Jayakar (1889) and Reinhardt (1894), who describe two sedentary dialects spoken in the northern part of the country.[13] Johnstone's decision, in fact, is not surprising: years later, Holes (1990, xii) would mention in the introduction to his Gulf Arabic grammar that "the sultanate of Oman is excluded from the main body of the description, since the Arabic spoken in the settled areas of this country […] is considerably different from that spoken in the Gulf states proper."

[13] The Sedentary/Bedouin labels applied to Arabic dialects belong to the set of traditional tools long employed by Arabists for the synchronic classification of these dialects—not only in the Peninsula. The distinction is based on phonological and morphological features, rather than on the lifestyle of speech communities. Nowadays, the line between the two is much more blurred, especially after the introduction of social media and the flourishing of various global communication means.

We still do not know exactly to what extent this 'difference' ranges, as Eades and Persson (2013, 343) state,

> most studies reporting on this divide have dealt with the phonology, morphology and, to some extent, lexis. Little is known, however, about the degree to which these dialectal groups differ from or correspond to one another in grammatical structure.

Investigating the reasons behind this marked difference is beyond the scope of this work, but still deserves scholarly attention. However, we will try to provide some analysis in regards to Oman.

Admittedly, the Arabian Peninsula has long proven difficult to access for foreign researchers, and the tough geographical environment did not facilitate exploration.[14] This partial isolation of the Peninsula from external influence ensured the retention in its dialects of more 'conservative' linguistic features "that distinguish them, as a group, from non-Arabian Arabic dialects" (Holes 2006, 25).[15] These traits are the ones most in danger of disappearance for the reasons explained in previous sections.

---

[14] Cf. Watson (2011a, 855): "The Arabian Peninsula has for various political, social and administrative reasons held on to its secrets for far longer than dialects spoken around the Mediterranean."

[15] Cf. also Watson (2011a, 852):

> The dialects spoken in the Arabian Peninsula are by far the most archaic. The depth of their history can only be guessed.... Isolated from the innovations caused elsewhere by population movement and contact, their ancient features were mostly preserved....

Geographically akin to an island, Oman also constitutes a linguistic enclave within the Arabian Peninsula. According to Holes (2017, 292), the Baḥārna, Omani, and south-Yemeni vernaculars share some features that represent "an older type than the Bedouin ʿAnazī type which,... has gradually spread to the Gulf coast from central Arabia via Bedouin migrations." The historical and socio-political reasons discussed above, in §§1.0–2.0, brought Oman to further isolate from the rest of the Peninsula, sparking the curiosity of researchers.[16]

In 1889, Jayakar wrote:

> In Oman learning has never flourished to the same extent as in other parts of Arabia, which may be observed by the almost total absence of any local literature, and although at one time a school of some eminence existed in Nezwa, the province has not produced any great poets or authors. The masses as a rule, as in other countries, are uneducated, but even the educated few are so regardless of the rules of Grammar, that they are constantly in the habit of using, both colloquially and in writing, forms and expressions which strike as strange to an outsider (Jayakar 1889, 649).

---

[16] Cf. Holes (1989, 447):

> The fact that Oman is a large country, about the size of France, with a varied topography which includes vast deserts, impassable mountain ranges and fertile coastal plains, with until recently no modern roads or communications to link them, makes it *prima facie* likely that a considerable degree of dialectal diversity would be found there. (italics in the original)

The isolation imposed by the geographical shape of the country and by the autocratic rule of Sultan Saʿīd bin Taymūr had at least one advantage from a dialectological point of view: the preservation of morpho-syntactic and phonological features which have disappeared elsewhere.[17]

One of the pioneering works on dialectal geography in Oman is Holes (1989), which analyses the features shared by all Omani dialects, with the exception of the Muscat area, Dhofar and Bedouin dialects spoken in central Oman. These features are:

- The 2FSG possessive/object suffix is -/š/, except in some Bedouin dialects of the North-East, where it is realised as -/č/, and the al-Wahība dialect, where it is not affricated and is realised as -/k/.
- An -/in(n)/- infix is obligatorily inserted between an active participle with verbal force and a following object pronoun. Some Omani speakers, in particular on al-Batinah coast, also insert this infix between the imperfect verb and the suffix object (Holes 1989, 448).
- The absence of the 'ghawa syndrome', particular to some central, northern, and eastern Arabic dialects—exceptions are some Bedouin vernaculars spoken in the areas on the UAE border (e.g., Buraymi).

---

[17] Cf. Holes (1998, 348): "The isolation of Oman from outside influences until twenty-five years ago probably explains the survival in its dialects of features, both morpho-syntactic and lexical, which have disappeared in virtually all non-Arabian dialects (and in many Arabian ones too)."

- Feminine plural verbal, adjectival and pronominal forms occur regularly.[18]
- The internal passive of verb forms I and II is of common occurrence.

In addition to this, Holes (1989) provides a detailed list of how the three OA[19] consonants **q*, **k*, and **ǧ*—usually adopted as discriminants in the Sedentary/Bedouin divide—are realised in various dialects of Oman:[20]

- The OA **q* is realised as: (a) [k] in some villages of the western and southern sides of Jabal Akhdar; (b) [g] in some dialects of al-Batinah coast (including Rustaq), but it is affricated in /ǧ/ in the dialects spoken in villages on the UAE border; (c) [g] in all other Bedouin dialects spoken in the western and southern part of the country, including Sur and Salalah; and finally, (d) it is retained as /q/ in sedentary dialects of Capital City, of the al-Batinah coast, and large mountain villages (including the al-ʿAwābī district).

---

[18] This feature is shared with some dialects of central and southern Arabia, distinguishing them from other Gulf dialects, where the gender distinction has been neutralised.

[19] The label OA (i.e., Old Arabic) is used by Holes (1989) to refer to the features which are supposedly the ancestors of the ones found today in spoken Arabic.

[20] We have already mentioned how these labels do not reflect any longer the lifestyle and/or the community type as it probably was 30 years ago, when Clive Holes wrote this article. Nevertheless, the list gives a general idea of the phonological features shared by some Omani dialects.

- The OA **k* is: (a) a velar occlusive in the Capital area and on the al-Batinah coast; (b) palatalised in some mountain dialects and affricated in /č/ in some others; (c) consistently affricated as /č/ with protruded vowels only in some Bedouin dialects spoken on the UAE border.
- The OA *ǧ is realised in all sedentary dialects as a velar occlusive [g]; in Bedouin dialects of the western and southern parts of the country it can be realised as [y] (as in Rustaq), or as an alveolar [ǧ] in the Sharqiyyah region and in some areas of al-Rubᶜ al-Khālī.

As described above in §2.0, recent political events and the acceleration of Oman's social transformation and development have brought about numerous phonological variations that can be traced everywhere in the Sultanate (cf. Davey 2016, 45). Furthermore, the greater freedom of movement fostered by the opening of the country in the 1980s has had significant impact on the linguistic landscape of Oman, affecting some of the traits that have been traced so far. In the course of this work, the diachronic variations in the Omani vernacular of the al-ᶜAwābī district will be presented, taking into consideration the traits exemplified in this section. In so doing, I hope to demonstrate the fast pace at which the dialects of Oman (and possibly of the whole Peninsula) are changing and the urgency of documentation.

5.0. Bibliographical Sources on Omani Arabic

On 23 July 1970, when Qaboos bin Saᶜīd bin Taymūr ascended the throne of the Sultanate of Oman, a new policy course was initiated. It was characterised by, among other things, opening to the West and to rest of the Arab world. Thus, when we talk about the state of the art in Omani dialectology, we cannot ignore this specific phase in the country's history, especially as it bore upon access to sources, which is necessary for thorough and accurate linguistic study.

The main studies on the languages and vernaculars spoken in Oman were the pioneering ones carried out between the end of the nineteenth and the beginning of the twentieth century. Particularly, the Indian surgeon Atmaram Sadashiv Jayakar—who lived in Muscat between 1868 and 1900—with his 1889 *The O'manee Dialect of Arabic*, analysed the dialect spoken by the sedentary population in the Muscat area. In his 1900 *Omani Proverbs*, he also worked on maxims and proverbs, which he described as,

> essential to the philologist, to whom they are invaluable as a storehouse of the dialectical and linguistic peculiarities exhibited in the expression of thoughts, while yet the nation was only in an early condition of civilization, as to philosopher who can often trace in them the inner springs of human action. (Jayakar 1900, 9)

The distinguished Semitist Nicolaus Rhodokanakis (1876–1945), professor in Graz for decades and specialist in Ancient South Arabian, focused his studies on the Arabic lexicon used as a poetic vernacular in Dhofar, contributing to Omani studies with his monumental two-volume *Der vulgärarabische Dialekt im Đofâr (Ẓfâr)*, consisting of the 1908 *Prosaische und poetische Texte, Uebersetzung und Indices* and the 1911 *Einleitung, Glossar und Grammatik*.

For a long time, Rhodokanakis's monumental work was one of the very few studies carried out in this area of the country, which is still considered remote and resistant to foreigners. Its proximity to Yemen makes Dhofar isolated, in terms of both lifestyle and language. Here one of more of the MSAL are spoken as main lanugages, and in the past the area experienced violent rebellions, which were harshly repressed.[21] However, in more recent years, Dhofari Arabic has been documented by Richard Davey in his 2016 *Coastal Dhofari Arabic: A Sketch Grammar*. In this work, the author analyses the phonology, morphology, local and temporal relations, adverbs and particles, and syntax of present-day coastal Dhofari Arabic. The book also presents a final chapter on the lexicon, following the semantic categories presented by Behnsted and Woidich (2011), although it does not aim to analyse it exhaustively.

Finally, Carl Reinhardt's 1894 work, *Ein arabischer Dialekt gesprochen in 'Oman und Zanzibar*, also belongs to the late nineteenth century. He focused on the grammar, particularly phonology and morphology, of the Banū Kharūṣī vernacular, spoken around Nizwa and Rustaq, but also among the elite of Zanzibar Island. The main purpose of his work was to provide a linguistic guide for the German soldiers quartered on the island and in the Tanganyka region, which were at that time briefly an imperial German colony. The material supplied by Reinhardt

[21] In 1965, a revolt supported by Southern Yemen and Russia erupted, lasting until 1975, when Great Britain and Iran intervened. The subsequent peace agreement was designed to promote economic and social growth in the region.

still plays an essential role for neo-Arabic linguistics and dialectology, since it constitutes the richest available description of Omani Arabic, although lacking a lexical repertoire.

More recent studies—i.e., those carried out between the 1950s and the 2000s—have emphasised either the dialectal variety of a specific town or population or have outlined an overall classification and organisation of those vernacular dialects.

Particularly relevant is Adrian Brockett's 1985 *The Spoken Arabic of Khābūra on the Bāṭina of Oman,* essential for technical rural and agricultural terminology used by the Khabura population in al-Batinah and which also includes discussion of some phonological and morphological traits.

Clive Holes, emeritus professor at the Institute of Oriental Studies, University of Oxford, is one of the major scholars of Arabic dialectology. Although he focused the majority of his studies on Arabic dialects of the Gulf and Bahrain, some of his works also dealt with Omani Arabic varieties. In the already cited 'Towards a Dialect Geography of Oman' (1989), Holes suggests a first and clear framework of features shared by all Omani dialects, from the perspective of dialectal geography. Relevant works by Clive Holes also include "Uman: Modern Arabic dialects' (2000), mainly on the morphology of these vernaculars; 'Quadriliteral verbs in the Arabic Dialects of Eastern Arabia' (2004), on this specific feature shared by Gulf and Omani dialects; and finally, 'Form X of the Verb in the Arabic Dialects of Eastern Arabia' (2005), on the behaviour of derived form X not only in Omani Arabic, but also in Gulf and Bahraini dialects. He also analysed some texts recorded in Sur in 'An Arabic Text from Ṣūr, Oman' (2013). Lastly, particularly valuable is the glossary based on his collection of ethnotexts in Bahraini Arabic in *Dialect, Culture, and Society in Eastern Arabia I: Glossary* (2000), accompanied by a clear explanation of methodology and by a discussion on the major languages of contact for that specific vernacular, some of which (Persian, Portuguese, Hindi, English) also left their mark on the Omani lexicon.

Domenyk Eades, during his teaching position at Sultan Qaboos University in Muscat, studied the dialectal variety of the Šawāwi community, in northern Oman, publishing 'The Arabic Dialect of Šawawi Community of Northern Oman' (2009), and some varieties of the Sharqiyyah region, stressing the distinction, far from clear, between Bedouin and Sedentary varieties in Oman.

Janet Watson, in collaboration with Domenyk Eades, published in 2013 the paper 'Camel Culture and Camel Terminology among the Omani Bedouin', which analyses the specific camel-related lexicon among the Bedouin population of Oman, comparing Omani camel terminology with the Mehri terminology used in Dhofar.

Although they have not been strictly considered for the present study, the works of Roger Webster and Dionisius Agius filled a substantial lexical gap in Omani dialectological studies. Roger Webster contributed to the study of Omani Arabic varieties with his 1991 'Notes on the Dialect and Way of Life of the al-Wahība Bedouin', providing a detailed analysis of the lifestyle of this Bedouin population, but also of a part of its lexicon specifically related to their pastoral way of life. Webster's work compares specific semantic fields of the Omani Bedouin lexicon with the same semantic field in the al-Murra tribe's vernacular (Saudi Arabia and Qatar).

Finally, Dionisius Agius's works, the 2002 *In the Wake of the Dhow: The Arabian Gulf and Oman* and 2005 *Seafaring in the Arabian Gulf and Oman: The People of the Dhow*, researched a lexical area, little studied so far in this macro-region: nautical terminology. Ships and the sea have always been a fundamental feature in the history of Oman, for both the commercial and economic development of the country, and for shipping routes and geographical discoveries. Even nowadays, these two elements play an important role, since fishing remains a major source of incomes for Omanis. Furthermore, Agius's monographs show the strong influence of English and Portuguese on the Omani nautical terminology. On the maritime lexicon of Oman, a new work was published in 2019 by Abdul Rahman Al Salimi and Eric Staples: *A Maritime Lexicon: Nautical Terminology in the Indian Ocean*. Their contribution to Omani literature is fundamental for the advancement of lexical research in Oman and in the Indian Ocean region as a whole.

A work co-written by Dionisius Agius and Harriet Nash, the 2011 'The Use of Stars in Agriculture in Oman', is also particularly important and innovative, although once again not strictly used for the present study. It focuses on the traditional use of stars in the *falaǧ* system of Omani agriculture.

In the past few years, new research conducted by early-career scholars have added fundamental insights into the field of Omani dialectology. This is the case of Bettega (2019a), which analyses in meticulous detail the categories of tense, aspect, and mood in Omani Arabic, the first monograph on this long-neglected subject in the field. Morano (2020; 2022) also contributed to the uncovering of interesting linguistic features in northern Oman.

What is clear from this state of the art, though, is that most of the studies carried out so far, despite some progress in the last fifteen years, are in specific areas of the country, leaving others uninvestigated. Moreover, the studies carried out by Clive Holes on dialectal diversification in Omani Arabic focus on phonological and morphological isoglosses, according to current dialectological practice. However, lexical diversification plays an important role as well, although it is less studied because of the absence of a reliable and comprehensive glossary of Omani Arabic.

6.0. Carl Reinhardt (1894): Strengths and Weaknesses

Carl Reinhardt's 1894 *Ein arabischer Dialekt gesprochen in 'Oman und Zanzibar* still plays a very prominent role in the fields of neo-Arabic linguistics and dialectology. The Omani variety that he describes is different both from the one spoken in the capital area (described by Jayakar, 1889) and the one spoken on the coast.

This subsection explores how the strength of Reinhardt's work—which lies in its being the only extensive description of an Omani dialect in the northern part of the country[22]—is partially neutralised by its weaknesses.

Reinhardt's biography (1856–1945) is interesting. He obtained a degree at a commercial school and then worked for several years in various trading houses as an accountant and correspondent in French, Italian, and English. In 1881, he started studying Egyptology, history, philosophy and Oriental languages in Berlin, Heidelberg, and Strasbourg. In 1885, he obtained his PhD, and then moved to Egypt. In 1888, he was appointed *dragoman* 'interpreter' to the consulate in Zanzibar, where he resided until 1893. It must have been in this period that he collected most of his data and thought about writing his main work (Hoffmann-Ruf 2013). After a short period back in Berlin, he started working at the consulate in Cairo in 1894.

In the introduction, Reinhardt states that it took him five years of hard work to collect all the material presented in the book[23] and that—due to illness—he would have given up if his teacher Professor Theodor Noeldeke, the famous orientalist, had not encouraged him to continue. According to Noeldeke, only Reinhardt's data provide a clear overview of Omani Arabic, despite the high value of Jayakar's repertoire.

The dialect described by Reinhardt is the one spoken in Wādī Banī Kharūṣ, today in the al-ʿAwābī district (northern

---

[22] At present, Davey's 2016 work on Dhofari Arabic represents the other extensive description of an Omani dialect, though this one is spoken in the southern part of the country.

[23] Reinhardt (1894, viii): "Mir kam, es lediglich darauf an, das grosse Material an Sprachstoff, welches ich in fünfjähriger schwerer Tropenarbeit gesammelt hatte."

Oman). The people he employed as informants (ʿAbdallāh al-Kharūṣī and ʿAlī al-ʿAbrī from al-ʿAwābī) were natives of Oman who had lived in Zanzibar for some time. Reinhardt relates that ʿAbdallāh al-Kharūṣī was an Omani from Rustaq, who worked with him at the consulate in Zanzibar, and knew how to read and write, and that whenever possible he consulted relatives and friends back in Oman. The second informant, ʿAlī al-ʿAbrī, was from al-ʿAwābī and was illiterate. Reinhardt mentions that he was very quiet and that it was therefore very difficult to extrapolate suitable material from his speech (cf. Reinhardt 1894, xii). Besides, the German author states that this vernacular was spoken at his time by the Omani court and by some two-thirds of the Arabs living in Zanzibar.[24] Thus, we can presume that it was sufficiently widespread to require the writing of a practical and quick guide for German soldiers quartered in the East African colonies.

Reinhardt's work is divided into four parts: 1. Phonology; 2. Morphology; 3. Remarks on the Syntax; and 4. Texts and Stories (including some war songs). The feature that distinguishes this book from other teaching material is the fact that it is almost exclusively written in the Latin alphabet, mainly for space issues (cf. Reinhardt 1894, viii). Reinhardt (1894, viii) admits that he is not an expert Arabist and that his aim is only to present the vernacular in the clearest possible way. Of these sections, however, the one which most detracts from the work's re-

---

[24] Reinhardt (1894, vii): "...dem Lernenden geordnet vorzuführen und ihn an der Hand einer reichen Sammlung von Beispielen mit den Regeln dieses herrlichen Dialekts bekannt zu machen."

liability is the lack of reference to syntax. Reinhardt deals only marginally with the syntactic features of the dialect, superficially examining noun phrases and verbal clauses (i.e., interrogative, relative, copulative, conditional, and hypothetical clauses), providing plenty of examples, but not an exhaustive analysis.

One of the weaknesses of Reinhardt's work—that he himself acknowledges[25]—is the lack of transcription, which was made by the author only afterwards and not during his stay in Oman and Zanzibar. This is one of the reasons why the data reported by Reinhardt are not always reliable from a phonological point of view. Moreover, he clearly states that he expects some criticism because he tried to present examples that would captivate students. His work, therefore, has more of a pedagogical than descriptive intent, which makes the entire monograph weaker for the broader field of Omani Arabic documentation than it could have been.

Another weakness of Reinhardt's data lies precisely in his informants. The two people he employed were too few in number and they worked for him, thus creating a relationship that is not ideal for a linguistic study.[26] Finally, he had no means of double-checking the data back in Oman, completely relying on the knowledge of his two informants.

---

[25] Reinhardt (1894, viii): "Diese immerhin verdientsvolle Arbeit habe ich jedoch aus dem Grunde nicht benutzen können, weil sie die Eigenheiten des Omani-(Maskat)-Dialekts nur oberflächlich streift und, abgesehen von manchen Irrthümern…"

[26] Reinhardt states that he paid "100 Mark" to ʿAbd Allāh al-Kharūṣī for his services, whereas ʿAlī al-ʿAbrī was more a sort of butler than an actual consultant for him (Reinhardt 1894, xi–xii).

While on the whole voicing appreciation for the usefulness of Reinhardt's work, the reviews published by experienced Semitic scholars and Arabists, such as Theodor Noeldeke (1895) and Karl Vollers (1895), pointed out a few obscure points in his description. Vollers (1895) devotes the first part of his review of Reinhardt's work to raising doubts on the reliability of the book because of its educational rather than descriptive purpose. He also reports an indigenous classification of the territory according to which the Banū Kharūṣī vernacular described by Reinhardt is the one spoken in the *'Omān* area by the sedentary rural population. On the contrary, Reinhardt states that his Omani variety is Bedouin and not Sedentary, which is opposite both to the statements of his informants and to Vollers's (1895, 491) idea of this vernacular being an isolated and conservative Neo-Arabic dialect of Southern Arabia.[27]

Nevertheless, Reinhardt gives us some interesting information about the Omani social and linguistic environment he worked in: he states that whilst in Egypt, Syria, and Algeria it was sometimes easy to find a local who spoke at least one European language, in Oman—and especially in Zanzibar—this was impossible.

About the work, Reinhardt (1894, viii) states that his grammar was born thanks to the huge amount of material he managed to collect: the texts are translated as literally as possi-

[27] On this, Vollers (1895, 491): "Um so weniger kann ich verstehen, warum R. [Reinhardt] im Widerspruche mit der Aussage seiner Gewährsmänner (VII) diese Sprache eher für beduinisch als für ḥaḍari halten will..."

ble into German, and some of these translations are supported by verses extracted from the *diwāns* of Ḥarīrī and Mutanabbī, who were very popular in Oman at that time.

The last section of the book is devoted to folkloristic stories, 200 proverbs and a few war songs. The stories tell about daily routines and common events; the proverbs are, according to Reinhardt, among the commonest in use; the war songs are usually preceded by explanatory comments and all of them come from ʿAlī al-ʿAbrī (Reinhardt 1894, xiv–xv). The only issue with the last section of Reinhardt's work is the fact that some of the grammatical features he reports are not common at all in the texts (e.g., the use of genitive markers; the use of the *bi*-prefix).

In conclusion, Reinhardt's work is an invaluable piece of study for the field of Omani dialectology. However, the premises of the work itself, the time that has passed since its publication, and the issues examined in this section show that the data examined in *Ein arabischer Dialekt gesprochen in 'Oman und Zanzibar* are in need of reinterpretation in light of a more detailed analysis of the type of Arabic spoken nowadays in the al-ʿAwābī district.

7.0. The al-ʿAwābī District: In Geographical and Historical Perspective

The al-ʿAwābī district is located in South al-Batinah and consists of al-ʿAwābī town—with a population of about 11,000[28]—and twenty-four small villages spread between it and Wādī Banī

[28] According to the 2020 census.

Kharūṣ. The district is 150 kilometres from Muscat, 36 kilometres from Nakhal (نخل), and 16 kilometres from Rustaq.

The ancient name of al-ʿAwābī town was Sūni. People in al-ʿAwābī say that Sūni is the name of the mountain at the entrance to Wādī Banī Kharūṣ. Wilkinson (1987, 14) identifies the 'Hisn al-Sawni', the fort which controls the access to Wādī Banī Kharūṣ as being the main objective for the ʿAbriyin tribe in the fight for control over the whole region. This also shows how strategic Wādī Banī Kharūṣ was, as one of the main access points to the interior of the country. The name of the town, then, changed to al-ʿAwābī at the time of the Imam Sayf bin Sulṭān al-Yaʿrūbī, and its origin may lie in the word *ʿawābi* (SG *ʿābye*), which is used in the district to mean 'cultivated soil, plot'.

The Wādī Banī Kharūṣ is a valley that goes deep into al-Hajar Mountains for about 26 kilometres, ending at Jabal Akhdar, and its main town is Stāl.[29] The population of the wadi is generally older than that of the town. Some of the villages are also populated by only one or two families, and people live mainly on agriculture and farming. Those villages are: al-Ẓāhir, al-Ẓahra, al-ʿAlya (the very last accessible village in the Wādī), al-Hawdiniyya, al-Hijā, al-Maḥḍūṯ, al-Maḥṣana, al-Marḥ, al-Wilayga, al-Ramī, al-Sahal, al-Ṣibayẖa, Dakum, Misfāt al-

[29] "...Wādī B. ʿAwf offers fairly easy access into Wādī B. Kharūṣ, an otherwise isolated wadi system belonging to the B. Kharūṣ, with their capital as Istal (var. Stal, not to be confused with Mistal) and its exit commanded by the important town of ʿAwābī" (Wilkinson 1987, 113).

Haṭāṭla, Misfāt al-Širayqīn, Šhū, Stāl, Ṣunaybʿ, Ṭawī al-Sayḥ, ar-Rajmah, Wādī Ṣufūn, al-Manẓūr, and Ṯaqub.[30]

The district is well known in Oman because of its historical heritage:[31] the Banū Kharūṣ played an important role throughout Omani history, and primarily in Ibadism. Descendants of the Yaḥmad tribe—a branch of ʾAzd—they moved to Oman during the pre-Islamic period, settling in a valley named after them as Wādī Banī Kharūṣ. The Yaḥmad provided most of the Ibadi imams of Oman until the arrival of the Yaʿrūbī dynasty in the seventeenth century (cf. Wilkinson 1987 and Rentz 2012). Wilkinson (1987, 206) mentions the Kharūṣ as "one of the major shaikhly clan" in the area, controlling a "strategic tribal position running from the major settlement of Sawni on to the Jabal al-Akhdar via the Wadi B. Kharus."

In the Wādī it is still possible to find inscriptions that testify to the lives and the deeds of these Imams. One of the best remembered still today is al-Warith bin Kaʾab, who "has been virtually sanctified in popular belief," and the only Imam carrying a shade of mythology (Wilkinson 1978, 211).[32] Finally, the al-Kharūṣī tribe played a fundamental role in the Omani *nahḍa*, by providing religious scholars throughout the nineteenth and twentieth centuries.

In this area, the tribe of al-ʿAbrī also found its strength: at the beginning of the twentieth century, it was the most power-

[30] Source: Sultanate of Oman, National Centre for Statistics and Information: https://www.ncsi.gov.om/Pages/NCSI.aspx.

[31] The symbol of the district is an inkpot and a quill, to signify that it is a place of knowledge.

[32] This is the Imam mentioned by S2 in ch. 4, example (64).

ful tribe in Oman, and its Imam was Salīm bin Rāšid al-Kharūṣī. The influence of the *ulema* from this tribe revitalised the Ibadi doctrine in all northern Oman.

Nowadays, al-ʿAwābī town is inhabited by two main tribes, namely the al-Kharūṣī and the al-ʿAbrī, which are native and are the same tribes found by Carl Reinhardt at the end of the nineteenth century. However, a few smaller tribes moved to al-ʿAwābī in more recent times from other regions of Oman. A custom of this district was to marry people from the same tribe, so that eventually it would have been the only tribe populating the area. In more recent years, however, this practice has been gradually abandoned by the younger population, because of inter-regional weddings among Omani people. The population of the town differs slightly from that of the Wādī more broadly, especially in terms of lifestyle and level of education: nowadays, many inhabitants go to college or university or work in the capital city, usually returning during weekends and festivities. Only a small percentage of them remain in the town, cultivating palm gardens and breeding goats. These cultural traits have been taken into consideration in the analysis of the data presented in this work, as will be explained in the next section on methodology.

8.0. Participants, Metadata, and Methodology

8.1. The Participants

Since Carl Reinhardt (1894) relied on just two speakers, who were natives of Oman, but had spent most of their life abroad and were working for him in Cairo, the present research is based on a wider range of speakers in order to gain a better picture of the dialect spoken and more suitable material for comparison. Hence, this research is based on the vernacular spoken by fifteen people who were all born and bred in the district. Table 1.1 provides a list of these fifteen participants, detailing their gender, age at the time of recording, provenance, level of education, and tribe of origin. These were not only crucial factors in the recruitment process, but also features of interest in the selection of examples in this work.

Table 1.1: Participant metadata

S	Gender	Age	Origin	Level of Education	Tribe
1	F	58	al-ʿAwābī	illiterate	al-Kharūṣī
2	F	45	Stāl (WBK)	illiterate	al-Kharūṣī
3	F	35	al-ʿAwābī	high school	al-ʿAbrī
4	F	60–70	al-Ramī (WBK)	illiterate	al-ʿAbrī
5	F	28	al-ʿAwābī	university	al-Kharūṣī
6	F	38	al-ʿAwābī	university	al-Kharūṣī
7	F	44	al-ʿAwābī	middle school	al-Kharūṣī
8	M	65–75	al-ʿAlya (WBK)	illiterate	al-ʿAbrī
9	F	32	Dakum (WBK)	university	al-Kharūṣī
10	F	55	al-ʿAwābī	middle school	al-Kharūṣī
11	F	45	Stāl (WBK)	high school	al-Kharūṣī
12	F	40	al-ʿAwābī	middle school	al-Kharūṣī
13	M	85–95	Stāl (WBK)	illitterate	al-Kharūṣī
14	F	50–60	Dakum (WBK)	middle school	al-ʿAbrī
15	F	80–90	al-ʿAwābī	illitterate	al-ʿAbrī

As Table 1.1 shows, three main criteria guided the choice of participants: age, provenance, and level of education. These criteria were chosen for two main reasons: firstly, since one of the scopes of this study is the analysis of diachronic variation in the district of al-ʿAwābī in comparison to Reinhardt's (1894) work, the criterion of age was deemed appropriate for comparison with the dialect he describes; secondly, level of education and provenance were chosen to see if the sociological factors mentioned above in §§3.0 and 7.0 had any impact on the variety spoken nowadays in the district, especially in the light of the process of 'Gulfinisation' that the Arabic varieties of this area are currently undergoing, and the increased use of social networks and the Internet in general, which put the younger generation in contact with the wider Arab world.

The first criterion is further divided into age groups to individuate three generations of speakers.

Table 1.2: Speaker age groups

Generation	Abbreviation	Age span	Speaker
Young	YS	28–40	3, 5, 6, 9, 12
Adult	AS	41–59	1, 2, 7, 10, 11, 14
Old	OS	60+	4, 8, 13, 15

This choice was made to have a clearer picture of diachronic variation in this dialect, expecting OS to have a type of speech closer to the one described by Reinhardt (1894) and YS to have a vernacular influenced by other neighbouring Arabic varieties or Standard Omani Arabic, social networks, and the language of broadcasting. Moreover, this age division was made while bearing in mind the historical phases of the Sultanate, as briefly traced above in §1.0–2.0: participants aged between 40 and 60 are people that lived their early years at the beginning of the new era established by Sultan Qaboos, and were able to witness the changes Oman went through afterwards; by contrast, participants aged 60+ have a better memory of the time prior to the rise of Sultan Qaboos, when Saʿīd bin Taymūr ruled Oman; younger speakers, finally, will potentially show the latest developments of the language, influenced by the media, by the type of Arabic used in education, and by the influence of supposedly more prestigious forms of Arabic. As Table 1.1 shows, for some of the speakers a possible age span is provided: that is because for the older generation—i.e., the generation born before the 1970s—it was not possible to give a precise age in terms of dates, since the registration of births started only later, with Sultan Qaboos.

The second criterion, provenance, is straightforward: it serves for examination of the geographical distribution of linguistic features, and it helps to check the differences in the speech of Wādī Banī Kharūṣ and al-ʿAwābī town inhabitants.

Finally, the third criterion, level of education, was deemed particularly appropriate from a sociolinguistic point of view: as classes are taught in Standard Omani Arabic, usually by Egyptian teachers, does this have any impact on the dialect spoken? And if yes, to what extent?

Gender could not be a criterion for informants' recruitment, since, with very few exceptions, access to male informants proved to be difficult for the author once in the field. Therefore, it has been excluded as a measure of analysis of the data.

One more factor deemed appropriate for the decision on informants' participation was tribe of origin. This was not counted as a main criterion; however, it was important to take tribal origin into consideration. Reinhardt's informants were from the al-Kharūṣī tribe and the al-ʿAbrī tribe, which were the only two that inhabited the al-ʿAwābī district at his time. At the present time, both tribes still live in the district, and, at least according to the consultants, remain the only two that live there, despite the recent tendency to marry people from other tribes or regions of Oman.

8.2. The Fieldwork

The data presented in this work were collected during two fieldwork trips conducted by the author: the first was made between February and April 2017, and the second in June 2018.

The transcription and translation of the texts, proverbs, and examples throughout this work were done *in situ* with the tireless help and diligent support of Iḫlāṣ Rašīd al-Kharūṣī, who patiently listened to several hours of recordings. In these sessions, I also added field-notes on linguistic structures of interest, and other local practices.

The second fieldwork trip was shorter and carried out during the month of Ramadan (i.e., June) in 2018. This trip had two main aims: first, a final check on some phonological and morphological features collected during the previous trip; and second, to collect stories, lexicon, and any other material related specifically to Ramadan and Eid celebrations in the district.

Both fieldwork trips were spent in the house of speakers 1 and 6, a house which was always overcrowded during the weekends, offering the opportunity talk to their relatives, siblings, and neighbours—some of whom became active participants in the research and are included in the list of participants.

8.3. The Data

The corpus[33] of data presented in this work is divided into three main groups, depending on the source of the material: the first group stands as the primary source for this monograph, and includes new data gathered during fieldwork (hereby called 'primary data'); the second group consists of secondary literature for comparative purposes; and, finally, the third group comprises sources related to neighbouring Arabic varieties, also for comparative purposes.

8.3.1. Group 1. Primary Data

The primary basis of this study consists of fifteen hours of recorded material I collected during the fieldwork trips in the al-ʿAwābī district. These fifteen hours also include four hours of WhatsApp[34] vocal messages, exchanged with participants both during fieldwork and at a distance. The WhatsApp vocal messages contain spontaneous speech from a group of seven women (i.e., speakers 1, 5, 6, 7, 10 and 12) from the al-Kharūṣī tribe, whereas the rest of the audio material is mainly the result of free-speech recordings.

---

[33] The term "corpus" is here intended as the collection of primary data presented in the course of this work and as it is employed in general linguistics, not in the specific meaning it has in the field of corpus linguistics.

[34] WhatsApp is a popular phone application that allows customers to chat via the Internet.

The free speech recordings were carried out in a variety of contexts and environments: of the remaining eleven hours, about five were recorded during the afternoon gatherings of women, usually in indoor places, where they exchange coffee, sweets, and stories; about four hours were recorded during Eid gatherings, usually outdoors, and weddings; finally, four more hours contain accounts of local stories, legends related to spiritual entities in the Wādī (i.e., *jinn*), changes in the local environment, and tribe-related events. The five hours recorded during the afternoon gatherings were not initiated by the author; rather, after asking for consent to record, the recorder was positioned at the centre of the circle of women and their conversation recorded. This was then analysed afterwards with the help of a native speaker. The same happened with the Eid celebrations and partly with local stories: once the participants acknowledged the scope of the research, they were always very keen to provide me with material for recording.

The remaining two hours are the result of elicitation of lexical items: these were partly collected in the Wādī with speaker 11, especially for plant names and medical terminology, and partly with speakers 2, 6, 7, and 12, especially for household terminology.

The recordings were conducted using an Olympus LS-12 Linear PCM Recorder, and all the files were saved in .WAV format at a sample rate of 16bit 44.100 kHz. The files were also stored on my personal laptop and on an external hard drive and analysed using the annotation programme ELAN.[35]

The other methodology employed in the collection of primary data was elicitation of samples that are not part of the audio material, but constitute a core of written notes. WhatsApp text messages were also useful in the elicitation of some syntactic features, such as negation structures, genitive markers, and different types of complex clauses: these WhatsApp examples are reported in their original Arabic script throughout this work, alongside transcription and glossing. In this elicitation process, three main methodologies have been used: first, submitting the sentence in English and asking informants to translate it—this worked especially well with university-educated speakers who knew English; second, sending the sentences in MSA and asking for differences with the dialect—this was helpful with people who did not have a full higher education, but had attended school for a few years at least; finally, employing the author's own knowledge of the dialect to write samples and asking informants for correctness judgements.

8.3.2. Group 2. Secondary Data

The second group includes the material presented by Carl Reinhardt (1894), which has been studied in detail and used for comparison purposes. If we take into consideration the importance of Reinhardt's material, as well as all the issues with his work— discussed in detail above in §6.0—the comparison

[35] ELAN is computer software used to annotate and transcribe audio and video recordings.

attains even more relevance. Since Reinhardt (1894) lacks an extensive analysis of the syntax of the Banū Kharūṣī dialect—with only marginal exceptions (e.g., genitive markers, sone clauses, and negation)—the material he presents will be displayed mainly in the morphology section (both nominal and verbal), where a few remarks regarding diachronic comparison are provided. In addition to Reinhardt's work, this group includes material presented by Brockett (1985) and Nakano (1995).

8.3.3. Group 3. Secondary Data from Other Arabic Dialects

The third group consists of samples taken from secondary sources on other Arabic varieties (i.e., Moroccan, Egyptian, Syrian, Najdi, Saudi, Gulf, Yemeni) used in the argument either to support a statement or, again, for comparison purposes.[36]

8.4. The Methodology

Taking into consideration these three groups of data and the methodology adopted, each chapter of this work is predominantly based on one or more of them: chapter two examines phonological features of the al-ʿAwābī district vernacular, reporting primary data elicited from the audio files, whilst Rein-

[36] For Moroccan, Egyptian, and Syrian Arabic dialects, the main sources used are Brustad (2000), Ouhalla (2008), and Eisele (1993; 1999); for Najdi Arabic, Ingham (1994); for Saudi Arabian dialects, Prochazka (1988); for Gulf dialects, Holes (1990; 2016) and Qafisheh (1977); finally, for Yemeni dialects, Watson (1993).

hardt's material is used only in specific instances for comparison purposes; chapter three, on morphology, uses as sources both primary data and Reinhardt's data, clearly divided and signposted, in order to visibly show the diachronic variation between them. Finally, chapter four, on syntax, is entirely based on primary data, since Reinhardt (1894) lacks an extensive syntactic description, with only a few exceptions; however, the chapter also takes into consideration syntactic features from neighbouring dialects for comparative or supportive purposes.

It is necessary to address a few limitations that this methodology and the range of participants pose to the research. First, the description presented has to be considered as based mainly on the speech of a limited number of women, of different ages and levels of education. Admittedly, having a wider range of speakers, including men, would have given a fuller picture of the linguistic and sociolinguistic situation of the district under investigation. Nevertheless, since male researchers in the past have suffered from the opposite problem—i.e., the difficulty of working with women, especially in Arab contexts—many linguistic studies carried out in Oman in the last century have considered dialectological material only from male speakers.[37] Hence, one of the limitations of this study might also be considered a strength and the starting point for a future widening of the description to include other variables.

Some may argue that another limitation of this work consists in the number of informants used. However, in recruiting

[37] See, for example, the work of Davey (2016), who had access to only three women out of a total of fourteen informants.

them, I tried to assemble a range of people as wide as possible vis-à-vis the criteria mentioned earlier in the section.

A recent tendency in Oman in general and, hence, in the al-ʿAwābī district, more specifically, is to marry people from outside one's tribe or one's region, whereas, up until a few decades ago, this practice was rare. This might pose another issue: to what extent do inter-regional or inter-tribal marriages impact on the dialect spoken today?

The extent of influence of other Omani varieties on this dialect, as a result of inter-tribal or inter-regional marriages and relocation of residents, is something that may be of interest to future researchers, but will not be addressed in this work. Here, the consultants' speech is described while taking into account the fact that all of them, if married, have local husbands, either al-Kharūṣī or al-ʿAbrī.

CHAPTER 2: PHONOLOGY

Phonological descriptions of Omani varieties are scarce. As regards the northern part of the country, Brockett's (1985) study deals with the agricultural terminology of Khabura, introduced with a brief phonological account of that dialect. Holes's (1989) overview of Omani dialects does not report any specific phonological traits—with the exception of reflexes of the OA consonants /q/, /ğ/, and /k/. Other recent descriptions—such as the ones mentioned in §5.0—deal only in part with phonology and do not present an exhaustive account for comparison.

Reinhardt's (1894) description of Banū Kharūṣī phonological traits covers the first chapter of his work, and examines consonants, vowels, diphthongs, assimilation, and word stress. His account on this matter, however—as mentioned in §6.0—is not completely reliable, due both to the lack of transcription on his part and to the nature of his informants, i.e., they were Omanis who had lived outside of Oman for most of their lives. Moreover, Reinhardt provides no details about their pronunciation, which was likely to have been influenced by other Arabic varieties (e.g., the Egyptian variety of Cairo, where they lived after leaving Oman), or other languages (e.g., Swahili in Zanzibar).

The phonological description in this chapter considers primary data elicited from the spontaneous speech of the participants and analysed with PRAAT[1], whereas the broader theoret-

[1] PRAAT is computer software used for speech analysis in phonetics.

 https://doi.org/10.11647/OBP.0298.02

ical discussion of phonological processes uses as reference sources the works of Cantineau (1960), McCarthy (1979), Hayes (1995), Levin (1998), and Watson (2002).

1.0. Consonants

The al-ʿAwābī district consonantal inventory contains 27 segments, all of which can appear in all word-positions, with the exception of the glottal stop (/ʾ/) and the glides, which are weakened or deleted altogether in certain positions. All consonants may be geminated, with the sole exception of *hamza*.

Table 2.1: Consonantal inventory of the al-ʿAwābī district

Transcription	Description
/ʾ/	voiceless glottal stop
/b/	voiced bilabial stop
/t/	voiceless alveolar stop
/ṯ/	voiceless interdental fricative
/g/	voiced velar stop
/ḥ/	voiceless pharyngeal fricative
/ḫ/	voiceless velar fricative
/d/	voiced alveolar stop
/ḏ/	voiced interdental fricative
/r/	voiced alveolar tap
/z/	voiced alveolar fricative
/s/	voiceless alveolar fricative
/š/	voiceless postalveolar fricative
/ṣ/	emphatic voiceless alveolar fricative
/ḍ/	emphatic voiced alveolar stop
/ṭ/	emphatic voiceless alveolar stop
/ʿ/	voiced pharyngeal fricative
/ġ/	voiced velar fricative

/f/	voiceless labiodental fricative
/q/	voiceless uvular stop
/k/	voiceless velar stop
/l/	voiced alveolar lateral approximant
/m/	voiced bilabial nasal
/n/	voiced alveolar nasal
/h/	voiceless glottal fricative
/w/	voiced labiovelar approximant
/y/	voiced palatal approximant

Reinhardt's (1894, 4–6) section on consonants examines their realisation, frequently referring to the German system of sounds—perhaps to facilitate the understanding of the German soldiers for whom the work was intended. His phonological description is supported by lexical examples for each consonant, reported in both Arabic script and transcription. Reinhardt (1894, 8–11) also provides lexically determined variants of some consonants, some of which are still valid today. In the following list, the lexically determined variants of consonants found in the primary data are presented, providing examples from recent recordings, and adding, when necessary, remarks on Reinhardt's notes.

1.1. *Tā* (ت)

**t* can be realised as *dāl* via assimilation when adjacent to a voiced consonant, e.g., *kidf* < *kitf* 'shoulder', pl. *kdūf*. The same is reported by Reinhardt (1894, 9).

1.2. *Qāf* (ق), *kāf* (ك), and *ǧīm* (ج)

**q* is realised as the voiceless uvular stop [q].

**k* is realised in all cases as the voiceless velar stop [k]. In the primary data, there is one lexeme recorded in al-ʿAlya (Wādī Banī Kharūṣ) from an old illiterate male speaker (i.e., speaker 8) where the velar stop is affricated as [č]—i.e., *seččārā* 'drunkards' < سكارى.

**ǧ* is generally realised as the voiced velar stop [g]. The same variables are reported by Reinhardt (1894, 4–6), who adds that in the case of other Omani tribes, the voiced velar stop /g/ is affricated as [ǧ].[2]

1.3. The Liquid Consonants: *Rāʾ* (ر) and *lām* (ل)

In the primary data, these two consonants appear to be somewhat interchangeable, and the same is reported by Reinhardt (1894, 10). The primary data include a few examples: words like *sulṭān* 'sultan' and *inglezi* 'English' are realised respectively as *surṭān* and *ingrezi* by all consultants.

1.4. The Emphatic Consonants: *Ṭā* (ط), *ẓā* (ظ), *ṣād* (ص), and *ḍād* (ض)

*ḍ and *ẓ are merged in one sound /ḍ/.

Reinhardt (1894, 7) reports four emphatic consonants—/ṣ/, /ṭ/, /ḍ/, and /ẓ/—but later states that the two sounds *ḍ

[2] Reinhardt does not specify the relevant tribe(s).

and *ẓ merged into /ḍ/. In the primary data, there is no distinction between *ḍ and *ẓ, and the reflex for both is /ḍ/.

*ṣ and *ṭ retain their emphatic sound in all cases in the primary data.

1.5. The Interdentals: *Ṯā* (ث) and *ḏāl* (ذ)

Reinhardt (1894, 10) states that the voiced interdental fricative *ḏ is realised as either /ḍ/ or /d/, and that the voiceless interdental fricative *ṯ is realised as /t/, providing, however, only one or two examples for each case.

In the primary data the interdentals /ṯ/ and /ḏ/ are retained in all cases.

1.6. *Hamza* (ء)

Reinhardt's (1894, 8–9) analysis of *hamza* in the Banū Kharūṣī dialect is very detailed, although not supported by enough examples. Nevertheless, the behaviour of the *hamza* in the vernacular under investigation did not seem to have undergone change.

In the primary data, *hamza* is not retained in *initial position*:

- in words like *ḫit* < *ʾuḫt* 'sister'; *sum* < *ʾism* 'name'; *hel* < *ʾahl* 'family'; *mrā* 'woman' < *ʾimrā*

- **ʔ* can also be realised, in specific words, as: *ʿayn*, e.g., *ʿaṣl* < *ʾaṣl* 'origin'; *wāw*, e.g., *bedwe* 'beginning'; and *yā*, e.g., *yāsīr* < *ʾasīr* 'prisoner'.[3]

In *medial position*, *hamza* is not retained and some nouns show compensatory lengthening of the vowel (e.g., *bīr* < *biʾr* 'well'; *rās* < *raʾs* 'head').[4]

In *final position*, the *hamza* follows the same rules applied to III-ء and III-ى verbs: it is not retained and is realised as either /a/, e.g., *qarā/yiqra* 'read', or /i/, e.g., *meše/yumši* 'walk'.

1.7. *Tā Marbūṭa* (ة)

The *tā marbūṭa*—a distinctive feature of feminine nouns and some masculine plurals—is often realised as [e] in this dialect, raised from /a/ according to the rules of *imāla*. Reinhardt (1894, 9) does not mention the behaviour of the feminine ending in the speech of his informants, reporting only the case of بدأة *bedwe* 'beginning', which also presents a final *hamza*.

In this work, the *tā marbūṭa* will be transcribed as either [e] or [a], based on the pronunciation of the specific word in the district.[5]

---

[3] This phenomenon is also reported by Brockett (1985, 13) for the dialect of Khabura, in al-Batinah.

[4] The lengthening of medial *hamza* in pre-consonantal position can be found in most modern Arabic dialects, with the exception of various Yemeni dialects (Watson 2002, 18).

[5] In the literature, *tā marbūṭa* is usually transliterated *-ah*, but here it will be transcribed as the simple vowels *a* or *e* to reflect the informants' sound production.

1.8. *Wāw* (و) and *yā* (ي)

In the primary data, **w* and **y* retain their consonantal nature only when in syllable-onset position, e.g., حياة *hayā* 'life'; دواء *duwā* 'medicine'.

2.0. Vowels

Reinhardt's (1894, 7–8) section on the behaviour of vowels is very short, briefly mentioning their sounds in specific consonantal environments. Here the description of vowels as it appears in the primary data is reported.

The vowel inventory of the al-ʿAwābī district consists of

- three short vowels: /a/, /i/, /u/;
- five long vowels: /ā/, /ē/, /ī/, /ō/, /ū/;
- two diphthongs: /aw/ and /ay/.

Short vowels differ in their realisation, depending on their syllabic environment: medial /i/, for example, is usually lax and retracted, e.g., [gɪld] 'skin'; in word-final position, it is tenser, higher, and more front, e.g., [bɪnti] 'my daughter'; before /b/, /m/, /f/, /r/, /q/, and the emphatics, it is backed and rounded, e.g., [zaːhʊb] 'ready'; with velars and pharyngeals, it is lowered and centralised, e.g., [jħəbːo] 'he likes him' (cf. Holes 2008, 480). The short vowel /u/ has the back mid rounded allophone [o] when preceding or following an emphatic sound.

The short vowel /a/ has two allophones in this variety: it is a low back unrounded [ɑ] next to an emphatic or a uvular consonant; and it is raised to [e], usually when gutturals and emphatics are absent, according to the rules that regulate *imāla*.

Short high vowels in unstressed non-final position undergo reduction or deletion. This phenomenon is known as *syncope*, and in other Omani varieties is of common occurrence, especially in rapid speech (Glover 1988, 61; Davey 2016, 61). In the primary data, syncope seems to occur in the first syllable only when the vowel is high, e.g., *gˈbin* < *gibin* 'cheese', and not when it is low, e.g., *ˈgamal* 'camel' (cf. Jastrow 1980, 110). Reinhardt (1894, 41, 146) does not mention syncope in his work, although his lexical data clearly show its occurrence, in both nouns and verbs, e.g., *rgíl* < *rigil* 'foot'; *lbís* < *labis* 'wear, dress').[6] The occurrence or non-occurrence of syncope can also be explained through metrical stress theory (see present chapter, §5.0).

The primary data show that OA **ū* and **ī* are retained in most positions as independent phonemes, e.g., فلوس *fulūs* 'money' and بيض *bīḍ* 'eggs'. The long vowel /ū/ also has the allophone [ō], when preceding an emphatic sound or a stop or following a parhyngeal sound, e.g., *qōṭi* 'tin', *nōbe* 'also'; *ʿōq* 'sickness, disease'.

2.1. *Imāla*

The term *imāla*, literally 'inclination', has been used since the time of the medieval Arab grammarians to indicate the fronting and raising of long /ā/ towards /ī/.[7] In the ancient sources, not

[6] See also Reinhardt's (1894, 135) list of strong verbs.

[7] "And the sense [denoted by] the [term] *ʾimāla* is that you incline the *ʾalif* in the direction of *yāʾ*, and the *fatḥa* in the direction of the *kasra*" (Ibn Sarrāğ, cited in Levin 1998).

much is said about the same phenomenon for short /a/, for which *imāla* is found, for example, in the vernacular under investigation. According to the medieval grammarians, *imāla* is a phenomenon conditioned by certain phonological factors: in particular, it can occur because of an etymological *yā* in the root, or the *kasra* of an adjacent syllable which can incline /a/ towards [i] (Cantineau 1960, 97). If it is true that strong *imāla*, i.e., the realisation of /a/ as [i], is not a common occurrence, it is also true that the inclination of /a/ towards [e], both in medial and final position, is a widespread phenomenon in Eastern Arabic dialects.[8]

The realisation of the *imāla*, both of /ā/ and /a/, depends on specific phonological factors, and in particular on the nature of the consonants that cluster around the vowel. In the primary data, it occurs in medial and final position, usually in the absence of gutturals or emphatics: in this case, short vowel /a/ is raised to either [e] or, more rarely, [i], e.g., *kelb* 'dog', *gebel* 'mountain', *šill* 'take', *siyyāra* 'car', *misgid* 'mosque'. *Imāla* in final position is very common in nouns with the feminine ending ة or ى, e.g., نوبة *nōbe* 'also'; خمسة *ḫamse* 'five'; *bedwe* < بدأة 'beginning', and in the 3FSG possessive pronoun -/ha/, which is realised as -/he/ in cases such as *ḥobbōt-he*[9] 'her grandmother',

[8] Cantineau (1960, 99) writes: "[...] l'ɔimāla allant jusqu'à *e* est largement attestée: en Orient son domaine couvre la majeure partie du Liban et le G. ed-Drūz; on le constate aussi dans l'oasis de Palmyre. En Afrique du Nord, la région de Bōne connaît aussi une ɔimāla allant jusq'à *e*."

[9] The first short vowel /o/ in *ḥobbōt-he* is one of the rare examples in the primary data of progressive vowel harmony.

whilst in others as -/ha/, e.g., *ʿumr-ha* 'her age'. The variation between the two depends once again on the consonantal environment: it is realised as -/ha/ when following a fricative or one of the sonorants *r*, *l*, *n*, and -/*he*/ after the epenthetic unrounded front vowel [i], e.g., *šufti-he* 'I/you (2MSG) saw her'.

Whilst the occurrence of *imāla* for the short vowel /a/ is supported by numerous examples in the primary data, the raising of long vowel /ā/ to /ē/ is found only in the conjugation of geminate, hamzated, and weak verbs (see ch. 3, §§2.2–4); no evidence is traceable in the lexicon.

In Oman, the *imāla* occurs in Dhofari Arabic (cf. Davey 2016) and in other dialects of the al-Batinah and Sharqiyyah regions, usually in communities living on the seaward side of the al-Hajar Mountains (cf. Holes 2008, 481). In terms of areal distinctions in the district under investigation, the *imāla* always occurs in the speech of informants from al-ʿAwābī regardless of their age and level of education. In Wādī Banī Kharūṣ, on the contrary, the *imāla* is found in the speech of AS and YS, either with a lower or a higher level of education, but is not found in the speech of OS, who had no—or very little—access to education or exposure to the speech of the town.[10]

2.2. Diphthongs

In the Semitic languages, the term diphthong normally refers to a falling diphthong, i.e., one that is formed by a short vowel fol-

---

[10] An exemplification of areal distribution of *imāla* in the district based on the informants' speech is given in Table 2.3 in the next section.

lowed by a glide, i.e., /w/ or /y/. In many modern Arabic dialects, the CA diphthongs **aw* and **ay* are not preserved.[11]

In the primary data, the long vowels [ō] and [ē] are the result of a process of monophthongisation of the OA diphthongs, as well as being allophones of /ū/ and /ā/, respectively. According to Youssef (2013, 186), "monophthongisation is an active synchronic process that fails to apply in particular environments, both phonological and morphological." Few studies have dealt with the behaviour and analysis of diphthongs in Gulf and Peninsular dialects, and it is difficult to formulate a clear explanation for the anomalous forms of diphthongs in the al-ʿAwābī district vernacular.

Reinhardt (1894, 8) states that diphthongs are retained only in monosyllabic words and in words with a geminate glide, whereas in all other cases they are lengthened. However, this is not entirely true today, since the primary data show that the retention of diphthongs varies depending on its position in the word, as exemplified in the following lists.[12]

---

[11] Cantineau (1960, 103) writes:

> Dans les dialectes arabes, la conservation phonétique complète des anciennes diphtongues est un fait rare. En Orient, cette conservation est attestée au Liban.... Au Maghreb, la conservation complète et inconditionnée des anciennes diphtongues est un fait fort rare, sinon inexistant.

[12] Admittedly, given the small number of informants consulted by Reinhardt and the consequent access to a limited amount of data, it might well have been that these rules also applied to diphthongs at his time.

2.2.1. Glide as C_1

Diphthongs in the first syllable of the word are retained when the glide is the antepenultimate consonant in the word, irrespective of where the consonant occurs in the root. This happens in (a) comparative adjectives, (b) passive participles, (c) verbal nouns, and (d) broken plurals:

(a)	*awsaʿ*	'wider'	*awsaḫ*	'dirtier'
	awgaʿ	'more painful'	*awṯaq*	'more solid'
(b)	*mawṯuq*	'reliable'	*mawgūd*	'existent'
(c)	*tawbīḫ*	'blame'	*tawrīb*	'double meaning'
	taysīr	'simplification'		
(d)	*awlād*	'children'	*awṭān*	'countries'

2.2.2. Glide as C_2

Diphthongs in medial position are retained in words with a geminate glide, which is consistent with Reinhardt (1894, 8), e.g., *jaww* 'weather', *ḥayy* 'neighbourhood', *ṣawwar* 'he photographed', *dawwar* 'he searched', *taww* 'now'.

Monosyllabic words that otherwise end in *-wC* or *-yC* in this position may undergo monophthongisation.

Table 2.2: Monosyllabic nouns where the diphthong is subject to monophthongisation in informant speech

Diphthong	Monophthong	Gloss
fawq	*fōq*	up, above
kayf	*kēf*	how
bayt	*bēt*	house
šayb	*šēb*	old man
zayn	*zēn*	good, well
ġayr	*ġēr*	different
layl	*lēl*	night

ayn	*ēn*	where?
sayl	*sēl*	flood
zawg	*zōg*	husband
sayf	*sēf*	sword

However, there are exceptions to this rule. The following monosyllabic nouns retain their original diphthong: *zayt* 'oil', *ṭayr* 'bird', *ṣawt* 'voice'. The noun *ʿayš* 'rice' is realised as *ʿīš* in al-ʿAwābī by YS and AS, regardless of their level of education. The case of *šay* 'thing' is also peculiar: it is realised variously as [šay], [šey]—with clear occurrence of *imāla*—and as the monophthongised form [šī].

Diphthongs in loanwords are retained when in final position, e.g., *bāw* 'wood', but can be subject to monophthongisation in other cases. The word *layt* 'light' is often monophthongised as *lēt* in the speech of YS from al-ʿAwābī—regardless of their level of education—and it is always monophthongised in the plural form, i.e., *lētāt*.

In Table 2.3, an account of the distribution of the occurrence of both *imāla* in the realisation of the word شيء 'thing' and monophthongisation in the word لايت 'light' is given.

Table 2.3: Occurrence of *imāla* and monophthongisation in informant speech

شيء **'thing'**	لايت **'light'**	**Speaker**
šey	*leyt*	1, 2, 10, 11
šey	*lēt*	3, 7,12, 15
šay	*layt*	4, 8, 13, 14
šī	*lēt*	5, 6, 9

A few conclusions can be drawn from the data presented in this table. First, *imāla* occurs in the speech of all al-ʿAwābī informants, regardless of their age or level of education. Second, in the instances of YS with a high level of education (i.e., university), we can see that شيء is monophthongised and raised to [šī]. Third, *imāla* occurs in the speech of AS and YS from Wādī Banī Kharūṣ, but not in that of the OS. Finally, with regards to the monophthongisation of the word لايت, we can see that speakers who have a strong occurrence of *imāla* in their speech often monophthongise /layt/ to /lēt/ or raise /a/ to /e/, as in [leyt]. The examples reported above also show that the raising is specifically perceptible in the speech of two illiterate AS (i.e., speakers 1 and 2)—from Wādī Banī Kharūṣ and al-ʿAwābī, respectively—as well as in that of one from al-ʿAwābī with a medium level of education (i.e., speaker 10). In all other cases, لايت is monophthongised in the speech of AS and YS in both areas under investigation.

2.2.3. Medial Glide in Monosyllabic Words

Diphthongs are retained in word-final syllables, e.g., *māy* 'water', *šāy* 'tea', *bāw* 'wood'.

2.2.4. Dual Endings

The dual ending *-ayn* always undergoes monophthongisation to *-īn*, e.g., مرتين *martīn* 'twice',[13] سنتين *santīn* 'two years'.

2.3. Assimilation

Assimilation is a widespread process in Arabic dialects and in CA. It happens with the definite article *al-*, which is always as-

[13] This example also shows a degemination phenomenon.

similated when followed by a coronal consonant (a consonant produced with the tip or blade of the tongue), i.e., ت, ث, د, ذ, ر, ز, س, ش, ص, ض, ط, ظ, ل, and ن.

In the primary data, t-prefixes of the non-past form of the verb and -t-suffixes of the past form show assimilation with the consonants /t/, /d/, and /ḍ/, e.g., *ḍḍann* 'she thinks' < *tḍann*; *tmarraḍḍ* 'I was ill' < *tmarraḍt*.

2.4. Metathesis

Metathesis refers to the rearranging or the switching of two contiguous segments within a word.

Reinhardt (1894, 14) dedicates a paragraph to this phenomenon with a few examples which the consultants did not recognise. Other examples in the data are *ḫumra* < *ḫurma* 'a type of date' and *karhabā* < *kahrabā* 'electricity'.

2.5. *Ghawa* Syndrome

The *Ghawa* Syndrome takes its name from the Arabic word for coffee *qahwa* (in some dialects pronounced *gahwa*) and refers to the rearranging of the tonic syllable CaG to CGa, where G stands for 'guttural', e.g., CA *qahwa* 'coffee' is realised as *ghawa* in Bedouin dialects of Najd; in certain cases, a stressed vowel is inserted after a velar or a pharyngeal consonant, i.e., CaGáC, resulting in forms like *qaháwa/gaháwa*. In some dialects of Oman this phenomenon is still productive (Holes 2008, 481), but it does not seem to occur in the primary data.

3.0. Syllable Inventory

A syllable is "a unit of sound composed of a central peak of sonority (usually a vowel), and the consonant that cluster around this central peak."[14] In the majority of Arabic varieties, syllables always start with a consonant (or in some cases two) followed by a long or a short vowel, and usually only a certain combination of syllables is allowed.

The syllable inventory of the al-ʿAwābī district vernacular consists of three main syllable types that can occur in any position of the word (CV, CVV, and CVC) and two syllable types which appear in word-final position only (CVVC and CVCC). In addition to these, the vernacular spoken by the informants presents four forms that are outcomes of vowel elision or foreign loan. For purposes of stress assignment, syllables can be divided according to their weight in terms of light, heavy, and superheavy.[15] The following table shows syllable structure based on stress and weight, according to the classification made by Watson (2002, 56–61).

---

[14] Online access at https://glossary.sil.org/term/syllable.

[15] A light syllable is formed by a consonant and a short vowel, i.e., CV, or, in some instances, by two consonants and a short vowel, i.e., CCV; a heavy syllable is usually formed by a consonant and a long vowel, i.e., CVV, or a branching rime, i.e., CVC; finally, a superheavy syllable is formed by either a consonant followed by a long vowel and a coda, i.e., CVVC, or an onset followed by a coda consisting of two or more consonants, i.e., CVCC.

Table 2.4: Syllable inventory of the al-ʿAwābī district vernacular

Syllable	Weight	Monosyllabic	Polysyllabic	CV-template
CV	light	*fa* 'so'	*qawaya* 'iron'	CV-CV-CV
CVV	heavy	*mū* 'what'	*farāša* 'butterfly'	CV-CVV-CV
CVC	heavy	*ḫit* 'sister' *sum* 'name'	*gamal* 'camel' *zabda* 'butter'	CV-CVC CVC-CV
CVVC	superheavy	*zēn* 'good'	*fingān* 'coffee cup'	CVC-CVVC
CVCC/ CVVCC	superheavy	*kidf* 'shoulder' *ḫall* 'vinegar'	*rūḥ-t* 'I went'	
CCV	light		*štaġal-t* 'I worked'	CCV-CVCC
CCVC/V	heavy	*mrā* 'woman' *ṣdur* 'chest'	*mgummaʿ* 'broom' *mḥaṭṭa* 'station'	CCV-CCVC
CCVV	heavy		*drīwal* 'driver'	CCVV-CVC
CCVVC	superheavy	*glās* 'glass'		

According to the Sonority Sequencing Principle,[16] a word must contain a sonority peak (often a vowel), preceded and/or followed by a sequence of segments (consonants) with progressively decreasing sonority values towards the word edge: the sonority hierarchy goes from vowels (4) to liquids (3), to nasals (2), and to obstruents (1). As Table 2.4 shows, the informants' speech does not always follow this principle: words like *gbin* 'cheese' and *bẓār* 'spices' begin with clusters of obstruent consonants. The phenomenon is the result of a process of syncope of the short vowel in the first syllable or of the deletion of initial *hamza*, e.g., *mrā* < امرأة).

4.0. CCC Cluster

In the primary data, CCC clusters may occur in word-medial position, as a result of suffixation or doubled verbs, even though

[16] The Sonority Sequencing Principle is a phonotactic principle that outlines the structure of a syllable in terms of sonority.

in some instances the speaker inserts an epenthetic vowel, [i] or [a], e.g., *šuft(i)-he* 'I/you (2MSG) saw her'. The CCC cluster can also occur in monosyllabic words with suffixed pronouns, e.g., *ṣdr-o* 'his chest'. This type of cluster can also result from the adaption of loanwords to the Arabic pattern, e.g., *hanqrī* 'rich' (< Hindi).

5.0. Stress

Reinhardt (1894, 15–18) presents a long section on stress in the Banū Kharūṣī dialect. He states that stress follows different rules when compared to other dialects in the Peninsula.[17]

In the primary data, the following stress rules apply:

(a) Stress a final superheavy syllable CVCC, CCVVC, and CVVC, if present, e.g., *krīm* 'kind', *katábt* 'I wrote', *šrúbt* 'I drank'.

(b) If no superheavy syllable is present, stress the rightmost non-final heavy syllable CVV or CVC, e.g., *safāra* 'embassy', *zábda* 'cotton'.

---

[17] Reinhardt (1894, 15) writes:

> Der Accent weicht, was die durch denselben bedingten Lautverschiebungen im Worte betrift, im Oman-Dialekt von den übrigen bekannten arabischen Dialekten vielfach ab, giebt demselben theilweise sein charakteristisches Gepräge und beeinflusst das Verständniss der Sprache so, dass nicht omanische Araber Schwierigkeit haben, einem gewohnlichen Oman-Mann genau in seiner Rede zu folgen.

(c) In all other cases, stress the leftmost light syllable CV, e.g., *báqara* 'cow'.

It is never possible to stress farther left than the antepenultimate syllable, e.g., *madrásat-he* 'her school'.

Reinhardt (1894, 16) reports that stress falls on the penultimate syllable also when the word has the negative clitic *-ši*, the interrogative clitic *-i*, or the possessive or object pronouns are suffixed. In the primary data, his statement has been confirmed with respect to suffixed pronouns only, whereas the negative and the interrogative clitic did not occur in informant speech, save one exception (see below, ch. 4, §3.1, for further details).

Metrical stress theory examines two types of metrical feet, namely the iamb and the trochee:[18] "the maximal and canonical iamb consists of a light syllable followed by a heavy syllable" (Watson 2011, 7), whereas a trochee consists of a long syllable which carries the stress followed by a short unstressed one. This type of metrical analysis based on iambs and trochees implies two different types of stress, namely iambic stress and trochaic stress. Trochaic stress is when in a CVCVC pattern the first syllable is stressed, i.e.,ˈCV-CVC, whereas iambic stress occurs in a CVCVC pattern, when the last syllable is stressed, i.e., CV-ˈCVC.

---

[18] The foot is the basic unit in metrical theory and usually contains one stressed syllable and at least one unstressed syllable. On metrical theory applied to Arabic dialects, see the works of Hayes (1995) and Watson (2011b).

The Omani varieties for which we have documentation tend to exhibit iambic stress.[19] In Dhofari Arabic, for example, a word like *gebel* undergoes final vowel lengthening and first vowel deletion, i.e., *gbāl,* because of iambic stress (Davey 2016, 64). A similar tendency to syncope is shown in Muscat Arabic, where all unstressed short vowels in open syllables can undergo reduction or deletion (Glover 1988, 61).

Analysis of the primary data collected shows that in CVCVC patterns there is a tendency for the first light syllable CV to carry stress, e.g., *ˈgamal* 'camel', *ˈgebel* 'mountain'. The behaviour of words like *ˈgamal* and *ˈgebel* shows that -CVC syllables in final position count as light and, therefore, do not attract stress. This phenomenon is also found in other Arabic dialects, e.g., Cairene and Sanʿani (McCarthy 1979; Watson 2002; 2011b) and it is due to extrametricality rules. Abu-Mansour (1992, 52) describes this phenomenon for Makkan Arabic, where the last consonant of the pattern CVCVC does not count in assignment of word stress. Cf. Hayse (1995, 56): "An extrametricality rule designates a particular prosodic constituent as

---

[19] In Dhofari Arabic, forms with a final syllable -CVC or -CCVC, show a strong tendency to lengthen the short vowel, thereby creating superheavy -CVVC or -CCVVC that always attract the stress (Davey 2016, 63). In addition to this, Glover (1988, 71) states that

> in OA [Omani Arabic]... there is a tendency for stress to move to the end of the word, so that a two-syllable word like /ráṭab/ 'fresh date', for example, is also commonly pronounced /ráṭáb/, with stress on both syllables, or /raṭáb/, which is then subject to reduction and may become /răṭáb/, and in faster speech /rṭáb/.

invisible for purposes of rule application: the rules analyse the form as if the extrametrical entity were not there." This statement explains why a CVC syllable in final-word position is light, but heavy in non-final position: C_2 is extrametrical and, therefore, ignored for stress assignment.[20]

The vernacular under investigation, in contrast to the dialects described by Glover (1988) and Davey (2016), shows a strong tendency to trochaic stress and extrametricality, placing it closer to the Arabic dialects of Egypt or North Africa, for example.

The extrametricality rule also explains why in the primary data syncope is not of common occurrence, whereas it is in Glover's and Davey's data: since syncope affects only unstressed short vowels, if the initial syllable is stressed, the vowel cannot be deleted. It remains to investigate further if this is the case in other dialectal varieties spoken in northern Oman.

---

[20] There are some restrictions to the application of extrametricality rules: (a) Constituency indicates that only constituents can be marked as extrametrical; (b) Peripherality states that in order for these constituents to be extrametrical, they need to be at the edge of the domain (left or right); (c) Edge Markedness indicates that "the unmarked edge for extrametricality is the right edge"; (d) Nonexhaustivity states that extrametricality is not applied, if it would make the whole domain extrametrical (Hayes 1995, 57–58).

CHAPTER 3: MORPHOLOGY

This chapter is devoted to the description of al-ʿAwābī district vernacular morphology. It is divided into sections on nominal morphology (§1.0) and verbal morphology (§2.0). This division facilitates comparison with Reinhardt's material and enables the reader to be guided through any linguistic changes that have occurred over time.

Reinhardt (1894) devotes the second part of his work to the analysis of both nominal and verbal morphology in the Banū Kharūṣī dialect. He starts by analysing the pronouns, the noun—in both its basic and derived forms—definiteness, adjectives, gender and number, the numerals, prepositions, and adverbs. A concluding section in Reinhardt's morphological description reports a small number of foreign loanwords he found in the speech of his informants.

In order to gain a clearer picture of the diachronic changes that have occurred over time, the organisation of this chapter is based, on the one hand, on the structure given by Reinhardt in his work and, on the other hand, on the structure found in other works that analyse the morphological structure of Arabic dialects (e.g., Davey 2016). Moreover, to stay true to the aim of comparison with Reinhardt's material, the following sections present examples from the primary data collected during fieldwork along with Reinhardt's annotations, which are signposted whenever applicable. The primary data provided in this chapter were collected through both elicitation—particularly for the account of plural formations—and spontaneous speech. In the

 https://doi.org/10.11647/OBP.0298.03

case of both nominal and verbal morphology, primary data provide sufficient similarities with Reinhardt's material.

In line with other descriptions and studies on Arabic dialects, this chapter divides the study of Banū Kharūṣī morphology into two parts, namely nominal and verbal. Nominal morphology is further subdivided into nine sections: the basic noun patterns (§1.1); pronouns (§1.2); verbal nouns (§1.3); gender and number (§1.4 and §1.5, respectively); definiteness and indefiniteness (§1.6); noun modifiers, that is the analysis of forms, e.g., adjectives, numerals, derived from nouns (§1.7); adverbs and quantifiers (§1.8); and finally, prepositions (§1.9).

The second part on verbal morphology includes the conjugations of strong (§2.1), hamzated (§2.2), weak (§2.3), and quadriliteral (§2.5) verbs. Derived verbs are analysed in §2.6, the future tense and imperative mood in §2.7 and §2.9 respectively, and the conjugation and behaviour of *kān* 'be' as a copula in §2.8. The active and passive participle are discussed in this chapter only with regard to their morphology, whereas an analysis of their uses and functions in the dialect is given in ch. 4 on syntax.

1.0. Nominal Morphology

1.1. Nouns

This category includes substantives, analysed in their basic and derived patterns.

There are a few nouns consisting of only two radicals, such as *sum* 'name', *bin* 'son', *ḏin* 'ear', *ṯum* 'mouth', *ḫit* 'sister', *sene* 'year'.[1]

Different CV syllable patterns are subject to various combinations to form nouns. Reinhardt's (1894, 39–40) list of basic noun patterns for the Banū Kharūṣī dialect is as follows:

- Nouns of minimal form: CCVC; CVCC; CVCVC.
- Stems[2] extended by:
  - lengthening the first vowel, i.e., CVVCVC;
  - lengthening the second vowel, i.e., CVCVVC;
  - doubling the second radical, i.e., CVCCVC;
  - doubling the second radical and lengthening the second vowel, i.e., CVCCVVC;
  - lengthening the first and the second vowel, i.e., CVVCVVC.

In addition to these, nouns can be formed:

- by extending the stem with prefixes:
  - with *a*, e.g., أَفْعَل, أَفْعال;
  - with *m*:

    to form names of place, time and instrument;
    to form the AP of derived forms of the verb, and the PP;

[1] Some of these are, however, the result of the deletion of initial or final *hamza*.

[2] Stem is intended here as the minimal unit of an Arabic word, also known as "root", to which affixes and suffixes can be added, or semivowels inserted.

to form verbal nouns of the III derived form.
- with *t*, to form verbal nouns of the II and V derived forms;
- with *n* or *st*, to form verbal nouns of the VII, VIII, and X derived forms;

- by extending the stem with suffixes:
  - with *ān*, e.g., فِعْلان, فُعْلان, فَعْلان;
  - with *e*, e.g., فعْلة;[3]
  - with the relative ending *i*, e.g., *āni*.

These patterns have been confirmed by the recent investigation conducted in the district of al-ʿAwābī, although a few more could be added.

1.2.1. Basic Noun Patterns

The following list displays the basic noun patterns found in the primary data, with at least one example for each type. These patterns consist of different combinations of CV syllables, as shown in the previous sub-section, to form lexemes. Most of the following syllabic combinations can also be found in Reinhardt (1894, 38–55). Consequently, some of the lexical items listed are similar: in these cases, the gloss [R. and PAGE NUMBER] accompanies the item in question. When Reinhardt's realisation appears different from the realisation of the lexeme in the primary data, his transcription is reported next to the page number.

---

[3] As mentioned above, ch. 2, §1.1, the *tā marbūṭa* is sometimes realised as [e] in this vernacular, and is henceforth transcribed in this way.

1. CVVC:[4] *rās* 'head, leader', *rīḥ* 'hernia', *ṯōr* 'bull', *sēl* 'flood'

2. CCVC:[5] *rgil* 'foot', *gbin* 'cheese' [R.41], *ṣġur* 'smallness', -*ḍhur* 'noon' [R.41]

3. CCVVC(V): *bzār* 'spices', *ḥmūḍa* 'heartburn'.

4. CVCC: *ḫall* 'vinegar', *nimr* 'tiger', *ḫubz* 'bread' [R.42], *durg* 'drawer'

5. CVCVC: *tabaġ* 'tobacco', *ʿadis* 'lentils', *qador* 'earthenware pot' [R.43]

6. CVVCVC: *ḫātim* 'finger ring' [R.43, *ḫātum*], *bākur* 'morning' [R.43], *zīlaq* 'noise' [R.44, *zēlaq*], *sīkil* 'bicycle', *mōtar* 'vintage car', *fōfil* 'nutmeg' [R.44, *fōfel*]

7. CVCVVC: *ʿaqāb* 'eagle', *ʿarīš* 'hut'[6], *ʿagūz* 'old woman', *gitār* 'guitar', *zibīb* 'raisins' [R.45, *zbīb*], *remōt* 'remote control', *ruṣāṣ* 'graphite'

8. CVCCVC: *farraḥ* 'popcorn', *ṯaʿlib* 'fox', *ḥigra* 'room', *gilgil* 'anklet' [R.54, 'bell'], *luġġa* 'gecko', *bulbul* 'nightingale' [R.54]

9. CVCCVVC: *šammān* 'honey melon', *sekkīn* 'knife' [R.49], *šangūb* 'grasshopper', *findāl* 'sweet potato' [R.55], *rummān* 'pomegranate' [R.48], *duktūr* 'doctor'

10. CVVCVVC: *sāmām* 'domestic appliances' [R.49], *tābūt* 'coffin' [R.49], *tītūn* 'newborn', *qūʿqūʿ* 'upside down' [R.55]

---

[4] This template can result from monophtongisation or lengthening of medial *hamza*.

[5] This template can result from syncope.

[6] 'Open hut made of palm-tree branches', found in Wādī Banī Kharūṣ.

1.2.2. Derived Noun Patterns

The primary data, in line with general Arabic language characteristics, show numerous nouns in derived patterns, in addition to basic forms. Some of these nouns are created from the basic form by addition of a prefix, e.g., *a-*, *mV-*, or suffix, e.g., *-ān*, *-ī*, *-āni*, or by extension of the basic stem via quantative changes to root consonants and/or vowels.

Stem Extended by Prefixes

The prefix *a-* is used in the primary data to form the comparative form of some adjectives, e.g., *awsaʿ* 'further', broken plurals, e.g., *feleg/aflāg* irrigation channel, stream', and the derived verbal form IV.

The prefix *mV-* assumes different patterns based on the meaning. The first set of examples from the primary data shows nouns following the maCCVC pattern, where the internal vowel is either /a/ or /i/. The vowel of the prefix can also be elided in some nouns for euphonic reasons, e.g., *mḥaṭṭa* 'station'. Lexical items that follow these patterns indicate names of places.

Table 3.1: Names of places, maCCVC pattern

maCCVC	**Example**
maCCaC	*maḫrag* 'exit' [R.49, *maḫreg*]
	maktab 'office'
	maṭbaḫ 'kitchen'
	maqbara 'cemetary' [R.50, *mqubra*]
	madrase 'school' [R.50, *mderse*]
maCCiC	*masgid* 'mosque'[7] [R.50, *misgid*]

The second set of examples from the primary data shows lexical items following the miCCVVC pattern, indicating names of instruments.

Table 3.2: Names of instruments, miCCVVC pattern

m(V)CCVVC	**Example**
miCCāC	*miftāḥ* 'key'
	minfāḫ 'fan, blower' [R.50]

Research findings also showed as names of instruments *mgummaʿ* 'broom', *mqamša* 'spoon', and *mwās* 'razor', which follow none of the patterns above and where the short vowel of the prefix is always elided.

Passive participles follow two main *m*-prefixed patterns in the data: maCCūC, e.g., *masmūḥ* 'allowed', *magnūn* 'crazy', *maʿrūf* 'known', *maḍbūṭ* 'excellent', valid for the first form of the verb, and a pattern prefixed by *mu-*, whose structure varies based on the derived form of the verb. The active participle, conversely, shows an *m*-prefixed pattern only in the derived forms.

[7] Also realised as [misgid], if the *imāla* occurs.

Stem Extended by Doubling of Second Consonant and Lengthening of the Second Vowel

Names of professions belong to this category and show the pattern CVCCVVC, e.g., *ḥaddād* 'blacksmith', *qaṣṣāb* 'butcher', *ḥaṭṭāb* 'carpenter', *ṭabbāḫ* 'cook'.[8]

Stem Extended by Suffixes

The suffix *-ān* is added to the basic stem to form both nouns and adjectives. In the primary data there are only a few examples of nouns and adjectives following this pattern.

Table 3.3: Suffix *-ān*

Nouns	Adjectives
qurān 'Quran' (< *qarā* 'read') [R.52, *qurʾān*]	*taʿabān* 'tired' (< *taʿab* 'become weak and thin')
	gūʿān 'hungry' (< *gawwaʿ* 'famish')

The suffix *-ī* (*-wi*, *-āwi*) and the relative ending *-āni* are used to indicate affiliation:

- countries, e.g., *miṣrī* 'Egyptian', *hindī* 'Indian', *pakistanī* 'Pakistani', etc.;
- Arab tribes, e.g., *Ḫarūṣī*, *ʿAbrī*, etc.;
- cities, e.g., *Nezāwi* 'from Nizwa', *Rustāqī* 'from Rustaq', etc.;
- generic, e.g., *ḥaḍrī* 'urban residents', *bedwī* 'Bedouin', *ibāḍī* 'Ibadi', etc.

[8] Cf. the form *faʿʿāl* in Reinhardt (1894, 48).

1.2. Pronouns

1.2.1. Personal

Personal pronouns can be divided into two main groups, i.e., independent forms and suffixed forms. In the primary data, they are as shown in Table 3.4; different forms reported by Reinhardt (1894, 21) are given in brackets.

Table 3.4: Personal pronouns

	Independent Pronouns	**Suffixed Pronouns**
1SG	*anā* ~ *ane* (R. *ene*)	*-nī* ~ *-ni*
2MSG	*nte*	*-ik*
2FSG	*ntī*	*-iš*
3MSG	*hūwa* (R. *hūwe, hūe*)	*-o/-hu*[9]
3FSG	*hīya* (R. *hīye*)	*-ha/-he*[10]
1PL	*naḥna/iḥna* (R. *ḥne*)	*-nā*
2MPL	*ntū*	*-kum*
2FPL	*nten*	*-kin/-kan*
3MPL	*hum/hma*	*-hum*
3FPL	*hin/hna*	*-hin*

(1) *anā* *kunt* *sağīra*

PRON.1SG was.1SG small.FSG

'I was young.' [S14]

[9] The realisation of the 3MSG suffix pronoun differs according to the phonological environment (as explained in ch. 2, §2.0).

[10] The different realisation of the 3FSG pronoun depends on the rules of *imāla* (see ch. 2, §2.1).

(2) *hūwa rega*ʿ *min el-baḥrein*

PRON.MSG came_back.3MSG from DEF-Bahrain

'He came back from Bahrain.' [S2]

(3) *gilsit* *ʿind-o* *arba*ʿ *sanuwāt*

stayed.3FSG around-PRON.3MSG four.M year.FPL

'She stayed with him for four years.' [S1]

1.2.2. Demonstratives

Demonstrative pronouns have distinct forms based on deixis, i.e., the proximity or distance of the object they refer to. In the data, they also distinguish for gender and number, and exhibit shorter or longer forms with no difference in use.[11]

Table 3.5: Demonstrative pronouns

	MSG	FSG	MPL	FPL
Proximal	*(ha)ḏā* ~ *hawā* (R. *hāḏe*)	*(ha)ḏī*	*(ha)ḏēlā* (R. *hāḏyle*, *hāḏēle*, *hāḏelāhum*)	*(ha)ḏēlā* (R. *hāḏylāhin*)
Distal	*(ha)ḏāk*	*(ha)ḏīk*	*(ha)ḏālēk* (R. *hāḏylāk*)	*haḏālēk* (R. *haḏylākhin*)

As Table 3.5 shows, Reinhardt's (1894, 31) forms differ from the primary data mainly in the plural, both masculine and feminine. I have checked them with the participants to this study and they have found no confirmation. Interestingly, though, it seems that the masculine and feminine plural forms in the primary data have lost the gender distinction preserved, instead, in

[11] Very similar forms are found elsewhere in Oman (cf. Davey 2016) and in the Baḥarna dialect described by Holes (2016).

Reinhardt's. Given the incontrovertible fact that Omani dialects are known for retaining gender distinction in pronouns—as mentioned in ch.1, §4.0—we may presume that the gender neutralisation here is the result of this dialect's exposure to neighbouring varieties where the gender distinction has already been neutralised, e.g., GA. Here follow some examples from the primary data on the use of the demonstrative pronoun.

(4) *haḏā* *l-fingān*
DEM.PROX.MSG DEF-coffee_cup.MSG
'this coffee cup' [S9]

(5) *haḏī* *l-ḥurma* *mā* *gīt*
DEM.PROX.FSG DEF-woman.FSG NEG arrive.3FSG
'This woman didn't arrive.' [S1]

(6) *haḏālēk* *seččarān*
DEM.DIST.MPL drunkard.MPL
'Those are drunkards.' [S8]

(7) *ḏāk* *il-yōm*
DEM.DIST.MSG DEF-day.MSG
'that day' [S7]

(8) *haḏēlā* *l-banāt*
DEM.PROX.FPL DEF-girl.FPL
'these girls' [S5]

1.2.3. Possessives

Possession in the vernacular under investigation can be expressed in different ways: with a synthetic genitive construction (i.e., *ʾiḍāfa*), using possessive suffixes, e.g., *zōg-i* 'my husband', or by means of a genitive marker, i.e., *māl*. A complete description of how possession is expressed in the vernacular under investigation is given in ch. 4, §1.1.2. Here, a list of the suffixed possessive pronouns used by my informants is presented, reporting Reinhardt's counterparts (1894, 22) in brackets when different.

Table 3.6: Possessive suffixes

Pronoun	Masculine	Feminine
1SG	*-ī* ~ *-i* (*-yī* after vowel)	*-ī* ~ *-i* (*-yī* after vowel)
2SG	*-ik* (R. *-ak*)	*-iš*
3PL	*-o/-hu*	*-ha/-he*
1PL	*-nā* (R. *-ne*) ~ *-na*	*-nā* (R. *-ne*) ~ *-na*
2PL	*-kum*	*-kin/-kan* (R. *-ken*)
3PL	*-hum*	*-hin*

In the primary data, monosyllabic words show syncope when the possessive pronoun is suffixed, e.g., *ẖt-ī* 'my sister' < *ẖit* 'sister'; *sm-ī* 'my name' < *sum* 'name'. The monosyllabic word *ab* 'father' shows a compensatory long /ū/ when a possessive pronoun is suffixed, e.g., *abū-hum* 'their (MPL) father'.

The *-iš* suffix for the second person feminine singular is a distinctive feature of peninsular Arabic dialects and it is widespread throughout the country.[12]

[12] The phenomenon of change **k* > *š* is known in the literature as *šinšinna* (cf. Holes 2018) and originally refers to the reflex /š/ of the 2FSG pronoun /k/ found in Yemeni dialects. Today, this is a "typical" southern feature (Holes 2018, 15). Modern Arabic dialects that show this feature include those spoken in northern Yemen and parts of Saudi Arabia, Bahrain, Qatar, and the UAE.

(9) *kēf* *ʿammūt-iš?*
how aunt-PRON.2FSG
'How is your aunt?' [S7]

(10) *regaʿ* *maʿa* *bint-o*
came_back.3MSG with girl.FSG-PRON.3MSG
'He came back with his daughter' [S4]

Some remarks on the possessive suffixes:

- When the possessive is suffixed to nouns ending with a vowel, the latter tends to lengthen, e.g., *šifā-k* 'your (MSG) recovery' < *šife* 'recovery'.
- The feminine ending ة (/a/ or /e/) becomes /t/ when a possessive is suffixed, e.g., *ġurfat-i* 'my room' < *ġurfe*, and the same happens with feminine nouns ending in *-āwe*, e.g., *benāwit-he* 'her stepdaughter' < *benāwe* 'stepdaughter'.
- The feminine noun endings *-we* or *-ye* become *-ūt* and *-īt*, respectively, e.g., *bedūtī* 'my beginning' < *bedwe* 'beginning', *mešīt-ne* 'our walk' < *mešye* 'walk'.

1.2.4. Indefinites

Indefinite pronouns are used to refer to non-specific beings, objects, or places. The table below shows the indefinite pronouns found in the primary data.

Table 3.7: Indefinite pronouns

'someone / anyone'	*ḥad*
'something / anything'	*šey* ~ *šī*
'somewhere'	*makān*
'anywhere'	*ēyy makān*
'sometime'	*marra*
'no one'	*mā ḥad* ~ *ḥadši*

Reinhardt (1894, 28–30) reports a full list of indefinite pronouns that includes those listed above, while also adding a few more. Among these, he documents: the formula *kemmīn wāḥi min* followed by a plural noun for 'some', which does not occur in the primary data, *baʿaḍ* + plural noun being used instead; the indefinite *ḥadši* for 'no one, anyone', still rarely used and further discussed in ch. 4, §3.1; and the noun *flān* (M)/*flāne* (F) for 'someone specific', used, according to Reinhardt (1894, 29), "wenn der Betreffende bekannt ist" [= 'if the person is known'], which is not found in the speech of my informants, but frequently occurs in Reinhardt's texts.

Here are some examples from the primary data on the use of the indefinite pronouns.

(11) *mā ḥad šūf-kum*

NEG person saw.3MSG-PRON.2MPL

'No one saw you.' [S11]

(12) *tʿaqq il-bint ēyy makān wa*

throw.3FSG DEF-girl.FSG any place.MSG CONJ

maʿ ēyy ḥad w-trūḥ

with any person CONJ-go.3FSG

'She leaves the daughter anywhere and with anyone and then goes.' [S1]

1.2.5. Interrogatives

Interrogative pronouns in the speech of my informants are given in Table 3.8.

Table 3.8: Interrogative pronouns

'Why?'	*amū/lēš*
'What?'	*mū*[13]
'When?'	*matā*
'Where?'	*ēn* ~ *wēn* ~ *hēn*
'Who?'	*min/bū*[14]
'How?'	*kē* ~ *kēf*
'How many?'	*kam*

The form *amū* for 'why?' is mainly used by OS and it is interesting to note that Reinhardt (1894, 32) documents the form *ḥamhū* for 'why?', as well as *ʿolām* and *māl* (as in *mā* + *l-*). None of these is confirmed by the primary data. The form *lēš* (also found in Dhofar, cf. Davey 2016, 108) is instead used by YS and AS.

1.2.6. Reflexives

This class of pronouns is formed from the word *nafs* 'soul', which is used to mean 'self' when a pronoun is suffixed, e.g., *nafs-o* 'himself', *nafs-i* 'myself'. It is also used in constructions with the word *šay* 'thing' to mean 'the same thing', e.g., *nafs*^{e}*-šay*.

[13] According to Reinhardt (1894, 282), this form is originated from the MSA interrogative pronoun *mā* and the 3MSG *-hu*.

[14] Some speakers use the relative pronoun *bū* as a general relativiser also in questions (see ch. 4, §1.1.3).

Alongside this form, in the primary data the numeral 'one', i.e., *wāḥid,* followed by the possessive suffix also appears to indicate 'alone', e.g., *wāḥd-ha* 'by herself', *wāḥd-i* 'by myself', etc.

(13) *wāḥd-ik* *fī* *hadā* *l-makān*
one-PRON.2MSG in DEM.PROX.MSG DEF-place.MSG
'All by yourself in this place' [S7]

1.3. Verbal Nouns

In the primary data, the verbal nouns of derived verb forms are predictable, in line with those in other forms of Arabic more generally: they follow a pattern specific for each form. Basic verb forms are, conversely, unpredictable. Reinhardt (1894) presents no specific section on verbal nouns in his work, but rather reports 'infinitiva' forms for each syllable combination he lists. The primary data show two main syllabic patterns for verbal nouns:

- CVCC: *terk* 'leaving' [R.41], *ḍarb* 'knocking', *ḥilf* 'oath', *ṭilbe* 'petition' [R.42], *šurb* 'drink, drinking', *šuġl* 'job' [R.42]
- CVCVC: *selef* 'borrowing', *ḫagel* 'blushing' [R.43], *ʿafid* 'jump' [R.43], *rakuḍ* 'running', *ketub* 'writing' [R.43]

1.4. Gender

As happens in other Arabic dialects, nouns have either marked gender, i.e., a suffix indicating the gender, or unmarked gender, i.e., inherent gender. Broadly speaking, masculine nouns are unmarked, whereas feminine nouns can be marked or unmarked. The gender of unmarked inanimate nouns can be detected only via agreement.

Unmarked feminine gender has not been studied thoroughly. Indeed, very few works can be found on this topic.[15] Reinhardt (1894, 55–56) reports the following list of inherent feminine nouns, which are confirmed by the primary data:

- proper nouns relating to females, e.g., *Mōze, Rabʿa, Šiẖẖa, Manal, Iẖlāṣ,* etc.;
- nouns denoting feminine entities or adjectives denoting female-related activities, e.g., *umm* 'mother', *ẖit* 'sister', *ʿarūs* 'bride', *sennūr* 'female cat', *ʿagūz* 'old woman', *ḥāmil* 'pregnant';
- plants, e.g., *nargīl* 'coconut palm',[16] *naẖal* 'date palm';
- countries and cities, e.g., *Miṣr* 'Egypt', *ʿUmān* 'Oman', *Mombei* 'Bombai', etc.;
- paired body parts, e.g., *yid* 'hand', *rgil* 'foot', *ʿēn* 'eye', *ḏin* 'ear', *ṣboʿ* 'finger'.[17]

Table 3.9 gives unmarked feminine nouns from elicited primary data.

---

[15] One of the very few is the article by Prochazka (2004).

[16] However, in the primary data *nargīl* 'coconut' is masculine. The same phenomenon can also be found in other languages. In Italian, for example, it is the other way around: the feminine is used to indicate the fruit, e.g., *la mela* 'the apple' and the masculine to indicate the tree, e.g., *il melo* 'the apple tree'.

[17] The case of *ṣboʿ* is interesting. According to Prochazka (2004, 240), it is included in this category, because in a human body there are two-times-five fingers, so a finger is considered a paired entity.

Table 3.9: Unmarked feminine nouns

Arabic	English	Arabic	English
arḍ	'ground, Earth'	*ṭarīq*	'road, street'
sekkīn	'knife'	*ṭawi*	'well'
korš	'stomach'	*ḫanger*	'dagger'
kubd	'liver'	*rūḥ*	'ghost'
bākor	'tomorrow'	*nefs*	'soul'
šams	'sun'	*ʿaqrab*	'scorpion'
nār	'fire'	*rīḥ*	'wind'
faʿā	'snake'	*qador*	'earthenware pot'

These nouns correspond to the ones reported by Reinhardt (1894, 56–57), with minor exceptions: e.g., *rumḥ* 'spear' and *legil* 'pond', which did not occur in the primary data.

It is interesting to note that, although the term for 'wind' is feminine, the names of the specific winds are usually masculine: *šemāl* 'east wind', *ġarbī* 'west wind', *kōs* 'south wind', *ezyēb* 'north wind' (cf. Reinhardt 1894, 57).

Moreover, not all paired parts of the body are feminine. Exceptions in the primary data are *marṣaġ* 'wrist', *zend* 'forearm', *maġḍan* 'knee joint', *ṣīm* 'leg', *kidf* 'shoulder', *kōʿ* 'elbow', *ġallūg* 'lobe', *gumʿ* 'fist', *ʿarš* 'back/top of the hand'. Also masculine are *ḫinṣor* 'little finger', *bhīm* 'thumb', *binṣor* 'ring finger', *ferkūn* 'knuckle'. Other marked feminine body parts are *loḫme* 'calf', *msebbḥa* or *sebbābe* 'middle finger' and *mōḫra* 'nose'. This list of nouns corresponds to that reported by Reinhardt (1894, 56), except for: *feskūl*, which, according to the informants, does not indicate the biological 'middle finger', but rather the 'middle finger' in a derogatory sense; *ġinz l fuqra* 'gluteus', which the informants did not recognise; and *faqš rrukaʿa* 'kneecap', for which the informants use the more general *rukbe* 'knee'.[18]

Feminine nouns excluded from any of the previous categories show a suffix *-a*—often pronounced [e]—in the singular form (i.e., MSA *tā marbūṭa*). Examples from the primary data are *banka* 'fan', *mkebbe* 'tin', *zabda* 'butter', *rōzne* 'shelf in the wall', *gaḥle* 'clay jug', *zibāla* 'rubbish', *ḫamse* 'five', *fazāʿa* 'scarecrow', *ṯallāga* 'fridge', *ġurfe* 'room', *ġarše* 'bottle' [R.57], *baḫše* 'envelope' [R.57], *qortāṣe* 'document' [R.57, 'paper'], *trīke* 'widow' [R.57], *delle* 'coffeepot' [R.58], *nemūne* 'type, kind', *drīše* 'window' [R.58].

The noun *dār* 'house' is feminine, although the terms *bēt* 'house' and *bāb* 'door' (which are feminine in many North African Arabic dialects; Prochazka 2004, 244–45) are masculine in the primary data.

In some cases, marked and unmarked nouns coexist in the primary data, but they are not semantically interchangeable, e.g., *bank* (M) 'bank', *banka* (F) 'fan'; *stār* (M) 'banister', *stāra* (F) 'curtain', *durg* (M) 'drawer', *durga* (F) 'stair'.

1.5. Number

Number includes singular, plural, and a dual reserved for nouns numbering two. The singular form of the noun with regards to the Omani vernacular under investigation has already been discussed above in the present chapter, §1.1.

---

[18] These nouns are reported in accordance with Reinhardt's transcription.

In the informants' speech, the dual is formed by adding the suffix *-īn*[19] to the basic noun form, e.g., *ḥrumtīn* 'two women'. This suffix is the result of the monophthongisation of the CA **-ayn* ending. In the primary data, the dual is quite rare and is mostly found in temporal expressions, such as *šahratīn* 'two months', *santīn* 'two years', *martīn* 'twice'; to indicate the price of something, e.g., *ryalīn* 'two ryals'; and to express the numerals 200 (*mitēn*) and 2000 (*alfīn*).

Plural can be divided into sound plurals and internal plurals.

Since in the spontaneous speech of the consultants there was only a small number of plurals, a simple elicitation technique—based on Reinhardt's (1894, 67–77) material—was employed to check plural formation in their speech. Therefore, although some of the examples are similar to those listed by Reinhardt, they should be understood as those used by the present day speakers involved in this research.

1.5.1. Sound Plural

The sound plural is formed by adding one of two different suffixes according to the gender of the noun: *-īn* for the masculine[20] and *-āt* for the feminine.

---

[19] As opposed to Reinhardt's (1894, 66–67) dual form *-ēn*.

[20] The primary data show that the suffix for the sound masculine plural is homophonous with the dual ending, which, however, is the result of monophthongisation.

The following categories of nouns are based on the examples reported in Reinhardt (1894, 67–68) and have been confirmed by the primary data.

Sound plural ending in *-īn*:

- participles of all verbal forms, when referring to masculine entities, e.g., *mḥobbīn* < *mḥobb* 'friend, beloved', *mitkellemīn* < *mitkellum* 'eloquent', *muslimīn* 'Muslims', *misterrīn* 'delighted';
- most adjectives, except those with the فعيل form, e.g., *ḥelwīn* < *ḥelū* 'sweet', *zēnīn* < *zēn* 'good', *ḥoṣṣīn* < *ḥoṣṣ* 'dirty';
- the relative form *-wī* and *-āwi*, e.g., *benāwīn* 'stepsons';
- numerals from 20 to 90, e.g., *arbaʿīn* 'forty';
- diminutive masculine forms that denote rational living beings, e.g., *bneyīn* < *bnei* 'son, little boy';
- some unmarked feminine nouns, e.g., *belādīn* < *beled* 'country'.

Sound plural ending in *-āt*:

- the feminine of all participles and adjectives that form their masculine plural in *-īn*, e.g., *muslimāt* 'a Muslim woman', *mḥobbāt* 'beloved';
- nouns ending in *-a* or *-e*, though some of them may also present an internal plural, e.g., *wāldāt* < *wālde* 'mother', *raqqāṣāt* < *raqqāṣa* 'dancer';
- the names of some months, e.g., *ar-rabīʿiyāt* 'the two months of *rabiʿ al-awwel* and *rabiʿ al-āḫer*', *il-gemādiyyāt* 'the two months of *gemād al-awwel* and *gemād al-āḫer*', *il-faṭriyyāt* 'the two months of *šūwāl* and *el-qaʿade*'.

Reinhardt (1894, 68) also reports in this category the plural of diminutives. However, in the primary data, diminutives are uncommon and it is not possible to assess a gender category at this stage.

There are also other nouns that present the sound plural ending *-āt* (cf. Reinhardt 1894, 69): *ḫawāt* < *ḫit* 'sister', *benāt* < *bint* 'daughter, girl', *ḫērāt* < *ḫēr* 'good', *semāwāt* < *seme* 'sky', *briyāt* < *bra* 'pin, needle', *ṣalāwāt* < *ṣalā* 'prayer', *mwāsāt* < *mwās* 'razor', *smāmāt* < *smām* 'bridge', *sādāt* < *seyīd* 'mister', *sebālāt* < *sebāl* 'monkey', *mākūlāt* < *mākul* 'food'.

Finally, there is a category of nouns that form their plural in *-īye* (cf. Reinhardt 1894, 69–70). These are:

- names of professions and nationalities, e.g., *ḥammālīye* < *ḥammāl* 'carrier', *baḥārīye* < *baḥḥār* 'sailor, seaman', *ḥarāmīye* < *ḥarām* 'thief';
- names of tribes, e.g., *ġāfrīye* < *ġāfri*, *henāwīye* < *henāwi*;
- other nouns, such as *ʿobrīye* < *ʿobrī* 'passenger', *ibāḍīye* < *ibāḍī* 'Ibadi', *sinnīye* < *sinnī* 'Sunni'.

Some of the nouns reported by Reinhardt in this category do not occur in the primary data, since many of them are now obsolete or related to previous historical phases of Oman (e.g., slavery): e.g., *mqēmri/mqēmryje* 'necromancer', and *šrūzi/šrūzyje* 'slave dealer'.[21]

---

[21] These nouns are reported in accordance with Reinhardt's transcription (1894, 69–70).

1.5.2. Internal Plural

The internal—or broken—plural is so called because it presents a change of the consonant and vowel pattern from the singular form. Reinhardt (1894, 70–77) reports numerous lists of broken plurals according to their syllabic template. Each of the following tables gives the singular and plural patterns; the examples provided must be considered from the primary data. Reinhardt's form, if different, is given following the same glossing system used above in the present chapter, §1.0. In some instances, an internal plural corresponds to multiple singular forms, and in these cases the new singular pattern is given in bold.

Table 3.10: CCVC plural pattern

CVCC(V)	**CCVC**[22]	**Singular**	**Plural**
CaCC(e)	CCaC	*berze* 'meeting'	*brez* [R.70]
		naṭle 'anklet'	*nṭal* [R.70]
		šelle 'war song'	*šlel* [R.70]
		qarbe 'hose'	*qrab* [R.70]
CiCC(e)	C(i)CaC	*fitne* 'dispute'	*ften* [R.70]
		silʿa 'product'	*slaʿ* [R.70]
		ʿisqa 'beam of dates'	*ʿisaq* [R.70]
CuCC(e)	CCaC	*ġurfe* 'room'	*ġraf* [R.70]
		gufra 'hole'	*gfar* [R.70]
		rukbe 'knee'	*rkeb* [R.70]
		boqʿa 'stain'	*bqaʿ* [R.70]
CVVCC(V)			
CūCC(e)	CCaC	*būme* 'entranchment'	*bwem* [R.70]

[22] The forms فُعُل, فِعِل, and فعَل in Reinhardt (1894, 70).

CVVC(V)			
CāCe	CCaC	*qāme* 'profile'	*qyem* [R.70]
		šēle 'woman's coat'	*šyel* [R.70]
CVVCVC			
CāCuC	CCuC	*sēḥor* 'magician'	*sḥor* [R.71]
C(V)CVVC			
C(a)CīC	CCuC	*qfīr* 'basket'	*qfor* [R.71]
		ḥaṣīr 'mat'	*hṣor* [R.71]
C(a)CīC	CCiC	*medīne* 'city, town'	*mdin* [R.71][23]
C(i)CāC	CCuC	*kitāb* 'book'	*ktub* [R.71]

Table 3.11: CVCC plural pattern

C(V)CVVC	**CVCC[24]**	**Singular**	**Plural**
CaCīC	CuCC	*ṭarīq* 'street'	*ṭurq* [R.71]
CCāC	CuCC	*frāš* 'rug'	*furš* [R.71]
		lḥāf 'woman's veil'	*loḥf* [R.71]

Table 3.12: CCVVC plural pattern

CVCVC	**(V)CCVVC[25]**	**Singular**	**Plural**
CaCaC	(a)CCāC	*feleg* 'irrigation channel'	*aflāg* [R.71]
		tefaq 'rifle'	*tfāq* [R.71]
		weled 'child'	*awlād* [R.71]
		nefer 'person'	*enfār* [R.72]
CaCiC	CCūC	*ḫatim* 'finger ring'	*ḫtūm*

[23] Reinhardt (1894, 75) also reports the form *medāin*, but no evidence of this is found in the primary data.

[24] The form فُعْل in Reinhardt (1894, 71).

[25] The forms فِعال, فُعال, and فعول in Reinhardt (1894, 71).

CVCC(V)			
CaCC(e)	CCāC	*šagre* 'tree'	*šgār* [R.71]
		baġle 'mule'	*bġāl* [R.71]
		raqbe 'neck'	*rqāb* [R.71]
		melle 'bowl'	*mlāl* [R.71]
		delle 'coffee-pot'	*dlēl*
CVCCVC			
CiCCaC	CCāC	*riggāl* 'man' [R.71, *reggāl*]	*rgāl* [R.71][26]
CVVC			
CāC	CCāC	*ġēm* 'cloud'	*ġyām* [R.71]
		bāb 'door'	*bwāb* [R.71]
CīC	CCāC	*rīḥ* 'wind'	*riyāḥ* [R.71]
CūC	CCāC	*ṯōb* 'dress'	*ṯiyāb*
		nūn 'woman's breast'	*nwān* [R.71]
CVVCVC			
CāCuC	CCāC	*šāʿor* 'poet'	*šʿār* [R.71]

Table 3.13: C(V)CVVC plural pattern

C(V)CVVC	**C(V)CVVC**[27]	**Singular**	**Plural**
C(a)CīC	C(a)CāC	*ʿaṣīl* 'noble'	*ʿaṣāl* [R.71]
		kbīr 'big'	*kbār* [R.71]
		ṯqīl 'heavy'	*ṯqāl* [R.71]
		ṭwīl 'long'	*ṭwāl* [R.71]
		ṣġīr 'small'	*ṣġār* [R.71]
		krīm 'kind'	*krām* [R.71]
	C(i)CāC	*gṯīl* 'fat'	*giṯāl* [R.71]
	C(u)CāC	*ḫabīṯ* 'poor, bad, mean'	*ḫubāṯ* [R.71]
		ʿaqīl 'reasonable'	*ʿuqāl* [R.71]
		uṣēm 'thin'	*uṣām* [R.71]

[26] Reinhardt (1894, 76) also reports the form *ragāgīl* as a broken plural for *raggāl*, but no evidence of this is found in the primary data.

[27] The forms فِعال, فُعال, and فعول in Reinhardt (1894, 71).

CVCC(V)			
CaCC	CCāC	*baṭl* 'brave'	*bṭāl* [R.71]
		baḥr 'sea'	*bḥūr* [R.71]
	CCūC	*ḥaff* 'camel hoof'	*ḥfūf*
		raml 'sand, desert'	*rmūl* [R.72]
CiCCe	CCūC	*šidfe* 'tree stump'	*šdūf* [R.72]
CVVC			
		ḫēl 'horse'	*ḫiyūl* [R.72]
CāC[28]	C(i)CūC	*bēt* 'house'	*byūt* [R.72]
		gēb 'button'	*gyūb* [R.72]
CVCVC			
CaCiC	CuCūC	*melik* 'king'	*mulūk* [R.72]

Table 3.14: CVCCVVC plural pattern

CVVCVC	**CVCCVVC**	**Singular**	**Plural**
CāCiC	CuCCāC	*ṭāriš* 'courier'	*ṭurrāš* [R.72]
		ʿāmil 'employee'	*ʿommāl* [R.72]
CāCuC	CiCCāC	*ḥakūm* 'ruler'	*ḥukkām* [R.72]

Table 3.15: (V)CCVVC plural pattern

CVC(V)C	**(V)CCVVC[29]**	**Singular**	**Plural**
CaC(a)C	aCCāC	*waqt* 'time'	*awqāt* [R.72]
CVVC			
CūC[30]		*lōn* 'colour'	*elwān* [R.72]
		yōm 'day'	*iyyām* [R.72]

[28] This form is the result of monophtongisation of **ay*.

[29] The form افعال in Reinhardt (1894, 72).

[30] This form is the result of monophtongisation of **aw*.

Table 3.16: C(V)CVVCC plural pattern

C(V)CVVC(V)	C(V)CVVC(V)C[31]	Singular	Plural
CCīCe	CaCāyC	*trīke* 'widow'	*terāyuk* [R.73]
		drīše 'window'	*derāyš* [R.73]
CaCīCe	CaCāyuC	*gezīre* 'island'	*gezāyor* [R.73]
		farīḍa 'salary'	*ferāyoḍ* [R.73]

Table 3.17: CCVVCVC plural pattern

CVVCV(C)	C(V)CVVCVC[32]	Singular	Plural
CūCaC	CwāCiC	*kōsel* 'consul'	*kwāsil* [R.73]
		rōšen 'shelf'[33]	*rwāšin* [R.73]
CāCi	C(a)wāCi	*ḥāši* 'young camel'	*ḥawāši* [R.73]
		šāwi 'shepherd'	*šawāwi* [R.73]
aCC	awāCuC	*emr* 'order'	*ewāmur* [R.73]

[31] The form فعايل in Reinhardt (1894, 73). In the original form, there is a medial *hamza* (فعائل), now completely lost, as explained in ch. 2, §1.6.

[32] The form فواعل in Reinhardt (1894, 73)

[33] Speakers in the al-ʿAwābī district use it not to refer to conventional shelves, but to recessed shelves built into a wall.

Table 3.18: CV(V)CCVVC plural pattern

C(V)CVVC	**CVCCVVC**[34]	**Singular**	**Plural**
C(a)CāC	CiCCān	*ḥzāq* 'belt'	*ḥizqān* [R.73]
		ġazāl 'gazelle'	*ġizlān* [R.73]
	CuCCān	*ġrāb* 'crow'	*ġurbān* [R.73]
		sqēw 'chick'	*soqwān* [R.73]
C(i)CāC	CiCCān	*gidār* 'wall'	*gidrān* [R.73]
C(a)CīC	CiCCān	*ṣadīq* 'friend'	*ṣidqān* [R.73]
	CuCCān	*raġīf* 'roll'	*ruġfān* [R.73]
CVCV(C)			
CaCa(C)	CuCCān	*ʿarab* 'Bedouin'	*ʿorbān* [R.73]
		ʿado 'enemy'	*ʿodwān* [R.73]
		ṭawi 'well'	*ṭuwyān* [R.73]
CVVC	CVVCān		
CāC	CīCān	*tāg* 'crown'	*tīgān* [R.73]
		nār 'fire'	*nīrān* 'blaze' [R.73]
CūC	CīCān	*ʿōd* 'branch'	*ʿīdān* [R.73]
		ḫōr 'harbour'	*ḫīrān* [R.73]
		kōš 'shoe'	*kīšān* [R.73]
		ġūl 'snake'	*ġīlān* [R.73]
		lōḥ 'plank'	*līḥān* [R.73]

Table 3.19: CVC(V)CVV plural pattern

CVCVVC	**CVC(V)CVV**[35]	**Singular**	**Plural**
CaCīC	CuCaCā	*faqīr* 'poor person'	*fuqarā* [R.73]
		ʿaqīd 'official'	*ʿoqdā* [R.73]
		ḥarīṣ 'stingy'	*ḥorṣā* [R.73]
		ḥaqīr 'paltry'	*ḥuqarā* [R.73]

[34] The forms فُعْلان and فِعْلان in Reinhardt (1894, 73).

[35] The form فُعلى in Reinhardt (1894, 73).

Table 3.20: CVCCVplural pattern

CVCVVC	CVCCV[36]	Singular	Plural
CaCīC	CiCCe	*qatīl* 'killed'	*qitle* (but *qitlā-hum*) [R.74]

Table 3.21: CVCVVCV plural pattern

CVVCV	CVCVVCV[37]	Singular	Plural
CāCe[38]	CeCāCi	*lēle* 'nights'	*leyāli* [R.74]
CūCi		*hōri* 'boat'	*hewāri* [R.74]
CVCīye			
CaCīye	C(a)CāCe	*belīye* 'ruin'	*belāye* [R.74]
CuCīye		*wuṭīye* 'sandal'	*waṭāye* [R.74]
CVCCīye			
CuCCīye	CaCāCi	*ṣufrīye* 'pot'	*ṣafāri* [R.74]

Table 3.22: C(V)CVVC(V) plural pattern

CVCC(V)	C(V)CVVC(V)[39]	Singular	Plural
		ṭaraf 'palm leaf'	*ṭrāfe* [R.74]
CaC(a)C	CCāCa	*beden* 'boat'	*bdāne* [R.74]
		qalem 'pen'	*qlāme* [R.75]
CiCC		*nimr* 'tiger'	*nmāra* [R.75]
CaCCa	CCīC	*garra* 'jug'	*grīr* [R.74]
		kumme 'cap'[40]	*kmīm* [R.74]
CuCCe		*qorra* 'frog'	*qrīr* [R.74]
		qubbe 'dome'	*qbīb* [R.74]
CVCCVVC			
CuCāC		*ḥomār* 'donkey'	*ḥmīr* [R.74]
CVC(V)C			
CaC(a)C	C(u)CūCe	*ʿamm* 'uncle'	*ʿomūme* [R.74]
		sehem 'part'	*shūme* [R.74]

[36] The form فِعْلَى in Reinhardt (1894, 74).

[37] The formsفعالا and فعالِي in Reinhardt (1894, 74).

[38] This form is the result of monophthongisation.

[39] The forms فعيل, فعالة, and فعولة in Reinhardt (1894, 74–75).

[40] This refers to a typical Omani cap for males, made of white cotton and usually hand stitched.

Internal Plural of Quadriliterals and Compound Nouns

Quadriliteral and compound nouns also follow specific patterns for broken plural formation. Table 3.23 presents a sample of quadriliteral patterns and their plurals in compliance with Reinhardt's (1894, 75) list and the primary data.

Table 3.23: CVCVVCVC plural pattern

CVCCVVC	**CVCVVCVC**[41]	**Singular**	**Plural**
CaCCāC	CaCāCiC	*daftār* 'notebook'	*defātir* [R.75]
CiCCūC		*gindūb* 'grasshopper'	*genādub*
CVCCVC			
		derham 'coin'	*derāhum* [R.75]
		ḫangar 'dagger'	*ḫanāgor* [R.75]
CaCCaC	CiCāCuC	[R.75, *ḫanger*]	
		bandar 'bay'	*binādur* [R.75]

Names of instruments and names of places are formed with the affix *mV-* and, in terms of plural formation, they follow the quadriliteral root patterns.

Here are some examples from the primary data:

CVCCVC/CCVVCVC:[42] *maḥzem/mḥāzum* 'belt' [R.75], *merkeb/mrākub* 'ship' [R.75].

CVCCVC/CCVCC(V): *mderse/mdāris* 'school' [R.75].

CVCCVVC/CCVVCVVC: *mismār/msāmīr* 'nail' [R.76], *mugdāf/mgādīf* 'oar' [R.76].

Nouns with medial geminates also form plurals in the same way as quadriliteral nouns.

---

[41] The form فعالل in Reinhardt (1894, 75).

[42] The form مفاعل in Reinhardt (1894, 75).

Table 3.24: CVCVVCVVC plural pattern

CVCCVVC	CVCVVCVVC[43]	Singular	Plural
		qaṣṣāb 'butcher'	*qaṣāṣīb* [R.75]
CaCCāC	CaCāCīC	*qammāṭ* 'fishmonger'	*qamāmīṭ* [R.75]
		ṭabbāḫ 'cook'	*ṭabābīḫ* [R.75]
CaCCīC		*kettīb* 'writer'	*ketātīb* [R.76]
		dahrīz 'sitting room'	*dahārīz* [R.76]
		ferkūn 'knuckle'	*ferākīn* [R.76]
CaCCūC		*sannūr* 'cat'	*sanānir* [R.76]
		zerbūl 'stocking'	*zerābīl* [R.76]
CiCCān		*bistān* 'garden'	*bsātīn* [R.76]
CuCCāC		*dukkān* 'shop'	*dekākīn* [R.76]

Lastly, some collective nouns and irregular plurals follow none of the patterns presented above. Examples from the primary data are: *insān* 'mankind', *bōš* 'camels', *hōš* 'goats', *nās* 'people',[44] *ṯāme* < *ṯum* 'mouth', *nsē* < *niswe* 'woman'. Reinhardt (1894, 77) adds a few more nouns to this list, which have not found confirmation among the consultants, whether in the elicitation process or in spontaneous speech.

1.6. Definiteness and Indefiniteness

1.6.1. Definiteness

Definiteness in the al-ʿAwābī district vernacular, as in most Arabic dialects, is expressed via the definite article *il-* ~ *el-*, more

[43] The form فعاعيل in Reinhardt (1894, 75–76).

[44] According to the primary data, as it will be demonstrated in ch. 4, §2.4, *nās* does not behave syntactically like other collective nouns, but shows an irregular pattern.

often realised as *l-*, attached to any noun.[45] The article is assimilated by the so-called 'solar' letters as in CA, e.g., *en-nās* 'the people'.

1.6.2. Indefiniteness

In CA, indefiniteness is usually marked by the *tanwīn* 'nunation', a final nasal consonant vocalised with /u/, /a/, or /i/ according to case (respectively, nominative, accusative, or genitive).

In the present day, "nunation is found in all dialects of eastern and central Arabia, and in Bedouin dialects from outside the peninsula (Jordan, Syria, and parts of Iraq)" (Holes 2016, 131). It also still functions as an indefinite marker in some Bedouin dialects of the Tihāma in Yemen (Versteegh 1997, 149) and in Bahrain "it is mainly used as an indefiniteness marker applied to the noun in a noun-adjective phrase" (Holes 2016, 131).

In the Omani dialects for which there is documentation, nunation is almost completely absent. Indefiniteness is usually expressed via the simple lexical item not preceded by the definite article, e.g., *bint gamīla* 'a beautiful girl'. However, the numeral *wāḥid* (M) or *wāḥda* (F) preceded by the noun can also be used to emphasise indefiniteness, e.g., *riggāl wāḥid* 'only a man'; *bint wāḥda* 'only a girl'. The sole occurrence of *tanwīn* in the primary data has been elicited in the speech of an old illiterate

[45] The realisation of the article as *il-*, *el-*, or *l-* depends on the word that precedes it: by itself it is either *il-* or *el-*, but if the preceding word ends in a vowel, the article is realised as *l-*, e.g., *hadī l-bint* 'this girl', otherwise *sennūr il-bint* 'the girl's cat'.

man (i.e., speaker 13) and is the temporal adverb *marrin* 'once'. This form appears now to have been standardised and is no longer perceived as a case of nunation. Reinhardt (1894, 62) reports another form of indefiniteness in the Banū Kharūṣī vernacular, which is the use of *šay* followed by the particle *min* and the indefinite noun, e.g., *šay min duwāb* 'a beast', but no occurrence of this construction is found in the primary data.

1.7. Noun Modifiers

This section includes adjectives and their inflectional forms (comparatives and elatives), colours, diminutives, and numerals. Quantifiers and adverbs, although technically counting as noun modifiers, are investigated below in the present chapter, §1.8.

1.7.1. Adjectives

Adjectives are not morphologically marked. Therefore, their syntactic function and the two different patterns they show in gender distinction are the only criteria for identifying them as adjectives. As with nouns, they follow specific CV-templates. The following lists are based on Reinhardt's (1894, 62–63) examples, which have been checked with the informants:

- CVVCV(C):[46] *ġāwi* (F *ġāwiye*) 'beautiful' [R.62], *ʿāti* (F *ʿātiye*) 'disobedient' [R.62], *bārid* (F *bārde*) 'cold' [R.62], *ʿāqid* (F *ʿāqda*) 'ripe' [R.62], *zāhub* (F *zāhbe*) 'ready' [R.62], *ḫāfoq* (F *ḫāfqa*) 'low' [R.62].

[46] Form فاعِل (Reinhardt 1894, 62).

- CVCVVC:[47] *faṭūn* (F *faṭūna*) 'perceptive' [R.62], *ḫagūl* (F *ḫagūla*) 'shy, bashful' [R.62].
- CCVVC:[48] *šwīr* (F *šwīra*) 'high' [R.62].
- CCVC:[49] *šroḥ* (F *šorḥa*) 'cool, airy' [R.63], *wṣuḫ* (F *waṣḫa*) 'dirty' [R.63], *smoḥ* (F *sumḥa*) 'generous' [R.63], *ḥdeb* (F *ḥadbe*) 'hunchbacked' [R.63], *frad* (F *farde*) 'one-eyed' [R.63].

In addition to these, adjectives also show patterns extended by the suffixes *-āwi,* e.g., *hawāwi* 'careless', *dinyāwi* 'secular', *henāwi* 'loveable'), and *-ān*:

- CVCCān:[50] *ḫarbān* (F *ḫarbāna*) 'damaged', *kislān* (F *kislāna*) 'hypocrite' [R.62], *forḥān* (F *forḥāna*) 'happy' [R.62].

Adjectives formed from quadrilateral roots do not follow any of the patterns listed above, e.g., *hanqrī* (F *hanqrīye*) 'rich', *gurgur* (F *gurgra*) 'naked' [R.63].

In terms of number, most adjectives take a sound plural (either masculine or feminine), according to the gender of the noun they qualify; whereas some others, usually of form فعيل, show a broken plural pattern, e.g., *ṣġūr* 'small', *ṭuwāl* 'long', *kbār* 'big'.[51]

---

[47] Form فعول (Reinhardt 1894, 62).

[48] Form فعيل (Reinhardt 1894, 62).

[49] This pattern is the result of an original CVCVC pattern where the first syllable short vowel has undergone syncope. In the feminine form the elided vowel reappears due to phonological reasons (cf. form فعُل in Reinhardt 1894, 63).

[50] Form فعلان (Reinhardt 1894, 62).

[51] Some broken plural forms of adjectives are reported in Table 3.13.

Colours

Adjectives of colour are formed on the pattern C(a)CaC for the masculine singular and CV(V)CCa for the feminine singular. Table 3.25 reports the colour forms found in the primary data. Reinhardt's list (1894, 63) matches them closely, with the sole exception of the feminine *saude* 'black', which in the consultants' speech is always monophthongised to *sōde*.

Table 3.25: Colours

Colour	**Masculine**	**Feminine**	**Plural**
'black'	*swed*	*sōde*	*sūd*
'green'	*ḫaḍar*	*ḫaḍra*	*ḫḍur*
'red'	*ḥmar*	*ḥamra*	*ḥumur*
'white'	*byaḍ*	*bēḍa*	*būḍ*
'yellow'	*ṣfar*	*ṣafra*	*ṣufur*

In addition to these primary colours, the primary data also show others that follow this pattern, such as *dḫaw* (F *daḫwe*) 'grey', *ġbar* (F *ġabra*) 'ashy' (cf. Reinhardt 1894, 63), and a few that show a pattern with a final /-ī/, usually deriving from a specific noun, e.g., *banafsagī* 'violet', *burtuqalī* 'orange' < *burtuqāl* 'orange', *bunnī* 'brown' < *bunn* 'coffee bean', *nilī* 'dark blue' < *nīl* 'Nile', *ruṣāṣī* 'grey' < *ruṣāṣ* 'lead'. Colour shades are given by placing the adjectives *dākin* 'dark' and *fātiḥ* 'light' after the colour name, e.g., *ḥmar dākin* 'dark red', unless there is a specific dedicated form.

Comparatives and Superlatives

The comparative is formed on the template aCCaC, although the initial vowel is elided in some instances and does not distinguish between gender and number. It also carries an elative meaning, which denotes intensity or superiority compared to the base form, similarly to other Arabic dialects. The following table presents a sample of comparatives found in the primary data, which are in agreement with Reinhardt's (1894, 63–64) list.

Table 3.26: Comparatives, aCCaC pattern

Adjective	**Comparative**
kabīr 'big'	*kbar* 'bigger'
ḥasan 'good'	*ḥsen* 'better'
wāsoʿ 'far'	*awsaʿ* 'further'
wbaṣ 'bright'	*awbaṣ* 'brighter'
ġāwi 'beautiful'	*eġwe* 'more beautiful'
zēn 'good'	*zyen* 'better'
šēn 'ugly, bad'	*šyen* 'uglier, worse'

This pattern is shown also by a few nouns and adverbs, such as *efwaq* 'upper' < *fōq* 'up, above'; *etḥat* 'below' < *taḥt* 'under'; *ergel* 'manlier' < *riggāl* 'man'; *ested* 'more expert' < *ustād* 'master, expert'. The same forms are documented by Reinhardt (1894, 64). In the primary data these forms only occurr in the speech of OS, both in al-ʿAwābī and Wādī Banī Kharūṣ.

When the comparative pattern is not applicable, then *akṯar* following the adjective is used instead, e.g., *hanqrī akṯar* 'very rich'.

The compared noun is always preceded by the particle *min* 'from, than', as in (14) and (15).

(14) *zōg-i* *ekbar* *min-nī*

husband.MSG-PRON.1SG big.COMP than-PRON.1SG

'My husband is older than me.' [S2]

(15) *rustāq* *awsaʿ* *min* *el-wādī*
Rustāq far.COMP than DEF-wadi
'Rustaq is farther than the Wadi.'[52] [S1]

The superlative is formed by adding the definite article to the elative pattern aCCaC, e.g., *el-ekbar* 'the biggest', *el-ezyen* 'the best', *el-ešyen* 'the worst'. Here, the initial vowel of the elative pattern is reinstated to avoid a CCC cluster. The superlative usually functions as a substantival form of the comparative and, as such, does not inflect for gender, e.g., *anā l-ekbar* 'I am the oldest'; *il-ḫit el-ekbar* 'the elder sister'; *il-āḫ el-ekbar* 'the eldest brother'.

Diminutives

Nominals in some instances have a diminutive form, carrying the meaning of physical smallness and reduction. In the documented Omani vernaculars, there are different patterns in use. Davey (2016, 109), for example, reports the pattern CuCēC(a) in Dhofari Arabic, e.g., *kulēb* 'small dog' < *kelb* 'dog', and the same pattern is reported by Reinhardt (1894, 46). In the primary data, diminutives are not common, so further investigation is needed. It seems, however, that two additional patterns are in use, i.e., C(a)CayyC, e.g., *bṣayyaṭ* 'little rug' < *bṣāṭ* 'rug, carpet', and C(u)CūC, e.g., *ḥubūb/ḥubūba* 'little love, darling'. The former template is similar to the one followed by diminutives in other Peninsular dialects; cf. Bahrain (Holes 2016) and Yemen (Watson 2006).

---

[52] In this example, the speaker is referring to the distance of the two places from al-ʿAwābī town.

1.7.2. Numerals

Numerals can be divided into two categories: ordinal and cardinal numbers.

Cardinal Numbers

Numbers from 1 to 10 present two different forms according to the gender of the noun they refer to. The following table presents the cardinal numbers as they are found in the primary data, where they differ from Reinhardt's (1894, 82) list. Therefore, for each number Reinhardt's counterpart is given in brackets.

Table 3.27: Cardinal numbers

	Masculine	**Feminine**
1	*wāḥid* (R. *wāḥi*)	*wāḥda* (R. *woḥde*)
2	*ṯnīn* (R. *hintēn, ṯnēne*)	*ṯnīne* (R. *ṯnēn, ṯnīn*)
3	*ṯalāṯ* (R. *ṯelāṯe*)	*ṯalāṯa* (R. *ṯlāṯ, ṯelaṯ*)
4	*arbaʿ* (R. *ʿarbaʿa*)	*arbaʿa* (R. *rbaʿ, ʿarbaʾ*)
5	*ḫams* (R. *ḫamse*)	*ḫamse* (R. *ḫams*)
6	*sitt* (R. *sitte*)	*sitte* (R. *sitt*)
7	*sabaʿ* (R. *sabaʿa*)	*sbaʿa* (R. *seboʿ*)
8	*ṯamān* (R. *ṯemānye*)	*ṯamāniye* (R. *ṯemān*)
9	*tisaʿ* (R. *tisʿa*)	*tisaʿa* (R. *tsoʿ*)
10	*ʿašar* (R. *ʿašra, ʿašort*)	*ʿašara* ~ *ʿašra* (R. *ʿašor*)

It has already been mentioned above, present chapter, §1.5, that the numeral 'one' is used to emphasise indefiniteness and that it always follows the noun it refers to. The number 'two' behaves the same and the noun it refers to is in its plural form, although speakers may use the dual form to indicate the quantity of two in some instances, e.g., *madrasatīn* or *madāris ṯnīn* 'two schools'.

If the counted noun is indefinite, numbers 3 to 10 always precede it, and the noun appears in its plural form. In terms of gender agreement, they follow the polarity principle (i.e., the feminine form precedes masculine nouns and the masculine form feminine nouns):

(16) *aḏkur kān ṯalāṯ madāris*
remember.1SG was.3MSG three.M schools.FPL
fī-ṣ-ṣulṭana
in-DEF-sultanate.FSG
'I remember there were three schools in the Sultanate.' [S1]

(17) *anā gubt tisaʿa awlād*
PRON.1SG was given.1SG nine.F child.MPL
'I had nine children.' [S2]

If the counted noun is definite, the numeral usually follows it:[53]

(18) *ʿind-nā es-sanānīr ṯnīne*
to-PRON.1PL DEF-cat.PL two.F
'We have two cats.' [S5]

Numbers from 11 onwards do not have a distinction in gender. As shown in the table below, the numbers from 11 to 19 in the primary data are formed by adding to the unit the numeral ten, i.e., *ʿašar*. When counting, speakers always use the long form. In everyday speech and especially when followed by another noun, they tend to use the shortened form, e.g., *ṯalāṯʿaš*

[53] In some Peninsular dialects (cf. Holes 2016; Davey 2016), in a definite context the numeral can also take the definite article. However, there is no occurrence of this in the primary data.

sana 'thirteen years'.[54] Reinhardt (1894, 83–84) documents different shorter forms employed by his informants, i.e., *hedār* 'eleven', *ṯnār* 'twelve', *ṯlittār* 'thirteen', *rbātār* 'fourteen', *ḫmoṣtār* 'fifteen', *sittār* 'sixteen', *sabātār* 'seventeen', *ṯmintār* 'eighteen', and *tsātār* 'nineteen'. Not surprisingly, the transcriptions are ambiguous, and they do not occur in the primary data.

Table 3.28: Cardinal numbers 11 to 19

11	*ḥidʿaš(ar)* [R. *hedāʿšer*]	16	*sittaʿaš(ar)* [R. *sittāʿšer*]
12	*ṯnāʿaš(ar)* [R. *ṯnāʿšer*]	17	*sabaʿatʿaš(ar)* [R. *sabātāʿšer*]
13	*ṯalāṯʿaš(ar)* [R. *ṯlittaʿšer*]	18	*ṯamāntʿaš(ar)* [R. *ṯmintāʿšer*]
14	*arbaʿatʿaš(ar)* [R. *rbātāʿšer*]	19	*tisaʿatʿaš(ar)* [R. *tsātāʿšer*]
15	*ḫamsʿaš(ar)* [R. *ḫmoṣtāʿšer*]		

These numbers always precede the noun they refer to, which is in the singular form, e.g., *ḥidʿaš(ar) ṭafil* 'eleven children'.

Turning to the decades—the number 20 is formed by adding the monophthongised dual ending *-īn* to number ten, i.e., *ʿašrīn*, whereas the numbers from 30 to 90 are formed following the sound plural pattern of masculine nouns, i.e., by adding the *-īn* ending to the unit form. They are not dissimilar from those in Reinhardt's (1894, 84) list.

[54] The elision of the last consonant *-(a)r* is also common in other Arabic dialects of the Gulf (cf. Johnstone 1967, 64; Taine-Cheikh 2008, 449).

Table 3.29: Cardinal numbers 20 to 100

20	*ʿašrīn*	70	*sabaʿīn*
30	*ṯalāṯīn*	80	*ṯamānyīn*
40	*arbaʿīn*	90	*tisaʿīn*
50	*ḫamsīn*	100	*mie*
60	*sittīn*	1000	*alf*

The same happens for the numbers 200 and 2000, which add the dual ending *-īn* to *mie* 'hundred' and *alf* 'thousand' respectively, i.e., *mitīn* and *alfīn*. The numbers from 300 to 900 are formed using the unit followed by the noun *mie*, e.g., *arbaʿ mie* 'four hundred', *ḫams mie* 'five hundred', and so on. Similarly, the numbers from 3000 to 9000 show the unit followed by *alf*, e.g., *ṯalāṯ alf* 'three thousand', *arbaʿ alf* 'four thousand', and so on.

Ordinal Numbers

The ordinal numbers present forms only from 1 to 10 and are distinguished by gender; numbers from 11 onwards follow the pattern for cardinal numbers. In Reinhardt's (1894, 86) material, only the ordinal number 'first' differs from what has been recorded in the primary data, and it is reported in brackets.

Table 3.30: Ordinal numbers 1 to 11

	Masculine	**Feminine**
1°	*awwel* (R. *auwel, wel, auli*)	*ūlīye* (R. *aulīye*)
2°	*ṯāni*	*ṯānye*
3°	*ṯāliṯ*	*ṯālṯe*
4°	*rāboʿ*	*rābaʿa*
5°	*ḫāmis*	*ḫāmse*
6°	*sādis*	*sādse*
7°	*sāboʿ*	*sābaʿa*
8°	*ṯāmin*	*ṯāmine*
9°	*tāsoʿ*	*tāseʿa*
10°	*ʿāšor*	*ʿāšra*

Ordinal numbers behave like adjectives in terms of agreement. They can function adjectively for both definite and indefinite nouns, taking (or not) the definite article.

(19) *tzawwagit* *marra* *wāḥid* *ġēr-o* *ṯāliṯ*

married.3FSG time one.M other-PRON.3MSG third.M

'She married once again a third (man) other than him.' [S12]

(20) *bint-i* *il-ūlīye*

girl.FSG-PRON.1SG DEF-first.F

'My first daughter' [S3]

1.8. Quantifiers and Adverbs

1.8.1. Quantifiers

A quantifier is a word or phrase used to indicate amount or quantity. In the vernacular under investigation the following quantifiers are in use.

Table 3.31: Quantifiers

'all/each'	*kill*	'other'	*ġēr*
'every'	*ēyy*	'many'	*wāgid*
'everything'	*kill šey*	'some'	*baʿaḍ*
'everyone'	*kill ḥad*	'a few/a little'	*šweyya*
'every time'	*kill marra*	'everywhere/anywhere'	*min ēyy*

The quantifier *kill* has the double function of 'all' and 'each'. A distinction is made according to the number of the noun it is related to.

(21) *kill sana*

every year.FSG

'Every year' [S5]

(22) *kill-hum*

all-PRON.3MPL

'All of them' [S12]

(23) *kill rgāl*

all man.MPL

'All men' [S3]

(24) *kill ḥad gilis fi-bēt-o*

every person stayed.3MSG in-house.MSG-PRON.3MSG

'Everyone stayed in his house.' [S1]

When *kill* is followed by an indefinite singular noun, as in (21) and (24), it indicates 'each, every'. In (22), the quantifier is followed by the suffix pronoun *-hum*, which indicates the plurality of 'them', and, in (23), by the plural noun *rgāl*. In both cases it indicates a totality.

The quantifier *baʿaḍ* is usually followed by a plural noun, as in:

(25) *baʿaḍ buyūt*

some house.MPL

'Some houses' [S2]

1.8.2. Adverbs

An adverb is a word or phrase that modifies the meaning or the intensity of an adjective or a verb, expressing time, space, manner, or degree. For this reason, it is debated whether they should be categorised as nominal or verbal morphology. Nevertheless, since they are derived mainly from nouns, noun phrases, and adjectives (cf. Watson 2006, 22), they will be discussed in this section.

Adverbs can be divided into temporal and spatial adverbs and adverbs of manner and degree. In Table 3.32, the temporal adverbs found in the data are presented.

Table 3.32: Temporal adverbs

'now'	*taww*	'never'	*ebeden*
'later'	*baʿdīn*	'today'	*il-yōm*
'tomorrow'	*bukra*	'yesterday'	*ems*
'always'	*dēman*		

(26) *bukra ṣ-ṣabāḥ*

tomorrow DEF-morning

'Tomorrow morning' [S11]

Spatial adverbs are shown in the table below.

Table 3.33: Spatial adverbs

'here'	*hinā ~ hnā*	'there'	*hināk*[55]
'inside'	*dāḫil*	'outside'	*barrā/ḫārig*
'above, up'	*fōq*	'behind'	*warā*
'far'	*ġādi/safīl*[56]	'on the left'	*yasār*
'on the right'	*yamīn*	'under, below, down'	*taḥt*
'in between'	*bēn*	'in front of'	*qiddām*

Other spatial adverbs are nouns referring to the cardinal points and directions based on them. Among speakers from Wādī Banī Kharūṣ, there is widespread use of these forms, which differ from those used in al-ʿAwābī. Examples are *ʿālī/safīl* (Wādī) and *šamāl* (town) for 'north', *ʿilwa* (Wādī) and *ganūb* (town) for 'south'. 'East' and 'west' do not present any difference between varieties and are, respectively, *šarq* and *ġarb*.

(27) *taḥt, fī-l-kurfāya*
below in-DEF-bed.FSG
'Down(stairs), on the bed' [S8]

(28) *atīb qahwa hnā*
bring.1SG coffee here
'I bring coffee here.' [S15]

The adverbs of manner found in the primary data are seen in Table 3.34.

---

[55] Distance is indicated with the suffix *-k*, the same used in the demonstrative pronouns.

[56] There is a difference in the use of these two adverbs: *ġādi* is mainly used in al-ʿAwābī town, whereas *safīl* is considered more archaic and it is used by speakers in Wādī Banī Kharūṣ also to indicate "north".

Table 3.34: Manner adverbs

'almost, about'	*taqrīban*	'so, in such a way'	*kḏāk*
'slowly'	*šweya šweya*	'very, much'	*wāgid*
'good, well'	*zēn*	'well'	*tamām/ṭayyib*
'a little'	*šweya*	'quickly'	*bi-suraʿ*

(29) *baʿad ʿašar sanuwāt taqrīban*

after ten.M year.FPL about

'After about ten years' [S1]

The last category presented here is adverbs of degree, which add an augmentative or diminutive adverbial sense to the noun or phrase.

Table 3.35: Degree adverbs

'more, many, much'	*wāgid/hest*[57]	'more'	*ekṭar*
'perhaps'	*mumkin*	'enough'	*bess*
'that is'	*yaʿni*	'also'	*nōbe*

1.9. Prepositions

The most common prepositions found in the primary data are presented in Table 3.36.

[57] The adverb *wāgid* is commonly used throughout Oman with no distinction in terms of speaker gender, age, or level of education. The form *hest* is an old Persian loanword which occurs in Reinhardt's material, but which is now recognised by the informants as an archaic feature of the language, being used only by OS in the Wādī.

Table 3.36: Prepositions

fī	'in, on'	*bi-*	'with, in, into'
ʿind-	'at, to, by'	*li-*	'to, at'
maʿ	'with'	*bidūn*	'without'
lēn	'until, to'	*ʿala*	'on, at, around'
ʿan	'about'	*ʿašān*	'in order to'
ḥāl	'for'	*lā- ~ ilā*	'to, towards'
min	'since, from, by'		

Many of these prepositions can express a double value of temporal and spatial relations, e.g., *fī-l-ġurfa* 'in the room'; *fī-l-lēl* 'at night', and most of them introduce noun phrases and prepositional phrases, which, as such, are treated in ch. 4 of this work.

2.0. Verbal Morphology

Given the pedagogical intent of his work, Reinhardt (1894) provides the reader with verbal conjugations accompanied by numerous examples showing their use in different contexts. In his own words, his aim is to provide the student with captivating examples. This holds true for the verb conjugations as well. The main differences between Reinhardt's material and the primary data is seen in the frequency of syncope in the conjugation of Reinhardt's verbs, which now seems to be present only in the speech of some OS in Wādī Banī Kharūṣ (speakers 4, 8, and 13). It is interesting, though, that two of these speakers are males.

Because of the ongoing literary debate on Arabic TAM categories—i.e., tense, aspect, and mood—and so as not to infer any temporal or aspectual value in the verbs as they are presented in this chapter, I will employ the labels used by other

Semitic scholars for the main conjugations of the verb, namely s-stem (suffix-stem) and p-stem (prefix-stem) (Holes 1995; Persson 2008; Horesh 2009; and Eades and Watson 2013a). The s-stem, as the name implies, is formed by adding suffixes to the verbal stem to inflect for person, gender, and number. The p-stem, on the other hand, uses prefixes to distinguish person, gender, and number.

2.1. Strong Verbs

Strong verbs are those verbs whose roots do not present a glide, a *hamza*, or a geminate consonant. The strong verb is presented in its 3MSG form, according to standard Semitic practice. Table 3.37 presents the conjugation of the verb *keteb* 'write' accompanied by Reinhardt's forms, when different.

Table 3.37: S-stem and p-stem conjugation of the verb *keteb* 'write'

	s-stem	
	Singular	**Plural**
1	*keteb-t [R. ktebt]*	*keteb-ne*
2M	*keteb-t*	*keteb-to* [R. *ktebto*]
2F	*keteb-ti* [R. *ktebti*]	*keteb-ten*
3M	*keteb*	*ketb-o*
3F	*ketb-it*	*ketb-en*
	p-stem	
1	*e-ktub*	*nu-ktub*
2M	*ti-ktub* [R. *tuktub*]	*ti-kitb-o* [R. *tkitbo*]
2F	*ti-kitb-i* [R. *tkitbi*]	*ti-kitb-en* [R. *tkitben*]
3M	*yi-ktub* [R. *yuktub*]	*yi-kitb-o* [R. *ykitbo*]
3F	*ti-ktub* [R. *tuktub*]	*yi-kitb-en* [R. *ykitben*]

If we compare the conjugation in Table 3.37 to Reinhardt's (1894, 131), we see that in the latter syncope is more common in some persons than in the former (e.g., 1SG and 2FSG). Major differences, though, can be found in the p-stem conjugation (cf. Reinhardt 1894, 146).

The vowel pattern in the p-stem forms varies. This stem can have three different combinations of vowels, depending on both the consonants and the vocalic pattern of the s-stem: CaCaC verbs display /i/, when the s-stem form is third radical is /d/, /ṯ/, /t/, /ḏ/, /ẓ/, /s/, /š/, /n/, and /l/, e.g., *geles/yiglis* 'sit'; /u/, when the third radical is /b/, /f/, /g/, /k/, and /m/, e.g., *raqab/yirqub* 'wait for', *katab/yiktub* 'write';[58] and /a/ in all other cases, e.g., *šaʿar/yišʿar* 'sing, recite'. CiCiC verbs display /i/ in the p-stem, e.g., *gfil/yugfil* 'look after sth.' and CuCuC verbs display /a/ in the p-stem, e.g., *šrub/yišrab* 'drink'.

2.2. Geminate Verbs

A geminate verb is a verb in which C_2 and C_3 are the same, e.g., *šill* 'take', *šebb* 'grow old', *ḍann* 'think'. In the primary data, geminate verbs insert a long vowel /ē/ in the s-stem conjugation between the stem and a consonant-initial subject suffix; whereas in the p-stem conjugation, the prefix joins the stem directly—with *t-* of the second person and third person feminine singular undergoing assimilation when the first radical of the verb is an alveolar or interdental obstruent, as shown in Table 3.38.

---

[58] The vowel /u/ has an [o] allophone when the third radical is an emphatic, i.e., /ṣ/, /ḍ/, /ṭ/, or /r/ or /q/, for example, *raqaṭ/yirqoṭ* 'gather, pick up, *baġaḍ/yibġoḍ* 'hate'.

Table 3.38: S-stem and p-stem conjugation of *ḍann* 'think'

	s-stem		**p-stem**	
	Singular	**Plural**	**Singular**	**Plural**
1	*ḍannē-t*	*ḍannē-ne*	*e-ḍann*	*n-ḍann*
2M	*ḍannē-t*	*ḍannē-to*	*ḍ-ḍann*	*ḍ-ḍann-o*
2F	*ḍannē-ti*	*ḍannē-ten*	*ḍ-ḍann-i*	*ḍ-ḍann-en*
3M	*ḍann*	*ḍann-o*	*yi-ḍann*	*yi-ḍann-o*
3F	*ḍanni-t*	*ḍann-en*	*ḍ-ḍann*	*yi-ḍann-en*

2.3. Hamzated Verbs

A hamzated verb is a verb which presents a *hamza* in first, second, or third position, i.e., C_1, C_2, or C_3. As mentioned in ch. 2, §1.0, the *hamza* is not retained: in the primary data, verbs cognate with CA hamzated verbs show compensatory lengthening of the vowel or, when word initial, the *hamza* is completely deleted.

Hamzated verbs exhibit similar behaviour. As C_1, the *hamza* is not retained in the s-stem and is lengthened in the p-stem, e.g., *kel/yūkil* 'eat'. The verb *kel* is also phonologically interesting, since it displays compensatory lengthening of the final vowel in the s-stem conjugation for persons with a consonant-initial suffix (as shown in Table 3.39). Reinhardt (1894, 188–89) reports the same conjugation. It thus seems that no variation has occurred in this instance.

Table 3.39: S-stem and p-stem conjugation of *kel* 'eat'

	s-stem		p-stem	
	Singular	**Plural**	**Singular**	**Plural**
1	*kelē-t*	*kelē-ne*	*ekil*	*nū-kil*
2M	*kelē-t*	*kelē-to*	*tū-kil*	*tū-kl-o*
2F	*kelē-ti*	*kelē-ten*	*tū-kl-i*	*tū-kl-en*
3M	*kel*	*kel-o*	*yū-kil*	*yū-kl-o*
3F	*kel-it*	*kel-en*	*tū-kil*	*yū-kl-en*

In the primary data, there is only one occurrence of a root-medial *hamza* verb, i.e., *sāl* 'ask', which behaves like verbs with a medial glide. Verbs with final *hamza* lose the glottal stop and behave like final-glide verbs, e.g., *qarā/yiqra* 'read'.

2.4. Weak Verbs

Weak verbs are those that present a glide /w/ or /y/ in any position C_1, C_2, or C_3. The realisation of the glide can vary according to its position within the root and according to the rules mentioned in ch. 2, §1.0.

2.4.1. Verbs with an Initial Glide—/w/, /y/

This class of verbs tends to behave like strong verbs in the s-stem conjugation, retaining the initial glide. But in the p-stem conjugation, the glide is realised as its corresponding long high vowel.[59] Examples include *wgaʿ* 'hurt' and *ybas* 'dry'.

[59] This behaviour is shared with some Bedouin dialects of Bahrain (cf. Holes 2016) and with Dhofari Arabic (cf. Davey 2016).

Table 3.40: S-stem and p-stem conjugations of the initial-glide verbs *wgaʿ* 'hurt' and *ybas* 'dry'

	***wgʿ* 'hurt'**		***ybas* 'dry' (intransitive)**	
	s-stem	**p-stem**	**s-stem**	**p-stem**
1SG	*wgaʿ-t*	*ūgaʿ*	*ybas-t*	*ības*
2MSG	*wgaʿ-t*	*tū-gaʿ*	*ybas-t*	*tī-bas*
2FSG	*wgaʿ-ti*	*tū-gaʿ-i*	*ybas-ti*	*tī-bas-i*
3MSG	*wgaʿ*	*yū-gaʿ*	*ybas*	*yī-bas*
3FSG	*wgaʿ-at*	*tū-gaʿ*	*ybas-at*	*tī-bas*
1PL	*wgaʿ-na*	*nū-gaʿ*	*ybas-na*	*nī-bas*
2MPL	*wgaʿ-to*	*tū-gaʿ-o*	*ybas-to*	*tī-bas-o*
2FPL	*wgaʿ-ten*	*tū-gaʿ-en*	*ybas-ten*	*tī-bas-en*
3MPL	*wgaʿ-o*	*yū-gaʿ-o*	*ybas-o*	*yī-bas-o*
3FPL	*wgaʿ-en*	*yū-gaʿ-en*	*ybas-en*	*yī-bas-en*

2.4.2. Verbs with a Medial Glide—/w/, /y/

In the s-stem conjugation, medial /w/ is realised as [u], except for the third persons masculine and feminine, which exhibit long /ā/. Medial /y/, conversely, is generally realised as [o] in the s-stem conjugation and as [ā] in the 3rd persons masculine and feminine. In the p-stem conjugation, the medial glides /w/ and /y/ are realised as [ū] and [ī], respectively, but /w/ can also be realised as [ā] in verbs such as *ḫāf/yḫāf* 'fear', from the root *ḫ-w-f*. The following table presents the s-stem and p-stem conjugation of *rām/yrūm* 'be able to' and *sār/ysīr* 'go'.[60]

[60] Reinhardt (1894, 202) also reports the same conjugation, hence no diachronic variation has occurred in this instance.

Table 3.41: S-stem and p-stem conjugations of *rām* 'be able to' and *sār* 'go'

	***rām* 'be able to'**		***sār* 'go'**	
	s-stem	**p-stem**	**s-stem**	**p-stem**
1SG	*rum-t*	*erūm*	*sor-t*	*a-sīr*
2MSG	*rum-t*	*t-rūm*	*sor-t*	*t-sīr*
2FSG	*rum-ti*	*t-rūm-i*	*sor-ti*	*t-sīr-i*
3MSG	*rām*	*y-rūm*	*sār*	*y-sīr*
2FSG	*rām-it*	*t-rūm*	*sār-it*	*t-sīr*
1PL	*rum-ne*	*n-rūm*	*sor-ne*	*n-sīr*
2MPL	*rum-to*	*t-rūm-o*	*sor-to*	*t-sīr-o*
2FPL	*rum-ten*	*t-rūm-en*	*sor-ten*	*t-sīr-an*
3MPL	*rām-o*	*y-rūm-o*	*sār-o*	*y-sīr-o*
3FPL	*rām-en*	*y-rūm-en*	*sār-an*	*y-sīr-an*

Verbs with a medial glide and original final *hamza* inflect by lengthening the glide with no trace of the glottal stop in both paradigms. Table 3.42 gives the inflection of the verb *gā* 'come'.[61]

Table 3.42: S-stem and p-stem conjugation of the verb *gā* 'come'

	s-stem		**p-stem**	
	Singular	**Plural**	**Singular**	**Plural**
1	*gī-t*	*gī-ne*	*egī*	*ngī*
2M	*gī-t*	*gī-to*	*t-gī*	*t-giy-o*
2F	*gī-ti*	*gī-ten*	*t-giy-i*	*t-giy-en*
3M	*gā*	*g-yo*	*y-gī*	*y-giy-o*
3F	*gī-t*	*g-yen*	*t-gī*	*y-giy-en*

[61] The original root of *gā* is ǦYʾ, but it has been reduced to ǦY—usually pronounced as [gē] in the speech of the informants.

2.4.3. Verbs with a Final Glide—/w/, /y/[62]

The vocalisation of the final glide /y/ in the p-stem of this class of verbs is determined by the vocalic pattern shown by the s-stem: that is, /a/ in CCi > yiCCa, e.g., *bġī/yibġa* 'want'; *nsī/yinsa* 'forget', and /i/ in CeCe > yiCCi, e.g., *meše/yimši* 'walk'; *beke/yibki* 'cry'.

Table 3.43: S-stem and p-stem conjugation of *nsī* 'forget' and *meše* 'walk'

	***nsī* 'forget'**		***meše* 'walk'**	
	s-stem	**p-stem**	**s-stem**	**p-stem**
1SG	*nasī-t*	*e-nsā*	*mešē-t*	*e-mši*
2MSG	*nasī-t*	*t-nāsī*	*mešē-t*	*ti-mš-ī*
2FSG	*nasī-ti*	*t-nāsy-i*	*mešē-ti*	*t-mišy-i*
3MSG	*nsī*	*yi-nsa*	*meše*	*yi-mši*
3FSG	*nasī-it*	*ti-nsa*	*meš-it*	*ti-mši*
1PL	*nasī-ne*	*ni-nsa*	*mešē-ne*	*ni-mši*
2MPL	*nsī-to*	*t-nasy-o*	*mešē-to*	*ti-mšy-o*
2FPL	*nasī-ten*	*t-nasy-en*	*mešē-ten*	*ti-mšy-en*
3MPL	*nasy-o*	*y-nasy-o*	*mešy-o*	*yi-mšy-o*
3FPL	*nasy-en*	*y-nasy-en*	*mešy-en*	*yi-mšy-en*

2.5. Quadriliteral Verbs

2.5.1. Basic Form

The basic form of quadriliteral verbs in the primary data is structured on two different patterns: $C_1VC_2C_3VC_4$ with four dis-

[62] There is no occurrence of final /w/ verbs in the primary data, but according to Holes (2016, 210) they behave as final /y/ verbs vocalised in /i/.

tinct consonants, or the reduplicative $C_1VC_2C_1VC_2$. The last vowel of both patterns can be either [a] or [u], however it is not possible to assess a criterion on their occurrence since the primary data are not sufficient in this sense.

Table 3.44: Basic pattern of quadriliteral verbs found in the al-ʿAwābī district.

$C_1VC_2C_3VC_4$		$C_1VC_2C_1VC_2$	
Verb	**Meaning**	**Verb**	**Meaning**
belġam	'clear the throat (spitting mucus)'	*šaḫšaḫ*	'urinate frequently'
gerdef	'coerce'	*farfur*	'flutter'
daʿṯar	'confuse, mix up'	*kezkez*	'shiver'

The s-stem and p-stem conjugation of these verbs follow the same inflection of basic triliteral verbs, as shown in Table 3.45.

Table 3.45: S-stem and p-stem conjugation of *šaḫšaḫ* 'urinate frequently'

	s-stem		**p-stem**	
	Singular	**Plural**	**Singular**	**Plural**
1	*šaḫšaḫ-t*	*šaḫšaḫ-na*	*a-šaḫšaḫ*	*ni-šaḫšaḫ*
2M	*šaḫšaḫ-t*	*šaḫšaḫ-to*	*ti-šaḫšaḫ*	*ti-šaḫšaḫ-o*
2F	*šaḫšaḫ-ti*	*šaḫšaḫ-ten*	*ti-šaḫšaḫ-i*	*ti-šaḫšaḫ-en*
3M	*šaḫšaḫ*	*šaḫšaḫ-o*	*yi-šaḫšaḫ*	*yi-šaḫšaḫ-o*
3F	*šaḫšaḫ-it*	*šaḫšaḫ-en*	*ti-šaḫšaḫ*	*yi-šaḫšaḫ-en*

2.5.2. Derived Templates t-$C_1VC_2C_1VC_2$ and t-$C_1VC_2C_3VC_4$

The templates t-$C_1VC_2C_1VC_2$ and t-$C_1VC_2C_3VC_4$ are the only two derived forms for quadriliteral roots found in the primary data. A sample of each is given in Table 3.46.

Table 3.46: The t-$C_1VC_2C_1VC_2$ and t-$C_1VC_2C_3VC_4$ templates

t-$C_1VC_2C_1VC_2$	**Meaning**	**t-$C_1VC_2C_3VC_4$**	**Meaning**
tḥamḥam	'cough intermittently'	*tdelhem*	'get cloudy'
tlaġlaġ	'flood'	*tšaḥreg*	'have an oppressive cough'
tsemsem[63]	'swell up and itch'	*tġanḍar*	'faint'
tṭaḥṭaḥ	'drop'	*trengaḥ*	'sway, swing'

2.6. Derived Patterns of the Verb

2.6.1. Strong Verbs

In addition to the basic forms, the primary data show eight further forms of the verb (derived from the basic pattern) for the strong verb and slightly fewer for weak and geminate verbs. These derived forms take different patterns, including the gemination of existing radicals and the infixing and prefixing of consonants and vowels to the core pattern.[64]

[63] This is an instance of a derivative verb, originating from the word *samsūm*, which indicates a 'small black ant' in Oman whose bite provokes swelling and a strong itch.

[64] In CA, nine common forms derived from the basic stem are attested, each one following a specific pattern. The only attested form that follows the CA Form IV, i.e., ʾaCCaC, is *aḥsant*, used to mean 'thank you' (lit. 'you have done a good deed'; cf. Holes 2016, 125). In the informants' speech, *aḥsant* (M)/*aḥsanti* (F) is used as an intensifier to mean 'well done!'. With regard to Form IX, attested CA forms indicate colours and physical defects, e.g., *iḥmarra/yaḥmarra* 'blush, become red', *iʿwağğa/yaʿwağğu* 'become hunchbacked'. In the primary data, the only occurrences of IX Form verbs are *ḥmarr/yoḥmarr* 'blush' and *ṣfarr/yiṣfarr* 'be/get yellow' due to a disease, for example.

Second Derived Pattern – $C_1VC_2C_2VC_3$

This derived form shows gemination of the second radical, i.e., $C_1aC_2C_2aC_3$. Verbs in this pattern usually have a causative meaning with respect to the basic form, e.g., *daẖal* 'enter' vs *daẖẖal* 'let in'.

Some examples from the primary data are *sallem/yisellum* 'greet', *šarraf/yišarrif* 'visit someone', *ṣaffed/yiṣaffid* 'repair'. This class of verbs follows the same rules applied in the conjugation of strong verbs, for both the s-stem and the p-stem, as shown in Table 3.47.

Table 3.47: S-stem and p-stem conjugation of the verb *šarraf* 'visit someone'

	s-stem		**p-stem**	
	Singular	**Plural**	**Singular**	**Plural**
1	*šarraf-t*	*šarraf-na*	*e-šarraf*	*n-šarraf*
2M	*šarraf-t*	*šarraf-to*	*ti-šarraf*	*ti-šarraf-o*
2F	*šarraf-ti*	*šarraf-ten*	*ti-šarraf-i*	*ti-šarraf-en*
3M	*šarraf*	*šarraf-o*	*yi-šarraf*	*yi-šarraf-o*
3F	*šarraf-it*	*šarraf-en*	*ti-šarraf*	*yi-šarraf-en*

Third Derived Pattern – $C_1VVC_2VC_3$

This derived pattern shows insertion of a long vowel after the first radical of the basic stem, i.e., $C_1āC_2aC_3$. Verbs in this class usually indicate an action performed 'on or with' someone.[65] Some examples in the primary data are *kālem/yikālum* 'talk to someone', *sāmaḥ/yisāmiḥ* 'allow someone', *nāzaʿ/yināziʿ* 'fight with someone', *sāʿad/yisāʿid* 'help someone'. Table 3.48 shows

[65] Cf. also Holes (2016, 150) for Bahraini verbs.

the s-stem and p-stem conjugations of the verb *sāfar/yisāfir* 'travel'.

Table 3.48: S-stem and p-stem conjugation of the verb *sāfar* 'travel'

	s-stem		p-stem	
	Singular	**Plural**	**Singular**	**Plural**
1	*sāfar-t*	*sāfar-na*	*e-sāfir*	*n-sāfir*
2M	*sāfar-t*	*sāfar-to*	*ti-sāfir*	*ti-sāfir-o*
2F	*sāfar-ti*	*sāfar-ten*	*ti-sāfir-i*	*ti-sāfir-en*
3M	*sāfar*	*sāfar-o*	*yi-sāfir*	*yi-sāfir-o*
3F	*sāfar-it*	*sāfar-en*	*ti-sāfir*	*yi-sāfir-en*

Fifth Derived Pattern – $tC_1VC_2C_2VC_3$

This derived pattern is formed prefixing /t-/ to the second derived form, i.e., t-$C_1aC_2C_2aC_3$, and the meaning usually associated with it is a passive or reflexive analogue of Form II, e.g., *kassar* 'smash' vs *tkassar* 'be broken'. There are also verbs in this class that exhibit an active meaning, such as *tsebbaḥ/yitsebbiḥ* 'bathe'. Table 3.49 presents the s-stem and p-stem conjugations of the verb *tmarraḍ/yitmarraḍ* 'get ill'.

Table 3.49: S-stem and p-stem conjugation of the verb *tmarraḍ* 'get ill'

	s-stem		p-stem	
	Singular	**Plural**	**Singular**	**Plural**
1	*tmarraḍ-ḍ*[66]	*tmarraḍ-na*	*e-tmarraḍ*	*ni-tmarraḍ*
2M	*tmarraḍ-ḍ*	*tmarraḍ-ḍo*	*ti-tmarraḍ*	*ti-tmarraḍ-o*
2F	*tmarraḍ-ḍi*	*tmarraḍ-ḍen*	*ti-tmarraḍ-i*	*ti-tmarraḍ-en*
3M	*tmarraḍ*	*tmarraḍ-o*	*yi-tmarraḍ*	*yi-tmarraḍ-o*
3F	*tmarraḍ-it*	*tmarraḍ-en*	*ti-tmarraḍ*	*yi-tmarraḍ-en*

[66] In this example, the /-t/ of the s-stem assimilates to the emphatic /ḍ/ of the root, as discussed in ch. 2, §2.3.

Sixth Derived Pattern – t-$C_1VVC_2VC_3$

Verbs in this class are formed prefixing /t-/ to the third derived pattern, i.e., tC_1āC_2aC_3, and usually indicate reciprocity with respect to Form III, e.g., *bāwas* 'kiss' vs *tbāwas* 'kiss one another' (Holes 2016, 153). Table 3.50 shows the s-stem and p-stem conjugations of the verb *tqārb/yitqārab* 'approach'.

Table 3.50: S-stem and p-stem conjugation of the verb *tqārb* 'approach'

	s-stem		p-stem	
	Singular	**Plural**	**Singular**	**Plural**
1	*tqārb-t*	*tqārb-na*	*e-tqārab*	*ni-tqārab*
2M	*tqārb-t*	*tqārb-to*	*ti-tqārab*	*ti-tqārb-o*
2F	*tqārb-ti*	*tqārb-ten*	*ti-tqārb-i*	*ti-tqārb-en*
3M	*tqārb*	*tqārb-o*	*yi-tqārab*	*yi-tqārb-o*
3F	*tqārb-it*	*tqārb-en*	*ti-tqārab*	*yi-tqārb-en*

Seventh Derived Pattern – (i)n$C_1VC_2VC_3$

This pattern is built by prefixing /(i)n-/ to the strong form of the verb, i.e., inC_1aC_2aC_3, and is used to indicate passivation of the basic form, e.g., *nkesar/yinkasir* 'be broken, defeated' vs *kasar* 'break'.

Table 3.51: S-stem and p-stem conjugation of the verb *nkesar* 'be broken'

	s-stem		p-stem	
	Singular	**Plural**	**Singular**	**Plural**
1	*nkesar-t*	*nkesar-ne*	*e-nkasir*	*ni-nkasir*
2M	*nkesar-t*	*nkesar-to*	*ti-nkasir*	*ti-nkasr-o*
2F	*nkesar-ti*	*nkesar-ten*	*ti-nkasr-i*	*ti-nkasr-en*
3M	*nkesar*	*nkesr-o*	*yi-nkasir*	*yi-nkasr-o*
3F	*nkesar-it*	*nkesr-en*	*ti-nkasir*	*yi-nkasr-en*

Eighth Derived Pattern – (i)$C_1tC_2VC_3$

This derived pattern is formed by infixing a /-t-/ after the second radical of the basic form of the verb, i.e., (i)$C_1tC_2aC_3$. It conveys reflexive or medio-passive sense (Holes 2016, 157) with respect to the basic stem meaning, e.g., *ʿaraf* 'know' vs *iʿtarif* 'recognise'. Table 3.52 presents the s-stem and p-stem conjugation of the verb *iẖtalaf/yuẖtlif* 'make a difference, stand out'.

Table 3.52: S-stem and p-stem conjugation of the verb *iẖtalaf* 'stand out'

	s-stem		p-stem	
	Singular	**Plural**	**Singular**	**Plural**
1	*iẖtalaf-t*	*iẖtalaf-ne*	*e-ẖtalif*	*nu-ẖtalif*
2M	*iẖtalaf-t*	*iẖtalaf-to*	*tu-ẖtalif*	*tu-ẖtalif-o*
2F	*iẖtalaf-ti*	*iẖtalaf-ten*	*tu-ẖtalif-i*	*tu-ẖtalif-en*
3M	*iẖtalaf*	*iẖtalaf-o*	*yu-ẖtlif*	*yu-ẖtlif-o*
3F	*iẖtalaf-it*	*iẖtalaf-en*	*tu-ẖtlif*	*yu-ẖtlif-en*

Tenth Derived Pattern – (i)sta$C_1C_2VC_3$

This derived pattern is formed by adding the prefix /(i)sta-/ to the root stem and, in the primary data, shows considerative or augmentative semantics compared to the basic form, e.g., *ʿāš* 'live' vs *istaʿīš* 'earn a livelihood'; *ḥmuq* 'get angry' vs *staḥmaq* 'rage with anger'. The table below shows the perfective and imperfective conjugation of the verb *staʿgil/yistaʿgil* 'hurry'.

Table 3.53: S-stem and p-stem conjugation of the verb *staʿgil* 'hurry'

	s-stem		**p-stem**	
	Singular	**Plural**	**Singular**	**Plural**
1	*staʿgil-t*	*staʿgil-ne*	*e-staʿgil*	*ni-staʿgil*
2M	*staʿgil-t*	*staʿgil-to*	*ti-staʿgil*	*ti-staʿgil-o*
2F	*staʿgil-ti*	*staʿgil-ten*	*ti-staʿgil-i*	*ti-staʿgil-en*
3M	*staʿgil*	*staʿgil-o*	*yi-staʿgil*	*yi-staʿgil-o*
3F	*staʿgil-it*	*staʿgil-en*	*ti-staʿgil*	*yi-staʿgil-en*

2.6.2. Derived Forms of Non-strong Verbs

Verbs with a geminate consonant or a glide in their root also show some derived forms, but in the primary data they are not of common occurrence. The table below reports a few examples of derived forms of this class of verbs:

Table 3.54: Derived forms of weak, hamzated, and geminate verbs

Form	**Weak verbs /w/**	**Weak verbs /y/**	**Hamzated verbs**	**Geminate verbs**
II	*waqqaf/yiwaqquf* 'maintain'	*sawwa/yisawwi* 'make'		*gedded/yigeddid* 'renew'
III	*wāqaf/yiwāqof* 'agree with'			
V		*tenne/yitenne* 'be late'		
VII		*inšād/yinšīd* 'ask about something'		
VIII		*ištāk/yištīk* 'complain' *štarā/yištri* 'buy'		
X	*stawḥad/yistaḥad* 'be alone'	*staṭnā/yistaṭnā* 'rent'	*stāḫar/yistāḫor* 'be late'	

Reinhardt (1894, 158–207) provides an overview with numerous examples of derived forms for both strong and weak verbs. Some of these verbs are also found in the pimary data. The tables provided thus far are not, of course, intended to be exhaustive for the dialect under investigation. Rather, they merely act as examples of conjugations. It may well be that with a higher number of speakers and a greater variety of topics, more verbs of this kind would have been found.

2.7. Future

In the primary data, the future is given by the simple p-stem form or by the p-stem with *b(i)*-prefix. Reinhardt (1894, 149) reports the particle *ḥa-* as a prefix for the future, but in the primary data it occurs in only one example and is not strictly a future marker.[67] It remains to properly investigate the use and functions of the prefix *ḥa-* in Omani Arabic as a temporal marker, whereas it is well known in other Arabic dialects (e.g., Egyptian). Verbal prefixes used in the informants' speech are discussed further in ch. 4, §1.2.3.

The conjugation of the p-stem verb with the *bi-* prefix is as follows:

Table 3.56: Future conjugation of the verb *katab* 'write'

	Singular	**Plural**
1	*bi-ktub*	*bi-ni-ktub*
2M	*bi-ti-ktub*	*bi-ti-kitb-o*
2F	*bi-ti-kitbi*	*bi-ti-kitb-en*
3M	*bi-yi-ktub*	*bi-yi-kitb-o*
3F	*bi-ti-ktub*	*bi-yi-kitb-en*

[67] For more details on this, see ch. 4, §1.2.3.

When the verb starts with a vowel, i.e., 1SG, it is substituted by the vowel of the prefix, e.g., *bi-ktub* 'I will write', *bi-šrub* 'I will drink', *bi-kil* 'I will eat'; whereas, if the verb is glide-initial, i.e., /w/ and /y/, the prefix loses its vowel and takes the initial vowel of the verb, e.g., *b-ūṣal* 'I will arrive'.

2.8. *kān/yikūn* as a Copula

The verb *kān/yikūn* 'be, exist' functions as both a copula and an auxiliary in the primary data. The s-stem and p-stem conjugations of the verb *kān* follow the same rules applicable to medial glide verbs, as shown in Table 3.57.

Table 3.57: S-stem and p-stem conjugation of the verb *kān* 'be, exist'

	s-stem		**p-stem**	
	Singular	**Plural**	**Singular**	**Plural**
1	*kun-t*	*kun-ne*	*e-kūn*	*ni-kūn*
2M	*kun-t*	*kun-to*	*ti-kūn*	*ti-kūn-o*
2F	*kun-ti*	*kun-ten*	*ti-kūn-i*	*ti-kūn-en*
3M	*kān*	*kān-o*	*yi-kūn*	*yi-kūn-o*
3F	*kān-at*	*kān-en*	*ti-kūn*	*yi-kūn-en*

As a copula, *kān* marks a link of qualification or identity between the subject and something else (i.e., noun, adjective). Its main use as a copula is in the narration of past events, as shown in examples (30) and (31) below:

(30) *kānat* *id-dinya* *muḏlima*

was.3FSG DEF-world.FSG dark.PP.FSG

'The world was dark' [S1]

(31) *abū Iẖlāṣ kān ʿamr šēbe*

father Ikhlas was.3MSG age old_man.MSG

'Ikhlas' father was an old man' [S2]

The verb *kān* can also be used to indicate the existential 'there were, there was' in past contexts:

(32) *aḏkur kānat syūḥ fī ēyy makān*

remember.1SG was.3FSG empty_lot.PL in any place.MSG

'I remember there were empty fields everywhere' [S2]

The use and behaviour of *kān* as an auxiliary is investigated in ch. 4, §1.2.5.

2.9. Imperative

In the primary data, the imperative mood is formed from the p-stem template of the verb without the prefixes and adding fixed suffixes. It is restricted to the second person (masculine and feminine, singular and plural). Table 3.58 shows the imperative conjugations of Forms I–X,[68] as they are produced by my informants in the primary data.

[68] Forms IV and IX are missing because, as explained in fn. 68, they rarely occur in the informants' speech. Form VII does not present an imperative conjugation in the informants' speech.

Table 3.58: Conjugations of imperative mood of verb Forms I to X.

	Singular		Plural	
Form	**M**	**F**	**M**	**F**
I	*ktub*	*kitb-i*	*kitb-o*	*kitb-en*
II	*šarrif*	*šarrif-i*	*šarrif-o*	*šarrif-en*
III	*sāfir*	*sāfir-i*	*sāfr-o*	*sāfr-en*
V	*tmarraḍ*	*tmarraḍ-i*	*tmarraḍ-o*	*tmarraḍ-en*
VI	*tqārb*	*tqārb-i*	*tqārb-o*	*tqārb-en*
VIII	*ḫtalif*	*ḫtalif-i*	*ḫtalif-o*	*ḫtalif-en*
X	*staʿgil*	*staʿgil-i*	*staʿgil-o*	*staʿgil-en*

2.10. Participles

As Payne (1997, 38) defines it, "a participle is a widely understood term for verb forms that have reduced verbal properties, but which are not full nominalisations." In many Arabic dialects, participles have verbal force, in opposition to those used as adjectives or frozen forms, e.g., *lāzim* 'it is necessary, must' (Brustad 2000, 182).

Reinhardt's (1894, 137–39) description of the active and passive participles (hereby, AP and PP, respectively) is very brief and lacks a proper analysis of their syntactic behaviour. He states that they can be used as adjectives, in questions, and in adjunction with another verb. Nevertheless, the morphological forms for both the AP and the PP he provides are the same found as those in the primary data.

2.10.1. Active Participle (AP)

Generally speaking, in modern Arabic dialects the verbal force of the AP seems to be more widespread than the nominal use.[69]

Morphologically, the AP behaves as a noun, i.e., it inflects for gender and number, but not for person. In the primary data, two main patterns are in use:

- CāCiC, which has four different forms for gender and number, e.g., MSG *kātib* 'one who writes, writing'; MPL *kātibīn* 'writing'; FSG *kātiba* 'one who writes, writing'; and FPL *kātibāt* 'writing'.
- CiCCān, e.g., *nisyān* 'forgetting'.

Derived verbs, on the other hand, only affix an *m-* (sometimes followed by an epenthetic vowel) to the p-stem form of the verb, e.g., *mṣalli* (MSG)/*mṣallya* (FSG)/*mṣallīn* (MPL)/*mṣallyāt* (FPL) 'praying, one who prays', *munkasir* (MSG)/*munkasra* (FSG)/ *munkasirīn* (MPL)/*munkasirāt* (FPL) 'broken'.

Some of the features of a verb are still carried by the AP, like its diathetic properties (i.e., transitiveness and intransitiveness) and some of its aspectual values. Preserving the diathetic properties of the verb stem which the AP is derived from implies that the AP of a transitive verb can take direct object suffixes. When a direct object is suffixed to the AP, its pattern can undergo changes. Owens (2008, 544) divided Arabic dialects in three main groups, as concerning the behaviour of APs with a direct object suffixed:

---

[69] Cf. Holes (2016) for Baḥarna dialects of Bahrain and Brustad (2000), Owens (2008), and Qafisheh (1977) for Gulf Arabic.

- No change. An object suffixed is simply added to the AP + gender/number suffix: *kātib-a* + *ha* = *kātiba-ha* 'she has written it (FSG)' (< Cairene Arabic).
- Feminine *-it*. The feminine singular takes the construct form *-it*: *kātb-it-ha* 'she has written it (FSG)', with no further changes (< Eastern Libyan Arabic).
- Intrusive *-in(n)-*. An intrusive *-in(n)-* is added between the AP and the suffix: *kātb-inn-uh* 'he has written it (MSG)'.

Most Omani dialects so far documented and the vernacular under investigation belong to the latter group. According to Owens (2008, 544), dialects belonging to this group are rare, but there are a few other examples. Holes (2018, 124) reports a list of dialects (all in the Arabian Peninsula), where the use of this infix is attested. These include: all northern Omani dialects;[70] in southern Yemen, a dialect in an area west of the Ḥaḍramawt and in Ibb; in the United Arab Emirates, mainly the Abu Dhabi and the oasis of Al-ʿAyn dialects, on the border with Oman; and all Baḥārna dialects of Bahrain, rural and urban. In addition to these, the infix is largely used in one dialect of Western Sudani Arabic and in the isolated dialects of Khurasan and Uzbekistan.[71]

---

[70] Davey (2016), in fact, provides no information on the occurence and behaviour of the AP in Dhofari Arabic.

[71] The use of this rare infix in dialects that are so geographically and morphologically distant is used by Holes (2011) to prove that this is an originally old feature of some modern dialects, probably belonging to "a group of cognate dialects in a confined geographical area" (Holes 2011, 85).

In the morphosyntactic construction, the infix in this vernacular is obligatorily applied to plural APs of both genders. The /n/ of the infix is doubled when the direct object suffix starts with a vowel:

(33) *hadā* *l-masgid* *bānay<inn>o*

DEM.PROX.MSG DEF-mosque.MSG build.AP.MSG <IN> PRON.3MSG

l-imām *ben Kāb* *aw* *ibn-o*

DEF-imam ben Ka'ab CONJ son-PRON.3MSG

'This mosque has been built by the Imam bin Kaʾab or his son' (Morano 2020, 115)

The use of the infix is obligatory between the AP and its suffixed pronoun, also for APs of derived forms:

(34) *muqaṣṣir<in>he*

negligent.AP.MSG <IN> PRON.3FSG

'He was negligent towards her' (Morano 2020, 115)

Further evidence of how productive this infix is in the district when a pronoun is suffixed is given in the traditional song presented in the Appendix of this work, where three APs of this kind appear, i.e., *tā<ynn>o* 'he is bringing him', *šārā<ynn>o* 'he is buying him', and *dā<ynn>o* 'he is putting it'.

The last category of AP analysed in this section concerns various 'frozen' forms attested throughout the Arabic-speaking world, used as either adjectives or adverbs.

Forms like *dāḫil* 'inside', *ḫārig* 'outside', *wāgid* 'many, much', and *qādim* 'next, following' are of very common occurrence in the primary data, and work mainly as adverbs:

(35) *ēn* *māmā?* *dāẖil*

where mother.FSG inside

'Where is mum? Inside' [S3]

The AP form *gāy* is also used instead of *qādim* to mean 'following, coming', as in *il-ʿām il-gāy* or *es-sana l-gāya* 'next year'. However, *gāy* cannot be counted as a fully grammaticalised form, since it inflects for gender and number and is commonly used as an AP of the verb *gā* 'to go':

(36) *anā* *gāya* *maʿ-kin*

PRON.1SG go.AP.FSG with-PRON.2FPL

'I am coming with you' [S10]

A fully grammaticalised AP form is *lāzim* 'be necessary, must', used as a modal verb, i.e., 'ought to, should, must, have to'.[72]

Finally, the AP forms *bāqī/bāqīn* 'remaining' are not entirely grammaticalised forms, but are commonly used in the everyday speech of my informants:

(37) *anā* *gubt* *tisaʿa* *awlād,* *ṯnīne* *māt-o*

PRON.1SG was_given.1SG nine.F child.MPL two.F died.3MPL

w-bāqīn *sbaʿa*

CONJ-remain.AP.MPL seven.F

'I had nine children, two died and seven remain' [S2]

2.10.2. Passive Participle (PP)

In the primary data, the PP behaves syntactically as an adjective, agreeing in gender and number with the noun it refers to. The PP of strong verbs follows the pattern maCCūC, e.g.,

---

[72] For more details on *lāzim*, the reader is referred to ch. 4, §1.2.5.

masmūḥ 'allowed', *maʿrūf* 'known', whereas geminate and weak verbs show the pattern mCaCCi, e.g., *msawwi* 'made', *mabġi* 'desired':

(38) *ntī* *magnūna*
PRON.2FSG crazy.PP.FSG
'You are crazy' [S4]

(39) *anā* *mutāḥḥira*
PRON.1SG late.PP.FSG
'I am late' [S10]

As a consequence of the recession of the apophonic passive—as detailed in the next section—the PP is often used instead of a passive form of the verb to express the passive voice.

Form VII, which usually expresses passivation of the basic form, lacks a PP and shows only an AP with passive value:

(40) *ḏelā* *el-fanāgīn* *munkisirīn*
DEM.PROX.MPL DEF-coffee_cup.MPL broken.AP.MPL
'These coffee cups are broken' [S5]

Existentiality can also be expressed by the PP forms *mawgūd* (M)/*mawgūda* (F), as in:

(41) *mā* *mawgūd* *iš-šuwāraʿ*
NEG EXIST.PP.MSG DEF-road.PL
'Roads did not exist' [S2]

2.10.3. Participial Forms and Verbal Nouns of Derived Forms

Participial forms and verbal nouns of derived forms follow specific patterns that differ from the ones used for the basic form of the verb. In the Table below, the active and passive participle and the corresponding verbal noun is presented for each derived form, with the sole exception of Form VII, which lacks a PP form.

Table 3.55: Participial forms and verbal nouns of derived forms

Form	Passive participle	Active participle	Verbal noun
II	*mšarraf*	*mšarrif*	*tašrīf*
III	*msāfar*	*msāfir*	*musāfar*
V	*mtamarraḍ*	*mtammariḍ*	*tamarruḍ*
VI	*mtaqārab*	*mtaqārib*	*taqārub*
VII		*munkasir*	*nkasār*
VIII	*muḫtalaf*	*muḫtalif*	*ḫtilāf*
X	*mustaʿgal*	*mistaʿgil*	*stiʿgāl*

2.11. Passive

The so-called apophonic, or 'internal', passive—which involves a change in the vowel pattern of the basic verb both in its s-stem and p-stem forms—is often reckoned as one of the 'conservative' features ascribed to Peninsular dialects. In Oman, Holes (1998) analyses the occurrence of the apophonic passive in three sedentary dialects of the Sharqiyyah and Jabal Akhdar regions. The results show that the apophonic passive in these dialects "seems functional only in the imperfect tense and is common only in certain morphological categories of the verb—and only then in the 3rd person, with perfect examples seemingly limited to certain lexical items and fixed expressions" (Holes 1998, 359). Different views are presented by Eades (2009), who analyses the occurrence of the apophonic passive in the Bedouin dialect of the Hidyīwī tribe of northern Oman:

here, "the AP [apophonic passive] is significantly more productive than in the sedentary dialects described by Holes" (Eades 2009, 5). He supports the claim by bringing examples of the apophonic passive both in the s-stem and in the p-stem of verbs used by his informants, stating, however, that passive imperfect verbs are less frequently used (Eades 2009, 13). Interestingly, Eades (2009, 15–18) also reports an account of how the coastal dialects of Oman are, in his opinion, coping with the recession of the apophonic passive as "a functioning morphological category": their strategy is the employment of the affixed forms of the verb (i.e., Form VII).[73]

The difference in the use of one or the other form, according to Holes (1998, 354, italics in the text), is related to the subject of the passive verb: 'the Omani *majhūl* form is used to refer to an *action* whose agent is unknown or unspecified, while the affixational forms denote *the state of the patient* as a result of a preceding action, implied or stated'.

Reinhardt (1894, 154) reports the internal passive as the norm in the dialect spoken by the Banū Kharūṣ tribe; and Davey (2016, 152) states that the retention of the internal passive is one of the features most characteristic of the Arabic dialect spoken in Dhofar.

In the dialect spoken by present-day natives of the al-ʿAwābī district, the apophonic passive seems to be receding. I base this assumption partly on the evidence brought by primary

---

[73] On this, see Eades (2009, 15): "the affixed forms emphasise state of the patient, and the involvement of an agent is not necessarily implied."

data, where the apophonic passive appears only with certain verbs and in specific contexts, and partly on Reinhardt's statement cited above. If for the German author the apophonic passive was the norm, this is not validated by the primary data in this study. In its place, the primary data show that speakers employ either affixed forms or constructions with the PP, which is not encountered in the literature as a 'regular' form.[74]

In the primary data—when the apophonic passive occurs—the s-stem displays the vowel sequence *i-i* instead of *a-a* (or *e-e*, if the *imāla* occurs) or the *a-i* of the active form, e.g., *kitib* 'it was written'–*keteb* 'he wrote', whereas the p-stem displays the vowels *u-a* instead of the *i-u* of the active voice, e.g., *yuktab* 'it is written'–*yiktub* 'he writes', or *i-a* when the second vowel of the active conjugation is /a/, e.g., *yiṭbaḥ* 'it is cooked', thus being homophonous with the active p-stem verb form.

According to the primary data, the internal passive is limited to the verb 'to be born':

---

[74] Retsö (1983, 9):

> In Arabic the situation is more complex; from an intuitive survey of the possible 'passive' constructions in any Arabic dialect, it becomes clear that a 'passive' verb in Arabic may have several different morphological shapes. Although one or two of these is usually considered the 'regular' or 'normal' one and indeed is the most frequent, all known forms of this language have so many means of forming a 'passive' verb that the morphology of the passive must be taken into consideration and analysed closely.

(42) *wilidt* *fi-l-ʿawābī,* *illi* *mawgūda* *fi-l-baṭīna*
was born.1SG in-DEF-ʿawābī REL EXIST.PP.FSG in-DEF-Baṭīna
'I was born in al-ʿAwābī, which is in al-Batinah' [S15]

Or it is linked to specific contexts, such as description of processes:

(43) *il-ḥarmal* *yistaḫdam* *ʿala* *niṭāq* *wāṣiʿ*
DEF-plant_name is_used.3MSG for range.MSG wide.MSG
il-amrāḍ
DEF-disease.PL
'The Rhazya Stricta is used for a wide range of diseases' [S11]

In the example below, a speaker from Wādī Banī Kharūṣ describes the preparation of the *ḥarmal* (scientific name *Rhazya Stricta*), a plant used in traditional medicine to treat epilepsy and chronic headaches.

(44) *li-ṣ-ṣarʿ:* ***yiṭbaḥ*** *maqdār arbaʿ kīlō fī liter w-naṣf māy w-* ***yiṭbaḥ*** *giddan ḥattā yabqā liter wāḥid w-**yufaṭṭar** bi-hu al-muṣāb bi-sarʿa li-muddit ṯalaṯīn yōm maqdār milʿaqtīn fī ʿasal fa-inn es-sarʿa yazūl ʿind-o w-law kān mazmūnan.*
li-ṣudaʿ: ***yiṭbaḥ*** *maqdār aw qiṭʿīn min el-ḥarmal fī liter māy ṯum* ***yunāwal*** *al-muṣāb maqdār milʿaqa aṣ-ṣabaḥ w-ṯanye ḍ-ḍuhur w-ṯalṯe fī-lʿašā li-muddit il-usbūʿ fa-inn eṣ-ṣudaʿ ir-rās il-muzmin yazūl.*
'For epilepsy: an amount of four kilos is cooked in a litre and half of water and it is cooked well until it remains (only) one litre; then it is given to the infirm as breakfast (in the morning) as soon as possible for the period of thir-

ty days; the amount is of two spoons in the honey and then he will recover fast even when it is chronic.
For a headache: an amount of two pieces of *ḥarmal* is cooked in a litre of water, then it is given to the infirm (in the quantity of) one spoon in the morning, a second in the afternoon and a third at dinner for a period of one week; in this way, the chronic headache heals.' [S11]

Example (44) shows the passive form *yiṭbaḥ*, homophonous with its active counterpart. Such verbs can also be interpreted as 3MSG, i.e., 'he cooks', the passivity interpretable only through the context.

It is not possible, however, at this point, to give a full conjugation of the passive form in the dialect spoken by the consultants due to the lack of suitable data.

Other verbs, like 'be said', 'be believed' or 'be known' are frequently expressed through a 3MPL or 3MSG p-stem verb with an impersonal subject:

(45) *qālo* *inn* *al-walad* *ḥayy* *w-yaʕīš*
said.3MPL that DEF-boy.MSG alive.MSG CONJ-live.3MSG
fī-l-gebel
in-DEF-mountain.MSG
'It is said (lit. 'they said') that the boy is alive and lives in the mountains' [S6]

(46) *ʕarafna* *l-gaww* *byikūn* *akṯar* *ḥarr*
knew.1PL DEF-weather FUT.be.3MSG more hot.M
'It is known (lit. 'we came to know') that the weather will get hotter' [S4]

(47) *yaʿtaqido inn sanānīr tišūf il-ginn*
believe.3MPL that cat.PL see.3FSG DEF-ginn
'It is believed (lit. 'they believe') that cats see ginns' [S14]

The active impersonal form of the verb is usually employed when a specific subject is not mentioned. This is in accordance with what Eades (2009, 9) found in his data.

The PP can also be employed as one of the methods for expressing the passive voice in the district, though it patterns morphologically as an adjective.

(48) *al-ašgār masqāya*
DEF-tree.PL watered.PP.FSG
'The plants have been watered' [S6]

(49) *il-bēt mabnī min ḫams sanūwāt*
DEF-house.MSG build.PP.MSG from five.M year.FPL
'It's five years since the house has been built' [S12]

(50) *il-maʿrūf inn iḏā qarīti il-qurān wa-ntī*
DEF-know.PP.MSG that if read.2FSG DEF-quran CONJ-PRON.2FSG
marīḍa inšāllah tathāwen
sick.FSG inshallah get_better.2FPL
'It is known that if you read the Quran when you are ill, you will get better' [S10]

Admittedly, examples expressing passivity in the primary data are quite few and assessing a criterion for the use of one or the other form on the basis of the data available is almost impossible. We can perhaps postulate that the apophonic passive has undergone recession since Reinhardt's time due to the influence of other Arabic varieties in the area and exposure to the media and education among the younger generation, as has occurred in the case of other Arabic dialects in the Peninsula. Holes (1998) suggests linguistic and sociolinguistic factors that have threatened the use of the apophonic passive in Oman and in the Gulf. Among the linguistic factors, he mentions certain phonological changes in the active/passive patterns that blur the semantic distinction between the two: *yiṭbaḥ* in (44) is an example of morphologically identical patterns where passivity can only be inferred by the context. He reckons the apophonic passive as a sign of 'interior speech', and the recent economic and political development of coastal populations (and their dialects)—for example, the overwhelming growth of the capital Muscat and its port Matrah, but also of Salalah, Sur, and other coastal towns—favoured the loss of more archaic features, of which the apophonic passive is an example.[75]

In the light of sociopolitical observations made in the first chapter of this work, the al-ʿAwābī district is a developing centre whose population has grown exponentially over the last few decades. Its younger population, often fully educated, moves

[75] Holes (1998, 361):

> The recession of the AP verb, a typical marker of 'interior' speech, is thus just one small aspect of a much larger sociolinguistic change. Much the same thing can be said of the situation in Bahrain. The S-dialects here are under pressure from the dominant B-dialect, which, within Bahrain, is associated with the business elite and the ruling family, and, within the immediately surrounding area, shows a strong typological affinity with the B-dialects of the elites in Kuwait, Qatar and the UAE.

about freely within the region. Therefore, the recession of such a 'conservative' feature as the apophonic passive should not come as a surprise.

CHAPTER 4: SYNTAX

This chapter deals with the analysis and description of syntax in the variety of Arabic spoken in the district of al-ᶜAwābī. The primary data in this chapter come from the corpora of spontaneous speech recorded with the informants and the WhatsApp messages (presented in Arabic script) used for the elicitation of specific syntactic structures.

The third section, i.e., "Dritter Theil," of Reinhardt's (1894) work is devoted to the syntax of the Banū Kharūṣī vernacular. In the introduction to the section—which he concisely entitles "Remarks on the Syntax and general additions"—Reinhardt suggests that the beginner-level learner can generally refer to the same syntactic rules applied in CA, albeit encouraging the students to go through all the examples for more clarity. He continues by saying, however, that it is Omani practice to cut sentences short and use specific "Semitic expressions" that often force the listener to pay particular attention.[1] It is not clear what Reinhardt means by 'Semitic expressions', we may presume he refers to syntactic constructions that might have sounded more archaic to his ear.

[1] Reinhardt (1894, 261):

> Charakterisch für das Omani, namentlich der Unterhaltung, ist das Fehlen alles Bombastischen, die kurze und kernige, echt semitische Ausdrucksweise, welche den Horer zwingt, dem haufig bloss andeutungsweise Gesprochenen genau zu folgen resp. dasselbe selbstthatig auszudenken.

 https://doi.org/10.11647/OBP.0298.04

Reinhardt's section then passes to a brief analysis of agreement rules, word order, the verb, and various types of clauses. The discussion on verbs partly examines tense and aspect, although not explicitly acknowledged by the German author, and will be briefly mentioned in the discussion on tense and aspect later in this chapter. The section on clauses follows the verbs, providing limited analysis as such, but plenty of examples.

Overall, it seems that not much has changed in the main syntactic structures of the al-ʿAwābī district, but this chapter contributes a proper analysis and further examples extrapolated from the primary data. The comparison with Reinhardt's notes and remarks are signposted throughout to signal diachronic variation in the district.

In order to give a clear and concise explanation of how the syntax of this variety of Arabic works, the present chapter has been divided into two broad categories, namely phrases and clauses. This choice has been made following other theoretical works on syntax (e.g., Payne 1997) and works that analyse syntactic structures in other Arabic varieties (e.g., Watson 1993). Payne (1997) deemed it especially appropriate for the theoretical background in approaching the study of syntax.

The category of phrases includes noun, verb, and prepositional phrases.

Noun phrase analysis includes the description of rules that regulate the agreement with nouns, the 'construct state', the use of genitive markers, and the attributive clause, considered here as a modifier of the noun phrase. Verb phrases consider a brief discussion on TAM cateories related to the morphological form of the verb, the verbal prefixes, and the auxiliaries used in this variety of Omani Arabic. Finally, prepositional phrases include existentials (i.e., prepositions used to indicate the existence or presence of something) and possession.

The second broad category includes: simple nominal clauses, simple verbal clauses, and complex clauses. The first subsection will analyse the structure of nominal and locational clauses in the vernacular under investigation; the subsection on verbal clauses will deal mainly with agreement in verbal contexts and word order, whereas the subsection on complex clauses includes adverbial clauses and complement clauses. The former group is further subdivided in time, location, manner, purpose, reason,[2] and the conditional clause.

These two broad categories are then followed by a minor section on negation, which analyses it in both nominal and verbal contexts, adding some remarks on Reinhardt's (1894) negation system.

1.0. Phrases

A phrase is "any term which functions as a major predicator—predicand or predicate[3]—or as a complement, attribute or adverb, but which lacks the predicand-predicate structure typical

[2] According to the division made by Payne (1997, 317).

[3] "The predicate is the portion of a clause, excluding the subject that expresses something about the subject" (https://glossary.sil.org/term/predicate). Consequently, the predicand is the subject of a clause, what the predicate relates to.

of clauses" (Watson 1993, 15). Thus, a phrase is any part of a sentence that modifies the so-called head word (i.e., the nucleus that determines the syntactic category of that phrase), and is henceforth called modifier.

There are three major types of phrases: noun phrase, verb phrase and prepositional phrase.

1.1. Noun Phrases

Noun phrases are characterised by elements such as determination, gender and number, modifiers, different types of annexation structures, i.e., 'construct state', numerals, and demonstratives (Holes 2016, 218), and the analytic genitive. In this section, noun phrases and adjectival noun phrases, i.e., a head noun and a modifier, will be analysed (§1.1.1), followed by some remarks on nominal agreement (§1.1.2). After those, two major sections will analyse the use of construct state and genitive markers in the primary data (§1.1.3) and the behaviour of the attributive clause, considered here as modifier of the noun phrase (§1.1.4).

Determination of nouns is signalled by means of the definite article *(i)l-/el-* prefixed to the determined word, e.g., *il-bēt* 'the house', *el-madrasa* 'the school'. A noun is also definite when it is the first element in an annexation construction, e.g., *kitāb el-bint* 'the book of the girl, the girl's book' or when it is followed by a possessive suffix pronoun, e.g., *zōg-he* 'her husband', *yad-i* 'my hand'. A determined head noun constitutes a noun phrase on its own, but it can also optionally be followed by a modifier.

1.1.1. Adjectival Noun Phrases

If the modifier is an adjective acting as attributive modifier, it usually follows the noun and agrees with it in definiteness, e.g., *el-bint iṣ-ṣaġīra* 'the young girl', *bēt qadīm* 'an old house'. Theoretically, there is no limit to the number of adjectives that can modify a head noun in a noun phrase (although in the primary data only strings of maximum two adjectives appear):

(1) *is-sannūr iṣ-ṣaġīr il-byāḍ*
DEF-cat DEF-small.MSG DEF-white.MSG
'The small white cat' [S5]

On the other hand, if the modifier is a cardinal number, it usually precedes the noun when it is indefinite, e.g., *tisaʿ awlād* 'nine children', *ṯalāṯa ašhur* 'three months'.[4] If the modifier is a demonstrative pronoun, the following lexical item is always definite, e.g., *haḏā l-kitāb* 'this book'. Lastly, if the modifier is a quantifier, the head noun always follows the modifier, e.g., *baʿaḍ kutub* 'some books'.[5]

Adjectival noun phrases include also head nouns modified by *wāgid* ('many, much') and *šweyy* (MSG) / *šweyya* (FSG) ('a little, a bit'), with apparently no restrictions in the order of items:

---

[4] For more details on numerals, the reader is referred to ch. 3, §1.7.2.

[5] Quantifiers can be followed by a singular or a plural noun, depending on the quantifier itself. For more details, the reader is referred to ch. 3, §1.8.1.

(2) *il-gaww* *wāgid* *ḥarr* *il-yōm*

DEF-weather very hot.MSG DEF-day.MSG

'The weather is very hot today.' [S14]

(3) *bint* *uḫt-ī* *rabša* *šweyya*

girl.FSG sister.FSG-PRON.1SG naughty.FSG a bit.FSG

'My niece (lit. 'my sister's daughter) is a bit naughty' [S12]

1.1.2. Some Remarks on Agreement in Noun Phrases

Singular head nouns agree in gender and number with their attributive modifiers with no exceptions: feminine singular, e.g., *el-bint iṣ-ṣaġīra* 'the young girl', *siyyāra ḫarbāna* 'a broken-down car', and masculine singular, e.g., *eš-šabb iṣ-ṣaġīr* 'the young boy', *bēt gedīd* 'a new house'.

The discussion on agreement with plural head nouns in Arabic takes into consideration various factors: animacy (i.e., human vs non-human) appears to be a determining feature in assigning agreement patterns to Arabic heads, as well as 'individuation'.[6] Brustad (2000, 53) reports three main agreement systems for Kuwaiti Arabic:

> in the first, all plural nouns take masculine plural agreement; the second system distinguishes between human and non-human, and all non-human nouns take feminine singular agreement; and a third system combines rules

[6] Brustad (2000, 24) includes six main features that can affect the 'individuation' of a noun and that play a role when it comes to agreement rules: agency; definiteness; specificity vs genericness; textual or physical prominence; qualification; and quantification vs collectivity.

from the first two and allows either masculine plural or feminine singular agreement with non-human nouns.

These so-called systems, however, show great variation among speakers, and this is visibile also in the primary data presented in this study.[7] Brustad (2000, 54) justifies this variation by correlating it to the degree of individuation manifest by the Arabic head. This applies, for example, to collective nouns and plural heads identifying animate or non-animate entities.[8]

A major distinction to be made when talking about plural agreement is based on the aforementioned 'animacy' feature of some Arabic nouns and distinguishes between human and non-human lexical items. The non-human group can be further distinguished in subcategories of inanimate (e.g., objects) and animate non-human (e.g., animals).

We have already seen how Omani Arabic as a broad category retains feminine plural agreement in nouns, verbs, adjectives, and pronouns. This factor impacts on the agreement patterns chosen by the speakers in this study. Therefore, I chose to follow the distinction in 'strict' (i.e., PL–PL) and 'deflected' (i.e., PL–FSG) agreement, as reported by Holes (2016, 326).

In the primary data, noun phrases with inanimate plural heads tend to take deflected agreement, whereas noun phrases

---

[7] Brustad (2000, 53) rightly states that 'systems' might not be the approapriate term to use, if speakers can "freely alternate" between them.

[8] For more detailes on this topic in Omani Arabic, the interested reader is referred to Bettega (2017), who analyses various animate and inanimate plural controllers, taking into consideration such factors as definiteness, qualification, head type, specificity, and concreteness.

with human and animate non-human plural heads take strict agreement according to the gender of the head noun.

Human head nouns with strict agreement:

(4) *el-banāt* *el-mašġūlāt*
DEF-girl.FPL DEF-busy.PP.FPL
'The busy girls' [S3]

(5) *er-rgāl* *it-taʿbānīn*
DEF-man.MPL DEF-tired.MPL
'The tired men' [S4]

Inanimate head nouns with deflected agreement:

(6) *mustašfayāt* *saġīra* *ḫāṣṣa*
hospital.FPL small.FSG private.FSG
'Small private hospitals' [S1]

(7) *il-malābis* *il-gedīda*
DEF-clothes.MPL DEF-new.FSG
'The new clothes' [S10]

(8) *aṭbāq* *laḏīḏa*
dish.MPL tasty.FSG
'Tasty dishes' [S5]

(9) *ašgār* *masqāya*
tree.FPL watered.PP.FSG
'Watered trees' [S12]

The rules shown in examples (7)–(9) are in contrast with Reinhardt (1894, 265), who generically states that broken plurals—unless masculine by nature—have strict agreement.

Collective nouns can also be distinguished in terms of animate and inanimate, in referring to the agreement rules. Collective animate non-human nouns, such as livestock, e.g., *bōš* 'camels', *hōš* 'goats', and *baqar* 'cows', are grammatically treated as feminine plurals, as seems to happen in the primary data for animals in general:[9]

(10) *el-bōš* *el-qalīlāt*
DEF-camel.COLL DEF-few.FPL
'The few camels' [S4]

(11) *el-hōš* *yūklen*
DEF-goat.COLL eat.3FPL
'The goats are eating.' [S8]

(12) *baqar* *sūdāt*
cow.COLL black.FPL
'Black cows' [S14]

Inanimate collective nouns, e.g., 'hair', 'chickpeas', 'dates', show masculine singular agreement in the primary data.

(13) *hadā* *d-dengu* *ladīd* *wāgid*
DEM.PROX.MSG DEF-chickpea.COLL tasty.MSG very
'These chickpeas are very delicious.' [S10]

---

[9] Consider these examples: *al-faʿyān yaʿīšen fī-l-gibāl* 'Snakes are common (lit. 'live') in the mountains' [S5], or *hadēlā l-kullāb kabīrāt* 'these dogs are big' [S9]. Reinhardt (1894, 266) also reports that collective nouns referring to animals behave as feminine when it comes to agreement rules.

(14) *ḫt-ī* *šaʿar-he* *ṭawīl* *wa*
sister.FSG-PRON.1SG hair.COLL-PRON.3FSG long.MSG CONJ
swed
black.MSG
'My sister has long black hair.' [S9]

The words used to indicate dates vary according to the ripeness of the date, but the most general ones are *tumur*, *suḥḥ*, and *raṭab*. While *tumur* is a plural form (SG *tamr*) and, therefore, behaves as other plural nouns, *suḥḥ* and *raṭab* are collectives and show different behaviours when it comes to agreement. Consider the following:

(15) *is-suḥḥ* *el-ḥelū*
DEF-date.COLL DEF-sweet.MSG
'The sweet dates'

(16) *yišill* *ir-raṭab* *wa-yibīʿ-hum*
take.3MSG DEF-date.COLL CONJ-sell.3MSG-PRON.3MPL
'He takes dates and sells them'[10] [S2]

In (15), *suḥḥ* attracts masculine singular agreement for all the participants to this study.[11] The term *raṭab*, on the other hand, is definite and attracts masculine plural agreement (expressed through the suffix pronoun *-hum* 'them'). Further evidence of the anomalous behaviour of *raṭab* is provided in example (77)

[10] Although examples (11), (13), (14), and (16) are not noun phrases, they serve to support the argument about agreement with collective heads.

[11] Reinhardt (1894, 266) reports an example with *soḥḥ*, which also takes masculine singular agreement.

of this chapter: in that instance, *raṭab* is indefinite and attracts masculine singular agreement. The peculiar behaviour of *raṭab* might be explained by the fact that it is considered a collective noun only when indefinite and not when definite. If so, then individuation might play a role in identifying *raṭab* as a masculine plural noun, especially when looking at the features of specificity and definiteness. It would be interesting to investigate further how inanimate collective nouns are treated elsewhere in the district and in Oman or neighbouring countries, although often not systematically used.

Dual nouns take, in the primary data, plural agreement and agree in gender with the head noun:[12]

(17) *haḏēlā* *l-mustašfīn* *al-gadīdāt*
DEM.PROX.FPL DEF-hospital.FDL DEF-new.FPL
'These two new hospitals' [S1]

(18) *riggālīn* *zenīn*
man.DL good.MPL
'Two good men' [S3]

In (17), both the demonstrative pronoun *haḏēlā* and the adjective *gedīdāt* agree with the head noun, e.g., the dual form *mustašfīn*, as feminine plurals. This happens because a dual noun "indicates some degree of individuation, and hence usually does not provide collective reference" (Brustad 2000, 57).

[12] In accordance with Reinhardt's (1894, 267) data.

1.1.3. Synthetic and Analytic Genitive

In modern Arabic dialects, possession and ownership are variously expressed. The comparative study of possessive linkers by Eksell-Harning (1980) is a good starting point, as well as the work by Bettega (2019b), which the interested reader is referred to for more insights on the topic.

In the primary data, two main constructions can be found: the construct phrase (or synthetic genitive, known in Arabic as *iḍāfa*), which links together two nouns in a relationship of possessor and possessed, and the analytic genitive (henceforth, AG), which uses genitive markers to express possession or relationship between two nouns.

The synthetic genitive is a construction that consists of a noun and a modifier, usually linked by the definite article *(i)l-* /*el-* depending on the context:

(19) *bistān* *el-gīrān*
garden.SG DEF-neighbour.MPL
'The garden of the neighbours' [S15]

(20) *maṣnaʿ* *it-tumūr*
factory.SG DEF-date.PL
'Date factory' [S2]

(21) *markaz* *iṣ-ṣaḥḥa* *n-nisā*
centre.SG DEF-health.FSG DEF-woman.FPL
'Centre for women's health' [S7]

(22) *malkat* *nūr*
engagement.FSG Nur
'Nur's engagement' [S3]

These examples show how the synthetic genitive construction does not exclusively indicate a relationship of possession, but also a relationship of generic belonging or characterisation, despite displaying the same pattern as nouns in a genuinely possessive construction. This is the case in examples (19) and (22), whereas example (20) provides evidence of a relationship of characterisation or description specifying the type of factory. Lastly, example (21) shows a double construct state. Although in theory there is no limit to the number of possible coordinated components in a construct state if the juxtaposition is maintained, very long strings of synthetic genitive are almost null in the primary data; strings that count more than three elements are usually interrupted by employing an AG construction (see further in this section).

In the synthetic genitive phrase, nothing can come between the noun and the modifier, except for the definite article or a demonstrative pronoun, e.g., *šaʿar haḏī l-bint* 'the hair of this girl'—considered to be in apposition to the lexical item it precedes.

In the al-ʿAwābī district vernacular, it is possible to use the synthetic genitive construction for the following categories: alienable possession, such as in example (19) above, and inalienable possession, e.g., *yad el-bint* 'the girl's hand'; naming, e.g., *madīnat ir-rustāq* 'the town of Rustaq', where the first noun is a geographical noun and the second is a proper noun; container-contents, e.g., *fingān qahwa* 'a cup of coffee' and not 'a coffee cup', or example (20) above, where the first is a noun denoting an object and the second is a noun of substance;[13] and material, e.g., *ḫātim ḏahab* 'a gold ring', where the first is a concrete noun and the second is a noun of material. The primary data, however, show that for the latter category, the syntethic genitive and AG constructions are interchangeable irrespective of age, provenance, or level of education of the speaker, e.g., *ḫātim māl ḏahab* 'a gold ring'.

The synthetic genitive construction is always considered definite, if the second term of the annexation is determined, as in examples (19)–(21), and in the genitive relations of alienable/inalienable possession and naming. In the genitive relations of container-content and material, instead, the synthetic genitive can also be indefinite.

Another common example of synthetic genitive is the relationship of possession expressed through the possessive pronouns (see ch. 3, §1.2.3). Nouns that have "inherent possession"—in Payne's (1997, 105) terminology—use this type of construction. These include body parts, kinship, and terms referring to personal adornments, e.g., *bint-i* 'my daughter'; *yad-iš* 'your (FSG) hand; *kumm-o* 'his *kumma* (Omani hat)'.

The second type of possessive construction sees the use of genitive markers or exponents, i.e., grammaticalised nouns expressing 'property' or 'ownership', and it is known in the literature as the analytic genitive. Eksell-Harning (1980, 10–11)

[13] Watson (1993, 183) defines this genitive relation as "genitive of description," which are usually indefinite: "the sense of genitive of description can be rendered attributively by making the modifier a relational (*nisbah*) or other adjective."

states that "modern Arabic dialects show a tendency towards an analytic language structure," probably caused by the loss of the case endings and, in some cases, by the reduction of the categories of number and gender. The AG is, indeed, found throughout the Arabic-speaking world, although different dialects use different genitive exponents with different functions, scope, and limitations. In most of the dialects, both synthetic and analytic genitive constructions are used, "and the choice between them creates a dynamic process of language development" (Eksell-Harning 1980, 11).

According to the classification made by Eksell-Harning (1980, 158) in her comparative study, Omani Arabic varieties belong to the second group of dialects, where the AG occurs sporadically, the semantic categories of the AG cannot be structured, and formal factors are decisive for the choice of the AG. However, Eksell-Harning's sources for Oman were mainly Reinhardt (1894) for the northern part, and Rhodokanakis (1908, 1911)[14] for Dhofar, whereas more recent studies show different behaviours of genitive exponents in both areas.

The Omani dialects for which we have documentation present three main markers, all derived from nouns expressing possession and ownership in some way: in Dhofar, according to Davey (2016), *ḥaqq* 'right, entitlement' and *māl* 'property' are of common occurrence, with no difference in use or function;[15] a

[14] These works have not been used as sources for this study, since Davey (2016) gives a much more reliable and recent account of the Arabic dialect spoken in Dhofar today.

[15] Taking into consideration Eksell-Harning's use of Rhodokanakis (1908, 1911) as source for Dhofari Arabic, Davey (2016, 228) states:

third type is *ḥāl* 'state', reported also by Reinhardt (1894) and of common occurrence in the primary data presented in this study. The main problem with Reinhardt's (1894, 79) description of genitive markers is that, despite stating that *ḥāl* and *māl* are *häufig* 'common', they both appear very sporadically in the texts reported at the end of his work. The German scholar adds other grammaticalised terms apparently used as genitive markers in his informants' speech. These are the APs *rāy/rāyāt* 'seeing', *ṣāḥib* 'owner', and *bū* < ابو 'father'. The latter is also used as a relative pronoun. With the sole exceptions of *ḥāl* and *māl*, and partly of *bū*, none of the other markers reported by Reinhardt occur in the primary data.

Based on the primary data, the most common exponents in use are indeed *ḥāl* and *māl*. However, only *māl* conveys a genitive function, whereas *ḥāl* is instead syntactically a preposition used to convey a completely different type of relation in this dialect.

In contrast with Dhofari Arabic, *ḥāl* and *māl* are indeclinable forms, which means that they do not agree in gender and number with the noun they refer to, acting merely as linkers between the noun (N) and the modifier (M).

The phrase with an exponent usually follows this construction: N + *māl* / *ḥāl* + M, e.g., *dišdaša māl ir-riggāl* 'a men's dishdasha'; *hadīya ḥāl Nūr* 'the gift for Nur'. The modifier, as in

---

"the current data in this study does indeed reveal that the AGC [analytic genitive construction] is far more common in CDA [coastal Dhofari Arabic] than was previously thought, and can express a variety of different possessive relationships".

the case of the synthetic genitive, can be another noun, a participle, an adjective, a numeral, or an infinitive—and it is definite.

Examples with an indefinite modifier are rare in the primary data, but they can be found, for example, in the categories of material, e.g., *ḥigāb māl ḥarīr* 'a silk hijab', and of non-possessive qualification, e.g., example (25) below. This type of relationship can also be found in Sample Text 2—provided in the Appendix of this study—*ʕyšti māl gebel* 'my life in the mountains'. The latter example is particularly interesting because the term *gebel* seems to convey characterisation and certainly not possession. Using this phrase, the speaker intends to draw attention to the type of life he will talk about, i.e., the part of his life spent in the mountains. In these cases—although quite rare in the primary data—the exponenet conveys a relationship not of possession, but rather of description or qualification.

Similarly, this type of relationship is conveyed by the genitive marker *māl* in expressions of professions and specialisation, e.g., *duktur māl wasm* 'doctor of traditional medicine', *brofesūr māl l-adab il-ingrīziyya* 'professor of English literature'.

Brustad (2000) identifies formal and pragmatic factors that come into play when the speaker needs to choose between the synthetic genitive and the AG contruction. Among the formal motivations, Brustad (2000, 74) considers "multi-term annexation (three or more nouns), the presence of modifying adjectives and parallel phrases with more than one head noun." This is consistent with the primary data presented in this study, where *māl* can be used to cut the line of coordinated items in a construct phrase, as in

(23) *maktab il-qabūl* ***māl*** *el-madrasa*
office.SG DEF-admission.SG GEN DEF-school.FSG
'The admission office of the school' [S7]

Furthermore, the genitive exponent is preferred with foreign loanwords:

(24) *instagram* ***māl****-iš*
Instagram GEN-PRON.2FSG
'Your Instagram profile' [S5]

(25) *raqm-o* ***māl*** *whatsapp*
number.SG-PRON.3MSG GEN WhatsApp
'His WhatsApp number' [S9]

With nouns ending with a long vowel:

(26) *kursī* ***māl****-i*
sofa.SG GEN-PRON.1SG
'My sofa' [S7]

(27) *gūṭī* ***māl****-iš*
shoe.SG GEN-PRON.2FSG
'Your shoe' [S12]

and when the AG noun phrase is in predicative position within a nominal clause, e.g., *hadī is-siyyāra māl-i* 'this car is mine'.[16]

Words of foreign origin may or may not take the genitive marker: nouns like *tilifūn* 'telephone' or *tītūn* 'toddler'[17] seem to

[16] See current chapter, §2.1 for more details on nominal clauses.
[17] The form *tītūn* is a Swahili loanword.

prefer a synthetic genitive construction, e.g., *tilifūn-iš* 'your (FSG) phone', *tītūn-he* 'her toddler'. A possible explanation is that they are treated by the speaker as inalienable possessions and behave syntactically as such.

Among the pragmatic functions of the genitive exponent, Brustad (2000, 76) argues that "the exponent places a focus on the *possessing* noun not conveyed by the construct phrase" (italics in the original). This statement might explain the simultaneous use of the synthetic and analytic genitive constructions also found in the primary data. Thus, for example, a phrase like *kitāb el-bint* 'the book of the girl' can be replaced by *kitāb māl el-bint,* with no apparent difference in meaning, but a difference in function: *māl* emphasises the possessor, in this case the girl (*bint*).

This interchange in the constructions for expressing possession is valid for almost every kind of relation, except for terms having inherent possessive value, such as parts of the body and kinship. Thus, it is not possible to find in the primary data phrases like **umm māl-o* 'his mother', but always *umm-o*; or like **yad māl-iš* 'your (FSG) hand', but always *yad-iš*, irrespective of gender, age, provenance, or level of education of the speaker.

The exponent *ḥāl*, conversely, conveys a function different from that of *māl.* In accordance with the primary data collected, *ḥāl* cannot be considered a marker of genitive relation, but rather is a preposition, albeit carrying strong pragmatic values.[18]

[18] Davey (2016, 230) reports some examples where the genitive exponents *māl* and *ḥaqq* appear to be interchangeable, "with no resulting

If *māl* is used mainly to express a genitive relation of belonging, *ḥāl* is used in contexts that indicate a benefactual relation: in all the examples found in the primary data, *ḥāl* expresses a benefit for the modifier (the second item of the annexation, as stated above) and what in English translates as 'for, to'.

(28) *ẖaḏo* *awlād* *ʿamm-ha* *šey*
took.3MPL child.MPL uncle.MSG-PRON.3FSG something
w-bāqit ***ḥāl**-he*
CONJ-remain.AP.MSG PREP-PRON.3FSG
'Her cousins took something, and the rest was for her.' [S1]

(29) *haḏī* *l-hadīya* ***ḥāl**-iš*
DEM.PROX.FSG DEF-present.FSG PREP-PRON.2FSG
'This gift is for you.' [S7]

(30) *haḏēlā* *l-mšākīk* ***ḥāl*** *el-gīrān*
DEM.PROX.MPL DEF-skewer.PL PREP DEF-neighbour.MPL
'These skewers are for the neighbours.' [S10]

In example (28), the speaker is talking about the division of an inheritance and *ḥāl* expresses beneficial value for the modifier (in this case represented by the possessive pronoun *-he*, 'her'). In (30), the speaker is referring to the skewers that are traditionally brought to neighbours and relatives on the second day of Eid celebrations. We may thus presume that *ḥāl* again is intended to convey here benefit for the modifier.

---

change in meaning." Whatever the case may be, this does not seem to be possible in the speech of my informants, since *māl* and *ḥāl* convey distinct functions in the primary data.

Consider the following examples, which show how *māl* and *ḥāl* are not interchangeable in the informants' speech:

(a) هذا الكتاب مال البنت

haḏā	*l-kitāb*	*māl*	*el-bint*
DEM.PROX.MSG	DEF-book.MSG	GEN	DEF-girl.FSG

'This book belongs to the girl'

(b) هذا الكتاب حال البنت

haḏā	*l-kitāb*	*ḥāl*	*el-bint*
DEM.PROX.MSG	DEF-book.MSG	PREP	DEF-girl.FSG

'This book is for the girl'

These sentences were elicited from all the informants involved in this research. In all cases, regardless of age, provenance, or level of education, the speakers clearly used the two constructions to convey the two different functions. The same difference is found by Bettega (2019b), who states that *ḥāl* expresses a dative case in his data, thus being a marker of clausal relation rather than genitive. As far as the primary data in this study are concerned, *ḥāl* can be considered a preposition and not a genitive marker, also confuting Reinhardt's position.[19]

A third, more rarely used, genitive exponent is *bū* (< *abū* 'father'), which is also used as a relative pronoun in the primary data (for further details, see next section). Only two examples showing *bū* in its genitive functions appear in the primary data, and they were found in YS:

[19] "Dass das Genitiv-Verhältniss häufig durch die Wörter *māl Besitz* und *ḥāl Zustand*, mit Beibehaltung des Artikels umschrieben wird" (Reinhardt 1894, 79, italics in the original).

(31) *asmaʿ eṣ-ṣawt bū mmi-na*[20]
hear.1SG DEF-voice.SG GEN mother.FSG-PRON.1PL
'I hear our mum's voice.' [S5]

(32) *es-siyyāra bū aḥmad*
DEF-car.FSG GEN Aḥmad
'Aḥmad's car' [S6]

Unfortunately, the examples are not sufficiently numerous to support any theory on the use of *bū* as a genitive exponent, and further research is needed. From these two examples, it seems that *bū* can be used when the modifier is a human entity and for the categories of both alienable and inalienable possession.

Eksell-Harning (1980, 160) offers two main criteria to detect how and when the AG is preferred to the synthetic genitive: one is geographical, "in the western region the AG tends to be the ordinary way of expressing genitive," whereas "in the east the AG is a more or less extensively used complement to the SG [synthetic genitive];" the second criterion is socio-cultural, asserting that the AG is more widespread in urban dialects and less in the rural dialects and almost completely absent in Bedouin dialects. The reason lies in the marked heterogeneity of urban environments compared to rural realities. These statements are not entirely applicable to the vernacular presented here, since, as shown in this section, the AG is very productive, as it is also in other neighbouring dialects,[21] and it is not always used

[20] The form *mmi-na* lit. 'our mother' is the informal way children call their mother.

[21] Qafisheh (1977, 117) states that the genitive exponents in Gulf Arabic *ḥagg* and *māl* are often used to avoid structural ambiguity, i.e.,

as a complement to the synthetic genitive, but rather expresses different genitive relations based on pragmatic and functional factors.

With regards to the criteria chosen for this study, no difference has been found in the use of the analytic or the synthetic construction in respect of age, gender, or level of education of the speakers involved. Moreover, no difference has been found in respect of the different geographical areas which form the al-ʿAwābī district, i.e., Wādī Banī Kharūṣ and neighbouring villages.

1.1.4. Attributive Clause

Following Watson (1993), a relative clause functions as a modifier of a noun phrase, thereby becoming an attribute of the noun phrase. In a sentence like 'the boy who lived in the countryside', *the boy* represents the head (or noun phrase) and the relative clause *who lived in the countryside* is the modifier (Payne 1997, 325). The head and the modifier are linked together by the relative pronoun. In the primary data, the two relative pronouns *illi* and *bū* are used; both are indeclinable.

In the construction of a relative clause, it is important to distinguish between a definite and an indefinite head noun. The relative pronouns are used only when the head noun is definite;

---

when "both elements of a noun construct have the same gender"; *ḥagg* precedes "animate or inanimate nouns, while *māl* is used with inanimate nouns." In Bahraini Arabic, Holes (2016, 223) finds no particular differences in the use of *ḥagg* and *māl*, except that *ḥagg* is "used only where the relationship was one of part-whole or purpose, and not always in these cases."

if the head noun is indefinite, the relative clause lacks the relativiser and is unmarked.[22]

(33) *zōg-he* ***illi*** *hūwa* *er-raqm*
husband.MSG-PRON.3FSG REL PRON.3MSG DEF-number.SG
arbaʿa *muqaṣṣar<in>he*
four.F negligent.AP.MSG<in>PRON.3FSG
'Her husband who was the number four was negligent towards her.' [S1]

(34) *il-māy* ***illi*** *yimši* *fi-l-balād* *gāy*
DEF-water.M REL walk.3MSG in-DEF-village.FSG come.AP.MSG
min *el-gebel*
from DEF-mountain.MSG
'The water that flows into the village is coming from the mountain.' [S1]

As examples (33) and (34) show, there are no restrictions on the semantic typology of the head noun to which the relative pronoun refers: in (33) the head noun desigates a human entity, i.e., *zōg* 'husband', whereas in (34) the head is a non-human noun, i.e., *māy* 'water'.

When the head noun is indefinite, the relative pronoun is omitted, and the relative clause is unmarked, as in (35).

---

[22] The same is found by Davey (2016) for Dhofari Arabic and by Holes (2016) for Bahraini dialects. However, Holes (2016, 387–88) later states that "in the speech of some elderly and uneducated B-dialect speakers" other forms can be found (i.e., *iladi, illadi,* and *illi*), even if they occur rarely.

(35) *yištġil* *fī* *naẖal* *yistaṭnī*

work.3MSG in palm garden.FSG rent.3MSG

'He works in a palm garden (that) he rents.' [S2]

The relative pronoun *bū* is found in sedentary dialects of Oman (cf. Holes 2008), and it is rarely found in any other neighbouring Arabic dialects.[23] In the al-ʿAwābī district, *bū* is used in more informal contexts and especially among YS. Reinhardt (1894, 34–35) reports *bū* and its negative form *buššī*—which never appears in the primary data—as relative pronouns; there is no trace of *illi*. The relative pronoun *bū* might well have been the more widespread form in this region at Reinhardt's time, a fact that is also evidenced by the high occurrence of *bū* in Reinhardt's texts. It is highly possible that *bū* is now being replaced by the more mainstream form *illi* due to the phenomenon of linguistic homogenisation mentioned in ch. 1, §3.0.

(36) *er-riggāl* *bū* *yibīʿ* *al-ẖoḍarā*

DEF-man.MSG REL buy.3MSG DEF-vegetable.PL

ʿamm-i

uncle.MSG-PRON.1SG

'The man who buys the vegetables is my uncle.' [S5]

Another clue supporting *bū* as the original relative form of this dialect is the fact that it is also found in local proverbs:[24]

---

[23] In Gulf Arabic (Qafisheh 1977), in Ṣanʿānī Arabic (Watson 1993), and in Najdi Arabic (Ingham 1994) the main relative pronoun is *illi* (or *allaḏī*).

[24] The reader can find the complete list of proverbs collected in the al-ʿAwābī district in the Appendix.

(37) *bū yatkall ʿalā ġēr-o w-qallal*
REL depend.3MSG on other-PRON.3MSG CONJ-became_less.3MSG
ḫēr-o
good-PRON.3MSG
'Who relies on someone else loses his right'

Both *illi* and *bū* can also function as general relativisers, i.e., 'the one who, whoever', 'that which', etc. In this case, they introduce a non-attributive clause, i.e., they do not have a head noun to modify:

(38) *illi yrīd yiṭlaʿ ilā l-wādī banī ḫarūṣ*
REL want.3MSG go.3MSG to DEF-wadi Bani Kharuṣ
mamnūʿ baʿad il-maġrib yiṭlaʿ
forbidden.PP.MSG after DEF-sunset go.3MSG
'He who wants to go to Wādī Banī Kharūṣ is not allowed to go after the sunset.' [S1]

(39) *bū mā bāya ʿīš tšill es-samak faqaṭ*
REL NEG want.AP.FSG rice take.3FSG DEF-fish only
'She who doesn't want rice takes the fish only.' [S6]

(40) *bū fī masqaṭ trūḥ ilā l-maktab*
REL in Muscat go.3FSG to DEF.OFFICE.SG
'Whoever is in Muscat goes to the office.' [S9]

Neither *illi* nor *bū* show gender distinction; in (39) *bū* is followed by a feminine singular AP, since the question is addressed to a group made of only women.

1.2. Verb Phrase

A verb phrase is a phrase whose head is a verb. In its simple conjugated form, the verb may already contain all the information needed to complete the clause meaning—albeit a transitive verb usually needs a complement:

(a) *ekāl* 'I eat.'

(b) *šribti* 'You (FSG) drank.'

Arabic verbs have received much attention from linguists, who have tried to identify whether their binary opposition is based on temporal (i.e., past versus non-past) or aspectual (i.e., perfectivity versus imperfectivity) factors, or on a combination of the two (cf. Eisele 1999). The reality is that in modern Arabic dialects it is not always possible to draw a clear demarcation between these categories.

For a thorough analysis of TAM categories in Omani Arabic, the interested reader is referred to Bettega (2019a), who provides numerous examples from his corpus of northern Omani data and to Brustad (2000), Dahl (1985), Comrie (1976; 1985), Payne (1997), Eades and Persson (2013), and Ingham (1994), who deal either with the theory of TAM categories or how these categories apply to various Arabic dialects.

In the verb section of his description of syntax, Reinhardt (1894, 271) briefly speaks of *die Tempora*, a label that seems to include both tense and aspect. Admittedly, the German author's omission of TAM categories is understandable, firstly because these categories had not yet been thoroughly studied at his time, and secondly, because the book was merely considered teaching material and not a linguistic description as such.

Nonetheless, Reinhardt provides some useful information. He says that the *Perfect* indicates either an action completed in the past (especially in narrative contexts), an action that is taking place at the moment of speaking, or an action that will take place in the future. The latter is especially common, according to Reinhardt (1894, 271), in oaths and wishes.

The *Imperfect*, on the other hand, describes an unfinished action in the present and the future; it is often used in subordinate clauses and in narrations to express the *Unvollendete* 'unfinished' (cf. Reinhardt 1894, 272).

In the following subsections, I will examine the roles of each morphological VP form with supporting examples from the primary data, without the intention of going further into the debate on tense and aspect.

1.2.1. Tense, Aspect and the VP Morphology

The labels 's-stem' and 'p-stem' introduced in ch. 3, §2.0, are often used by scholars of the field to avoid implying any temporal and/or aspectual value to the morphological verb form. These forms, however, may carry temporal and aspectual values depending on their stems and/or the context of the utterance.

The S-stem VP

The s-stem is usually employed in a VP expressing a state or an action that was completed in the past and that is not relevant to the present situation. Thus, the time value of the s-stem is past and carries a perfective aspectual value.

The following example, narrated by a middle-aged illiterate woman from Wādī Banī Kharūṣ (i.e., S2), serves as an example of how s-stem verbs (highlighted in bold) are employed in past contexts and how their perfective value is conveyed:

(41) ***rūḥne*** *ilā masqaṭ w-**nasīt** kēf **uṣalne** hinăk baʿadīn zōgi **štaġal** fī is-safāra al-briṭannya w-**staqar** hinăk ḥawal ṯalāṯ sanuwāt baʿadīn **gīne** fī l-ʿawābī fī as-sabʿīnāt w-**ʿayšt** ʿindo fī l-ʿawābī wa **ḫaḏḏ**[25] haḏī l-mazrʿa l-kabīra baʿadīn **sawwēna** bēt w-anā **gubt** tisaʿ awlād, ṯnīn **māto** w-bāqīn sabaʿ. haḏī **kānat** ḥayyati*

'**We went** to Muscat, **I forgot** how **we arrived** there. Then my husband **worked** at the British embassy, and **he stayed** there for about three years. Then **we came** to al-ʿAwābī in the Seventies, and **I lived** with him in al-ʿAwābī and **I took** this big palm garden. Then **we built** a house. I **had** nine children, two **died** and seven have remained. This **was** my life.' [S2]

In (41) the speaker lists a sequence of events which are all connected one after the other by the adverb *baʿadīn* ('then'). The actions expressed by the VPs in (41) are all *punctual*, in that they start and finish in the past with no repercussions in the present state of events. In narrative past contexts of this kind, the s-stem is always preferred. Here are two more examples of narrative past:

---

[25] This form is the result of the assimilation of the /t/ suffix in خذت 'I took'.

(42) *marra wāḥid surt ʿind awlād-i*

time one.MSG went.1SG to child.MPL-PRON.1SG

w-šarraft il-makān w-rigaʿt

CONJ-visited.1SG DEF-place.MSG CONJ-came_back.1SG

'Once I went to my children, I visited the place, and I came back.' [S8]

(43) *darast fi-l-gāmiʿa sulṭān qābūs w-baʿadīn*

studied.1SG at-DEF-university.FSG Sultan Qaboos CONJ-then

ruḥt ilā baḥrīn w-galast hunāk sitte ašhūr

went.1SG to Bahrain CONJ-stayed.1SG there six.FSG month.MPL

'I studied at Sultan Qaboos University and then I went to Bahrain, and I stayed there for six months.' [S6]

According to primary data, the s-stem always appears in this context, although other uses are possible in different peninsular dialects (cf. Holes 2016).

The P-stem VP

For its part, the p-stem form is employed to describe an action as incomplete, carrying an imperfective aspectual value. This incomplete action can be depicted as durative, continuous, or habitual.

P-stem conveying durative action:

(44) *aʿyš maʿ uḫt-i wa umm-i*

live.1SG with sister.FSG-PRON.1SG CONJ mother.FSG-PRON.1SG

'I live with my sister and my mother.' [S9]

In (44), the speaker is talking about a situation—i.e., living with her mother and sister—that started prior to the time of the utterance and it will continue for the time being. The action expressed by the p-stem *aʿyš* is therefore *durative*.

P-stem conveying continuous action:

(45) الصغيرين يلعبو خارج

iṣ-ṣaġīrīn *yalʿabo* *ẖārig*
DEF-small.MPL play.3MPL outside
'The kids are playing outside.' [S5]

In (45), the p-stem *yalʿabo* expresses an action that is simultaneous to the time of the utterance, since the kids are in the process of playing. The VP, therefore, depicts *continuous* action.

P-stem conveying a habitual action:

(46) *kill* *yōm* *azūr* *gīrān-i* *w-ašrub*
every day.MSG visit.1SG neighbour.MPL-PRON.1SG CONJ-drink.1SG
qahwa *maʿ-hum* *w-baʿadīn* *argaʿ* *l-bēt*
coffee with-PRON.3MPL CONJ-then go_back.1SG DEF-house.MSG
w-aṭbaẖ *el-ġadā* *ḥāl* *iṣ-ṣaġīrīn*
CONJ-cook.1SG DEF-lunch for DEF-small.MPL
'Everyday I visit my neighbours and drink coffee with them. Then I go back home and cook lunch for the kids.' [S7]

In (46) the speaker is describing her daily routine; therefore, the actions can be depicted as *habitual*.

The p-stem, contrary to the s-stem, does not have a default time reference: it can refer to the present, to the past and to the future. Consider these examples:

(47) *aṣbaḥ* *zōg-he* *riggāl* *ġēr* *yišrub*
became.3MSG husband.MSG-PRON.3FSG man.MSG different drink.3MSG
ḫamr *yiḍrab-he* *yištum-he* *yitkallam*
wine beat.3MSG-PRON.3FSG insult.3MSG-PRON.3FSG talk.3MSG
ʿali-he *hūwa* *mā* *maḍbuṭ* *lā*
about-PRON.3FSG he not correct.PP.MSG not
yiʿṭi-he *malābis* *w-fulūs* *lākin* *tištiġil*
give.3MSG-PRON.3FSG cloth.PL CONJ-money.COLL but work.3FSG
šweyya *w-nās* *tḥarraqo* *ʿali-he*
a little CONJ-people suffer.3MPL for-PRON.3FSG
'Her husband became a different man. He would drink wine, beat her, insult her, and speak ill of her. He was not a good man. He wouldn't give her clothes or money. Although she worked a little, people suffered for her.' [S1]

(48) *agīb* *il-awlād* *ilā* *l-duktūr* *bukra*
bring.1SG DEF-child.MPL to DEF-doctor.MSG tomorrow
'I (will) bring the kids to the doctor tomorrow.' [S10]

In (48), the speaker is telling the story of a woman whose husband mistreated her. The s-stem *aṣbaḥ* sets the story time in the past, but the p-stem verbs bring the story forward, describing a set of habitual actions that lasted for some time. In this sense, the *habitual* function of the p-stem is also maintained in past context. Further evidence of the past context is given by the negative marker *lā*, which in the primary data negates only the s-stem or the past tense.[26]

[26] Negation in the al-ʿAwābī district is discussed in ch. 4, §3.0.

Brustad (2000, 186) calls the use of the p-stem in past context "historical present" and says that it arises from the need of the speaker "to be as close as possible to the audience." Something similar is mentioned by Holes (2016, 239), when he says that "the p-stem is often used to give a sense of drama and immediacy when narrating past events." Switching between verb forms in storytelling and narrations is also used by speakers to differentiate between actions in the background and actions that move the story forward.[27]

Often, the time reference of the p-stem is supported by the context of the utterance and/or the presence of an adjoining word, e.g., a temporal adverb, such as *bukra* 'tomorrow' in (48).

The AP

In the debate on tense and aspect in modern Arabic vernaculars, the AP plays a leading role, being the most disputed issue. Due to its nature intermediate between noun and verb, scholars have long argued over its temporal and aspectual values. For a thorough analysis of tense and aspect of the AP in Omani and Gulf Arabic, the interested reader is referred to the works by Bettega (2019a) and Eades and Persson (2013).

In the primary data, the AP commonly appears in everyday speech and narrative discourse with the whole spectrum of time values, i.e., past, present and future. Reinhardt's contribution to the role of the AP in the dialect spoken by his informants is that it often carries an adjectival value, as in *ir-riggāl māyt* 'the man is dead' (Reinhardt 1894, 272). This holds true for the

[27] On this see also, Brustad (2000), Holes (2016), and Persson (2015).

primary data, where the AP of stative verbs may have the syntactic role of an adjective, also in accordance with Eades and Persson (2013), e.g., *el-bint nāyma* 'the girl is asleep/is sleeping'.

With present time reference, the AP usually behaves as a normal adjective, as in (49), indicating an action simultaneous to the utterance time:[28]

(49) *in-naḫīl* *kibār* *w-šweyya* *min-hin* *ʿāyšāt*
DEF-palms.FPL big.PL CONJ-a_few.FSG of-PRON.3FPL live.AP.FPL
'The palms are old and only a few of them are living' (Morano 2020, 119)

In the example above, the AP *ʿāyšāt* presents strict agreement with the head *in-naḫīl* 'the palms', as a normal adjective.

The AP is also found in the primary data with past and future time reference. Consider the following examples:

(50) *abū-y* *rigaʿ* *ʿumān* *fi-s-sabʿīnāt*
father-PRON.1SG came_back.3MSG Oman in-DEF-Seventies
w-sāyd *es-surṭān* *fa-taṭawwur*
CONJ-help.AP.MSG DEF-sultan.MSG CONJ-advanced.3MSG
w-banā *ʿumān*
CONJ-built.3MSG Oman
'My father came back to Oman in the Seventies and has helped the Sultan to advance and build the country.' [S12]

[28] More examples are given in Morano (2020).

(51) *il-bīdār* *gāyb* *es-suḥḥ* *fī-l-ʿaṣr*
DEF-farmer.MSG bring.AP.MSG DEF-date.COLL in-DEF-afternoon
'The farmer will bring (lit. 'is bringing') the dates in the afternoon' (Morano 2020, 120)

When used in past contexts, as in (50), the AP often expresses an action that is relevant to the present time of the utterance. Therefore, whilst all the main VPs in (50) are in the s-stem, the action of 'helping' to build the new Oman is expressed by means of the AP *sāyd*. By doing so, the speaker moves the attention to the fact that Oman is the way it is today thanks in part to her father.

Example (51) shows the AP in a future time reference. This is found especially with the AP of motion verbs and is always accompanied by a temporal adverb.

The aspectual value associated with the AP is 'perfect', assigning to a past state some relevance with respect to the time of the utterance. When talking about aspect and AP, we cannot disregard the concepts of lexical aspect (or *Aktionsart*) and telicity, the former being the internal temporal constituency of verbal predicates and the latter being an inherent quality of VPs whose action or state may (or may not) lead to a conclusion.[29]

In the primary data, the AP can convey either a perfect or an imperfective aspect, and never the perfective one.

[29] Not many works to date deal with these concepts in Peninsular dialects. Nevertheless, the reader may find interesting the discussion on *Aktionsart* and telicity in GA and NA, respectively by Eades and Persson (2013) and Ingham (1994).

The recent work by Bettega (2019a), which analyses a corpus of 2200 verbs in Omani Arabic, found that 11.6 percent of it consisted of APs. Of these, he found that the number of participles of telic and atelic verbs were almost the same (i.e., 130 and 119 respectively), demonstrating that the AP does not privilege one type of verb stem over the other.

The AP of telic verbs like *qarā* 'to read' can bear only perfect aspect in the primary data, since it can only give the resultant reading 'having read' and indicates a past that has some relevance to the present time of the utterance (cf. Brustad 2000, 171).

However, telic stative verbs can also have a progressive reading in this dialect, i.e., concomitant with the time of the utterance, if accompanied by the semi-grammaticalised[30] AP form of the verb *galas* 'sit, stay', i.e., *gālis / gālsa / gālsīn / gālsāt*, followed by the p-stem verb (Morano 2020, 117):

(52)	*gālsa*	*aqrā*	*l-qurān*	*taww,*	*baʿad*	*ʿašar*
	sit.AP.FSG	read.1SG	DEF-quran	now	after	ten.M
	daqāyq	*arūḥ*	*ilā*	*l-maṭbāḥ*		
	minute.FPL	go.1SG	to	DEF-kitchen		

'I am reading the Quran now; I will go to the kitchen in ten minutes.'

[30] Grammaticalisation is the phenomenon by which words representing objects or actions, i.e., nouns and verbs, further develop as grammatical markers. The use of *gālis* as a marker of continuous aspect is well known in the Gulf area, as well as in other Arabic dialects (cf. Caubet 1991, for North African dialects).

(53) *gālis* *ašūf* *il-aḫbār* *taww*
sit.AP.MSG see.1SG DEF-news.PL now
'I am watching the news now.'

(54) *gālsa* *abḥaṯ* *dawra* *l-gāmiʿa*
sit.AP.FSG search.1SG course.FSG DEF-university.FSG
mumtaza *lākin* *ġālī* *giddan*
excellent.FSG but expensive.MSG very
'I am (still) searching for a good university course, but it is very expensive.' [S3]

In all examples, the AP of *galas* is followed by the p-stem form that agrees in gender and number with the subject. All these AP forms can be translated as 'I am sitting and reading the Quran', 'I am sitting and watching the news', and 'I am sitting and searching', i.e., as two simultaneous actions conveying continuous aspect. The verb *šāf* in (53) is an atelic action verb that cannot convey a progressive reading without the AP *gālis/gālsa*.

To sum up, in the primary data, the AP can have two main readings, i.e., either resultant or progressive, and therefore can be associated only with the 'perfect' or 'imperfective' aspects. According to the primary data, though, the 'perfect' aspect can only be related to the AP when it conveys a resultant reading; whereas when it conveys a progressive reading, the AP carries the 'imperfective' aspect. This reading depends on the combination of the *Aktionsart* of the verb involved and on the semantic properties of the verb in a given context.

In the primary data, APs of motion verbs tend to convey a progressive reading: AP forms such as *gāy* 'come' and *māši* 'walk' in all cases—regardless of age, provenance, or level of education of the speaker involved—convey progressive meaning. By contrast, telic motion verbs give a resultant reading in the primary data. Consider these examples, which show how telicity can affect the aspectual values of motion verbs:

(55) *sāyir* *martīn* *li* *l-mustašfi*
go.AP.MSG twice.DL to DEF-hospital.FSG
'I have been twice to the hospital.' [S8]

(56) *rāyḥa* *ilā* *l-dikkān*
go.AP.FSG to DEF-shop.MSG
'I am going to the shop.' [S11]

Sār in (55) is a telic motion verb, whereas *rāḥ* in (56) is an atelic motion verb. In the first case, the AP *sāyir* indicates a resultant state: the speaker has already been to the hospital, and he is seeking help in order not to go back there again. In the second case, the AP *rāyḥa* conveys a progressive reading and a continuous state relating to the present time of the utterance. In the primary data, there is no evidence of AP of *rāḥ* with a resultative meaning.[31]

Interestingly, Reinhardt (1894, 276) states that the dialect he describes employs three main strategies to indicate *im Begriffe sein* 'being in the process of': (a) the simple AP; (b) the Imperfect (i.e., p-stem verb); and (c) the AP *bāġi*. The latter, especially, is used—according to Reinhardt (1894, 226)—with the meaning of 'about to be' and therefore 'be in the process of becoming', as in this example: *ṣṣēf ḫāḏum ʿād bāġi yinḏeg* 'the fruit

[31] This is also noted by Brustad (2000, 170), who confirms that the verb *rāḥ* "cannot give a resultant meaning in some dialects."

already has seeds, it is about to be ripe' (Reinhardt 1894, 226). A more detailed analysis of the AP form *bāġi* in this dialect can be found in the next section. It seems, however, that in Reinhardt it keeps that futurity value which is at the origin of the verbal prefix *b(i)-*.

The aspectual value of 'progress' or 'being in the process of something' seems to be a feature of the AP of motion and stative verbs in the informants' speech, as exemplified so far.

1.2.2. Mood

Mood is a complex category in dialectal Arabic. Modern Arabic dialects show different structures and forms to express mood.

Payne (1997, 244) defines 'mood' as "the speaker's attitude towards a situation, including the speaker's belief in its reality." Thus, 'mood' can be intended as the belief of the speaker that the event is possible, necessary, or desirable. And in order to express this belief, VPs in the primary data may present a verbal prefix or the speaker may employ some modal verbs and expressions conveying 'potentiality', 'obligation', and 'desire' (see ch. 4, §1.2.5).

Amongst the unmarked moods (i.e., verbs with zero prefixes), the primary data show the indicative and the imperative. The indicative is used for statements and questions, whereas the imperative is used for commands or requests.

Consider these examples:

(57) *trīdi* *samak* *aw* *laḥam?*
want.2FSG fish.MSG CONJ meat.MSG
'Do you want fish or meat?' [S4]

(58) *il-ḥarīm* *yiṭbaḫen* *fi-l-masā*
DEF-woman.FPL cook.3FPL in-DEF-evening
'The women cook in the evening.' [S14]

(59) *ḥabbir-ni*
inform.IMP.2MSG-PRON.1SG
'Tell me!' [S14]

1.2.3. Verbal Prefixes

Admittedly, dialects of the Arabian Peninsula tend to show minor use of verbal prefixes to indicate mood—compared, for example, to Syrian or Egyptian dialects.[32] The most common of these prefixes and, probably, the most debated in the literature for its disputed modal values is *b(i)-*. The verbal *b*-prefix has been extensively investigated in the literature: numerous studies recognise it as a marker of future or condition in many Arabic dialects (cf. Brockett 1985; Ingham 1994; Brustad 2000; Eades and Persson 2013; Persson 2015; Holes 2016; Davey 2016).

---

[32] Cf. Brustad (2000, 241): "Kuwaiti, on the other hand, will receive less attention, because its modal system does not make extensive use of verbal prefixes"; and also, Persson (2008, 29): "The dialects of the Arabian Peninsula, however, are comparatively poor in terms of modal or temporal markers." Further on, she also states that "the temporal and modal system of Gulf Arabic appears to be quite rudimentary" (Persson 2008, 29).

In his analysis of a corpus of 2200 Omani verbs, Bettega (2019a) finds 302 occurrences of prefixed p-stem forms, the majority of which are prefixed by *b(i)-* and are used without an inherent modal value, but instead convey future time reference. The *b(i)-* prefix finds itself in a very blurred position between time reference and mood. This prefix often seems to carry a modal value of intention and volition, mainly because it is the result of the grammaticalisation of the root *BĠY 'to want',[33] ultimately having undergone phonological reduction to become *bi-*. Undeniably, the distinction between futurity and intention is not always clear-cut, as also reported by Bettega (2019a) and Persson (2008, 40), the latter of whom rightly states that "intention often comes with a tint of futurity." In their analysis of p-stem verbs prefixed by *b(i)-* in Omani and Gulf Arabic, respectively, both Bettega and Persson find that the occurrence of a predicate introduced by *b(i)-* and not expressing futurity is rare, and often found only in narrative discourse.

Davey (2016) reports that the prefix *ba-* in Costal Dhofari Arabic is often used for reference to the future, but that it can imply a modal quality if prefixed to *kān/yikūn* 'be'. In the primary data, though, this does not seem to happen and when used in future contexts, this prefix conveys a future that is intentionally planned or about whose occurrence there is some degree of certainty. Nevertheless, the *bi*-prefix in the primary data also appears in non-future contexts, especially in condi-

33 Cf. Ingham (1994), Davey (2016), Owens (2018), and Bettega (2019a).

tional clauses. It never appears as a prefix in the indicative mood.

The following examples demonstrate *b-* as a future marker:

(60) *bitgiyi* *ʿars* *manāl?*
FUT.come.2FSG wedding.MSG Manal
'Are you coming to Manal's wedding?' [S11]

(61) بجي البيت لساعة ١٢ تقريبا
bgī *l-bēt* *li-sāʿa* *ṯnāʿaš* *taqrīban*
FUT.arrive.1SG DEF-home.MSG PREP-hour twelve about
'I will be home around twelve.' [S5]

The difference in use between the p-stem verb alone and the *b(i)*-prefixed p-stem to express futurity in the primary data seems to be the planning or the likelihood of the future event happening: the *b*-prefix is used when the future event is planned or is about to happen, whereas a general future is indicated by the bare p-stem verb. In (61), for example, the speaker is giving a specific time of arrival, i.e., around 12 o'clock on the following day.

Consider this example:

(62) *il-awlād* *ygyio* *bukra* *maʿa* *l-banāt*
DEF-child.MPL arrive.3MPL tomorrow with DEF-girl.FPL
'The children will arrive tomorrow with the girls.' [S12]

Here, the speaker employs a 'plain future' expressed by the p-stem verb. The future time reference is inferable only on the basis of the presence of the temporal adverb *bukra* 'tomorrow'. In contrast to (61), the speaker in (62) is not given a specific time. Therefore, 'the children' can potentially arrive at any point during the following day.

In addition to *b(i)-*, other verbal prefixes found in Omani Arabic and partially in the primary data are *raḥ* and *ḥa-*, which are both used as a modal marker of future or realis/irrealis and prefixed to the p-stem verb. The verbal markers *raḥ* and *ḥa-* are attested in other Arabic varieties (i.e., Levantine, Egyptian, and some Gulf dialects; Brustad 2000, 241), and the latter, especially, is reported by Reinhardt (1894, 149) as the only prefix for the future in the Banū Kharūṣī vernacular. In the primary data collected and presented in this section, very few occurrences of *raḥ* or *ḥa-* have been found.

(63) رح اكون هناك في ديسمبر

raḥ akūn hunāk fī dīcimber

FUT be.1SG there in December

'I will be there in December.' [S5]

The verbal prefix *raḥ* is generally used as a marker of future in northern Oman (cf. Holes 1989; 2008), but in the primary data appears rarely.

The only occurrence of the *ḥa*-prefix is in the apodosis of a conditional clause, expressing a realis condition:

(64) *al-imām* *Wāriṯ bin Kāb al-Kharūṣi* *haḏā*
DEF-Imam.MSG Warith Bin Ka'ab al-Kharūṣi DEM.PROX.MSG
ʿālim *kabīr* *iḏā* *ẖaḏ* *el-ḥaṣā*
man_of_religion.MSG big.MSG if took.3MSG DEF-stone.FSG
ḥa-yimaššī-he *b-ʿūd* *el-qatt*
FUT-walk.3MSG-PRON.3FSG PREP-branch DEF-clover.SG
'The Imam Warith Bin Ka'ab al-Kharūṣi, this is a big man of religion. If he took a stone, he would have made it walk by the clover branch.' [S2]

In (64) the speaker is telling a story about one of the Imams of Wādī Banī Kharūṣ—Warith Ben Ka'ab—famous for moving objects and stones. Given the lack of other reliable examples, it is not possible at this stage to provide a full analysis of the *ḥa-* prefix in this (or other) Omani dialects, whether in a future or in a conditional context.[34]

Persson (2008) analyses the occurrence of the *b*-prefix and *raḥ* in Gulf Arabic and finds that *raḥ* is hardly ever used in a non-future context, whereas *bi-* is very extensively used in conditional clauses. The fact that the *b*-prefix functions both as a future and a conditional marker is explained by Persson (2008, 44), who remarks that "futures also often have a conditional trait in the sense that their fulfilment often depends on certain conditions." In the primary data presented in this study, we will see that the *bi*-prefix is used only in the first type of conditional clause—i.e., the one expressing a realis condition—supporting the modal value of *b(i)*- in the informants' speech.

[34] However, the interested reader can find further insights in Persson (2008).

1.2.4. The Case of *bāġi/bāya* 'want'

Ingham (1994, 93) classifies *bġī* as a dynamic atelic verb, since in Najdi Arabic it cannot be used as an AP. In the primary data, however, the AP of the stative verb *bġī* is extremely common and therefore deserves some analysis.

Interestingly, the AP *bāġi* shows the feminine counterpart *bāya* 'want', which represents the only gender differentiation found in the primary data. The form *bāya*—used exclusively by women—lacks a complete verbal conjugation and can be used only in contexts where the AP is acceptable, whereas the verb *bġī* presents s-stem and p-stem forms, i.e., *bġī/yibġa*.

One possible etymology of the AP *bāya* is the verb *abā/yabī* 'want', commonly found in the Arabic dialects of North Africa and the Levant (cf. Owens 2018). The fact that Retsö (2014) states that the *ba*-prefix found in South Arabia most likely developed from the verb *abā* rather than the verb *baġā* (realised in the ditrict as [bġī]) can be seen as evidence of the once widespread use of *abā* in the southern Arabian Peninsula (or at least parts of southern Oman). Moreover, the simultaneous occurrence in Oman of *bġī*, *bāya*, and the *b*-prefix—which all have different syntactic functions—supports this idea.

The primary data show various verbal predicates to mean 'want':

(65)	***trīdi***	*tūkli*	*šey?*	*lā,*	*mā*	***bāya***
	want.2FSG	eat.2FSG	thing	NEG	NEG	want.AP.FSG

'Do you want to eat something? No, I don't (want to).' [S5]

The same question could instead be posed using the verb *bġī*, i.e., *tibġi tūkli šey?*, without any difference in meaning and the answer would still be the same. For example, the formulation *lā, mā arīd* is acceptable in the answer, but several people I talked to in al-ʿAwābī told me that if I wanted to sound like an Omani from al-ʿAwābī, I had to use the form *bāya* to express 'want' (or, of course, *bāġi* for a male).

The forms *bāġi* and *bāya* are modal in that they are often used to express a wish or desire, although modality is expressed through their syntactic function rather than their morphological AP form.

The time reference of the APs *bāġi/bāya* is usually present, expressing a state of 'wanting, desiring' something simultaneous to the utterance time:

(66) *wāgid bāya arūḥ maʿ-kin bas il-yōm*
much want.AP.FSG go.1SG with-PRON.2FPL but DEF-day.MSG
mašġūla min el-ʿaṣr lēn is-sāʿat ʿašar
busy.PP.FSG from DEF-afternoon until DEF-hour.FSG ten.M
il-masā
DEF-evening
'I really want to go with you but today I am busy from the afternoon until 10 pm.' [S12]

(67) *bāya duwā wa mā arūm arūḥ ilā*
want.AP.FSG medicine.FSG CONJ NEG can.1SG go.1SG to
ṣ-ṣaydilīya
DEF-pharmacy.FSG
'I want a medicine, but I cannot go to the pharmacy.' [S7]

In both (66) and (67), the AP indicates a strong desire or a need for something. It expresses a state of wanting simultaneous to the utterance time. In the following example, *bāya* is used to express a wish:

(68) *bāya* *arūḥ* *lākin* *mā* *ʿind-i* *waqt*
want.AP.FSG go.1SG but NEG to-PRON.1SG time.MSG
'I would like to go, but I don't have time.' [S9]

In the example above, the AP *bāya* conveys the speaker's state of 'wishing' to be able to go, but the wish cannot be fulfilled because the speaker does not have enough time to go with the others.

Morphologically, as the above examples show, both *bāġi* and *bāya* are followed by the conjugated p-stem verb:

(69) *bāya* *tismaʿ* *kill* *šey* *ʿind-ik*
want.AP.FSG hear.3FSG every thing to-PRON.2MSG
'She wants to hear everything you have (to say).' [S11]

(70) *awlād-o* *bāġīn* *yibīʿo* *il-hōš*
child.MPL-PRON.3MSG want.AP.MPL sell.3MPL DEF-goats.COLL
'His children want to sell the goats.' [S15]The AP *bāġi* behaves in the same way.

It is only used by men[35] to convey a wish or a desire, as in:

35 Both examples (71) and (72) were elicited from male speakers. One was university-educated 32-year-old from Stāl in Wādī Banī Kharūṣ. The other was illiterate, aged about 55 from al-ʿAwābī. Both belonged to the al-Kharūṣī tribe. Thet are not on the list of speakers provided in ch. 1, §8.1, because they were employed for the sole purpose of eliciting the AP form of *bāġi*.

(71) *turīd* *ʿīš?* *lā,* *mā* *bāġi*

want.2MSG rice NEG NEG want.AP.MSG

'Do you want rice? No, I don't want it.'

(72) *bāġi* *arūḥ* *ilā* *d-dikkān*

want.AP.MSG go.1SG to DEF-shop.MSG

'I'd like to go to the shop'

In contrast with *abā*, the verb *bġī* shows a verbal conjugation and can be used in both s-stem and p-stem:

(73) *qāl* *haḏī* *ṣaġīra,* *mā* *abġ-ha*

said.3MSG DEM.PROX.FSG small.FSG NEG want.1SG-PRON.3FSG

'He said, "She is young, I don't want her."' [S1]

(74) *aqūl-l-iš* *anā* *mā* *abġ-ak*

say.1SG-to-PRON.2FSG PRON.1SG NEG want.1SG-PRON.2MSG

w-ṭallaq-ni

CONJ-divorce.IMP-PRON.1SG

'I tell you, I don't want you, divorce me!' [S2]

The conjugated verb *bġī* can be used, as shown in (73) and (74), both by men and women, as can the verb *arād*, e.g., *anā mā arīd-iš* 'I don't want you (FSG)'. From the samples collected, it seems that there is a tendency among high school- and university-educated speakers to prefer *arād* over *bġī*, e.g., examples (65) and (71). I noticed that it was more frequently used in formal contexts and in YS, whereas OS and speakers with little access to education in general prefer *bġī*, also in questions. At present it is not possible to assess for sure if the alternation between *arād* and *bġī* depends more on syntactical or sociolinguistic factors. It seems, however, that in all the syntactic contexts where the AP is acceptable—as per previous discussion—the forms *bāġi* and *bāya* are preferred. Moreover, since the VP *bġī/yibġa* can be used by both men and women, it seems that the gender distinction in speakers applies only to the participial forms of these predicates.

1.2.5. Auxiliaries and Modal Expressions

In the primary data, the most frequently used modal verbs and expressions include *lāzim* 'it is necessary, must', *yiḥtāg* 'it needs', *rām/yrūm* 'be able to', *qadar/yiqdar* 'can'. In addition to these, there are also auxiliaries that support the predicate in expressing its modal values.

kān/ykūn 'be, exist'

We have already seen the role of *kān* as a copula in ch. 3, §2.8.

As an auxiliary, *kān* modifies the aspect and tense in nominal clauses, when accompanied by a p-stem verb:

(75) *mā ḥad kān yišti̇ġil yōm ṭwōfi*
NEG person was.3MSG work.3MSG day.FSG died.3MSG
abū-hum
father.MSG-PRON.3MPL
'None of them used to work when their father died.' [S1]

(76) *kān* *abū* *Iḫlāṣ* *yištaġal*[36] *fī* *masqaṭ*

was.3MSG father Ikhlas work.3MSG in Muscat

'Ikhlas's father used to work in Muscat.' [S2]

(77) *kān* *ništrī* *raṭab* *min* *il-mazraʿ*

was.3MSG buy.1PL dates from DEF-palm_garden.FSG

il-qarībe *w-nšārik-o* *maʿa*

DEF-near.FSG CONJ-share.1PL-PRON.3MSG with

gīrā-nā

neighbour.MPL-PRON.1PL

'We used to buy dates from a farm nearby and share them with our neighbours.' [S14]

We have already seen how the p-stem VP is employed in past contexts to express the habitual past. In these contexts, the auxiliary *kān* can recur at the beginning of the narration as an aspect/tense marker, as in (75), (76) and (77).[37] Once the main story line has been set in the past at the beginning of the narration, the p-stem verb can be found even without repeating the auxiliary, as in (77).

Similar combinations of *kān* and the p-stem are not new to Arabic and are also found in CA and MSA (cf. Haak 2006).

However, the combination of *kān* followed by a s-stem verb is rarer. The primary data offers one example uttered by an illiterate AS:

---

[36] Examples (75) and (76) also show a different realisation of the 3MSG *yištaġal* 'he works': in Wādī Banī Kharūṣ there is no *imāla*, whereas in al-ʿAwābī there is.

[37] On the auxialiry *kān* as an aspect marker, see also Persson (2015).

(78) *ḏāk* *il-ayyām* *kān* *rāḥ* *ilā*
DEM.DIST.MSG DEF-day.MPL was.3MSG went.3MSG to
l-baḥrīn *bi-rgūla*
DEF-bahrain on-foot.PL
'In those days, one could go to Bahrein on foot.' [S2]

In (78), the speaker infers a possibility that ended at some point in the past: one could walk to Bahrain, but now it is no longer possible. More data on this subject are needed to be able to assess if this construction is still productive or used only sporadically. Suffice to say that I have found only one example here in 15 hours of recordings.

The syntactic construction of modal verbs and auxiliaries embedding s-stem verbs is unusual, but can be found, for example, in Levantine Arabic (cf. Brustad 2000; Wilmsen 2015). In the district of al-ʿAwābī asyndentically juxtaposed s-stem verbs are rare, but the primary data offer a few examples. Here is one with the verb *nsī* 'forget' in its auxiliary function:[38]

(79) نسيت اشتريت حليب للصغيرين
nasīt *ištrīt* *ḥalīb* *li-ṣ-ṣaġīrīn*
forgot.1SG bought.1SG milk to-DEF-small.MPL
'I forgot to buy the milk for the kids.' [S10]

[38] When *nsī* does not function as an auxiliary in the sentence, it is usually followed by a p-stem verb in asyndentic construction, as in *nasīt arīd ṯūb gedīd li-l-ʿīd* 'I forgot I wanted a new dress for Eid' [S9].

lāzim 'necessary, must'

lāzim is an impersonal modal expression, used to express 'necessity' or 'obligation'. It is an old AP form which underwent grammaticalisation in CA. It does not conjugate, thus the p-stem verb which follows it carries the grammatical functions (i.e., person, number and gender) specified in the sentence.[39]

(80)

lāzim	*yargaʿ*	*marra*	*ṯanya*
necessary.AP	come_back.3MSG	time	second.F

li-balād	*w-yinām*	*fi-l-ʿawābī*
to-DEF-village.FSG	CONJ-sleep.3MSG	in-DEF-ʿAwābī

'One had to come back again and sleep in al-ʿAwābī.' [S1][40]

(81)

lāzim	*aẖalliṣ*	*haḏā*	*l-kitāb*
must.AP	finish.1SG	DEM.PROX.MSG	DEF-book.MSG

'I must finish this book.' [S7]

In (80), the sentence has an impersonal subject, expressed with the third person masculine singular. In (81), conversely, the subject of the sentence is the first person singular and it is carried by the p-stem verb *aẖalliṣ*.

---

[39] *lāzim* can also occur in a nominal construction, i.e., with no verb involved, as in: *lāzim qabil il-maġrib* 'it was necessary before the sunset' [S1]. However, there are only two examples of this construction in the primary data.

[40] In the primary data, a verb with an impersonal subject is often realised as 3MSG, as in this example.

yiḥtāg 'it needs'

This verb governs the p-stem verb directly. An example of *yiḥtāg* as an auxiliary is:

(82) *aḥtāg* *arūḥ* *ilā* *d-dikkān*
need.1SG go.1SG to DEF-shop.MSG
'I need to go to the shop.' [S10]

rām/yrūm 'be able to' and *qadar/yiqdar* 'can'

The verb *rām/yrūm* appears to have an interesting function in the primary data. The root *RWM originally indicates 'be over, overlook',[41] but in the primary data it means 'be able to' and, according to my informants, is characteristic of the al-ʿAwābī district.[42]

rām/yrūm is generally followed by a p-stem form, which is conjugated in the same person, gender, and number as the main verb.

(83) ما تروم تساوق لان سيّارته خربانة

mā *trūm* *tusāwwiq* *l-inne* *siyyarat-he*
NEG can.3FSG drive.3FSG because car.FSG-PRON.3FSG
ḫarbāna
damaged.FSG
'She cannot drive because her car is damaged.' [S7]

(84) *mā* *yrūm* *yiṭlaʿ* *l-inne* *šīši* *darag*
NEG can.3MSG come.3MSG because NEG.EXIST stair.MSG

[41] The Sabaic noun *rym-m* means 'height'. Cf. RYM in Beeston (1982, 120).

[42] This root is also attested by Reinhardt (1894).

'He cannot go up because there are no stairs.' [S15]

(85) *aqdar musāʿid-iš?*

can.1SG help.AP.MSG-PRON.2FSG

'Can I help you?' [S12]

The main difference in the use of *rām/yrūm* and *qadar/yiqdar* is that the former indicates actual ability (or inability) of the subject to fulfill the action expressed by the verb, whereas the latter has a stronger modal value, similar to the English modal 'can'. In (83) and (84), the subjects are both physically unable to perform the action expressed by the subordinate verb because of external factors (i.e., the car damaged and the absence of the stairs). In (85), *aqdar* functions as a modal and does not involve any physical ability.

The verb *qadar/yiqdar* can also be found in asyndetic construction governing an s-stem verb, as in:

(86) *mā qadart ḥaṣalt waqt asawwi*

NEG could.1SG found.1SG time do.1SG

'I couldn't find time to do (it).' [S9]

'Potentiality' can also be expressed in the primary data by the impersonal non-past form *yumkin* followed by a p-stem verb usually agreeing with the referent, as in:

(87) *yumkin yrūḥ ilā l-wādī*

is_possible.3MSG go.3MSG to DEF-wadi

'It is possible for him to go to the wadi.' [S1]

This form, albeit not particularly common in the primary data, is strictly linked to the category of 'mood', since potentiality is expressed mainly through semantics.[43]

ḍall/yiḍall 'continue, keep on' and *dār/yidīr* 'start'

The auxiliaies *ḍall* and *dār* govern a p-stem verb directly:

(88) *w-ḍallit* *trabbi-hum*

CONJ-kept.3FSG take_care.3FSG-PRON.3MPL

'She kept on taking care of them.' [S1]

(89) *ḍall* *yiḫāf-he*

kept.3MSG scare.3MSG-PRON.3FSG

'He kept on scaring her.' [S2]

The verb *dār/yidīr* is an interesting case. It is not documented in any other Omani dialect,[44] but is a common feature of Moroccan Arabic. In the primary data, it often appears when 'start' is used as an auxiliary,[45] particularly in the speech of AS in Wādī Banī Kharūṣ with low or no education. In the examples, *dār* is always followed by a p-stem verb.

---

[43] This way of expressing 'potentiality' is also found in Najdi Arabic (cf. Ingham 1994, 129).

[44] This is according to all works on Omani Arabic already published and used as sources for this study.

[45] The verb *badā* is also attested in the primary data in non-auxiliary contexts, e.g., *badāt kitāb gedīd* 'I started a new book' [S7], *sulṭān qabūṣ badā dāḫil el-mašārīʿ aš-šuwāraʿ* 'Sultan Qaboos started inside (the country) projects of roads (highway projects)' [S1].

(90) *w-dār* *en-nās* *yištaġlo*
CONJ-started.3MSG DEF-people work.3MPL
'People started to work.' [S2]

(91) *dār* *hadā* *l-ʿālim* *yaqrā*
started.3MSG DEM.PROX.MSG DEF-man_of_religion.MSG read.3MSG
l-qurān
DEF-Quran
'This man of religion started to read the Quran.' [S2]

In examples (90) and (91), *dār* is in first position in the sentence, followed by the subject and then by the verb of the subordinate sentence. In (90), the auxiliary verb does not need to be conjugated, because, when the main verb is in first position, it needs to agree only in gender with the subject, but not necessarily in number; the secondary verb, however, agrees grammatically with the subject *nās* 'people', which takes the agreement as masculine plural, i.e., *yištaġlo*.

When the subject is not mentioned, or it is implied, the p-stem verb follows directly the main auxiliary verb:

(92) *dār* *yidris* *fī-l-gāmiʿa* *sulṭān*
started.3MSG study.3MSG in-DEF-university.FSG Sultan.MSG
qābūs
Qaboos
'He started to study at Sultan Qaboos University.' [S14]

Interestingly, Reinhardt (1894, 207) reports *dār* followed by the 'Imperfect' as indicating a commitment to something, and states that "it usually precedes verbs whose activities cannot be done all at once."

ḫallī 'let'

The verb *ḫallī* 'let' is also an interesting modal verb in this dialect. Ingham (1994, 124) reports it in Najdi Arabic, where it is used as "a regular marker of the 3rd and 1st person jussive." In the primary data, this verb is often found followed by a suffix pronoun, as in *ḫallī-ni* 'let me' or *ḫallī-he* 'let her'. It also has non-auxiliary use in the meaning 'stay, remain', as in *ḫallī-k hnā* 'You (MSG) stay here'.

1.3. Prepositional Phrase

Prepositional phrases are those phrases introduced by a preposition, e.g., *min, bi-, fī, ʿind-*[46], and *li-*. Prepositions are indeclinable, therefore lacking morphological inflection.

(93) *(grūb)* *min* *ṯnāʿaš* *ḥurma*
group.MSG of twelve woman.FSG
'(A group) of twelve women' [S14]

(94) *bi-alfīn* *ryāl*
PREP-two_thousand ryal.PL
'(At a price of) two thousand ryals' [S9]

(95) *fī* *s-siyyāra*
in DEF-car.FSG
'In the car' [S8]

The case of the prepositions *fī* 'in', *ʿind-* 'at', and *li-* 'to' needs to be explored in more detail. In the literature they are sometimes

[46] I am including *ʿind-* in the list of prepositions to express possession following the classification made by Prochazka (2008, 699–709).

referred to as 'pseudo-verbs', which is linked to the way they are translated in other languages.[47]

The preposition *fī* introduces the existential clause, whereas the prepositions *ʿind-* and *li-* introduce the possessive clause. In this work, following the classification made by Watson (1993, 224), the label prepositional phrases will be used throughout for phrases introduced by a preposition.

1.3.1. Existential Clause

It is possible to refer to existentials as those prepositions forming phrases that express the presence or the existence of something. In the primary data, the most common form of existentials is the preposition *fī* 'in' plus the 3MSG pronoun, in some cases followed by a locational or temporal adjunct:

(96) *fīh* *māy* *dāẖil* *iṯ-ṯallāga*

EXIST water inside DEF-fridge.FSG

'There is water in the fridge.' [S10]

(97) *fīh* *ṭawla* *barrā*

EXIST table.FSG outside

'There is a table outside.' [S14]

---

[47] Brustad (2000, 153): "In general, most pseudo-verbs consist of either prepositions that give locative or possessive meaning, or of nominally derived forms that give modal meaning. Pseudo-verbs are characterized by one or more semantic or syntactic features". One of the supporting characteristics for the label 'pseudo-verbs' is that both existentials and possessive clauses take the same negation as verbs. However, since in the primary data both nouns and verbs are negated by *mā*, the denomination used by Brustad is not appropriate in this study.

Consistent with Davey's (2016, 180) analysis of existentials in Dhofari Arabic and with Payne (1997, 123), the noun phrase following *fīh* is always indefinite. Moreover, the time reference expressed by the existential construction is always present (in relation to the time of the utterance). In fact, the primary data show the use of the verb *kān/yikūn* to express the existence or presence of something in the past (see ch. 3, §2.8 for examples).

'Existentiality' in the future is also expressed with *kān b(i)*-prefixed, sometimes accompanied by a temporal adverb, as in:

(98)

byikūn	*hunāk*	*ḫamsīn*	*šaḫṣ*	*fi-l-ʿurs*	*bukra*
FUT.be.3MSG	there	fifty	person.MSG	in-DEF-wedding.MSG	tomorrow

'There will be fifty people at the wedding tomorrow.' [S12]

In addition to *fīh*, the word *šey* 'thing' is also used:

(99)

šī	*fanāgīn*
EXIST	coffee_cup.MPL

'There are coffee cups.' [S11]

(100)

šey	*siyyarāt*
EXIST	cars.FPL

'There are cars.' [S1]

No criteria seem to be used in the choice of one form or another among the speakers: both *fīh* and *šey* are used by men and women, in YS, AS, and OS with no relevance to their level of education either.

1.3.2. Possessive Clause

The prepositions *ʿind-* 'at' and *li-* 'to', followed by a suffixed pronoun, are used to express possession:

(101) *li-š* *ṯūb* *gedīd*

to-PRON.2FSG dress.MSG new.MSG

'You have a new dress.' [S10]

The example above shows how in the possessive prepositional phrase the predicand is indefinite. In cases in which a subject is expressed, the preposition follows it and an anaphoric pronoun, agreeing grammatically with the subject, is suffixed to it, as in:

(102) *ʿamm-i* *ʿind-o* *siyyāra* *bēḍa*

uncle.MSG-PRON.1SG to-PRON.3MSG car.FSG white.FSG

'My uncle has a white car.' [S3]

(103) *el-bint* *ʿind-he* *sannūr* *ṣaġīr*

DEF-girl.FSG to-PRON.3FSG cat.SG small.MSG

'The girl has a kitten (lit. 'small cat').' [S12]

2.0. Clauses

A clause is a group of words consisting of a subject and a predicate (i.e., a referent expressing something about the subject). This sub-section has been divided into simple nominal clauses, simple verbal clauses, and complex clauses (i.e., adverbial clauses and complement clauses). In this work, any clause consisting of a predicand and a predicate that can be a noun phrase, an adjectival noun phrase, or a prepositional phrase is considered a nominal clause. Conversely, any clause including a finite verb (either in first or second position), followed by optional subject and complements is considered a verbal clause.

2.1. Simple Nominal Clause

A simple nominal clause is a sentence where the predicand is a noun phrase and the predicate can be another noun phrase, as in examples (104) and (105), an adjectival phrase, as in (106) and (107), or a prepositional phrase, as in (108) and (109).[48]

(104)	*ḏāk*	*ir-riggāl*	***ʿamm-i***
	DEM.DIST.MSG	DEF-man.MSG	uncle.MSG-PRON.1SG

'That man is my uncle.' [S14]

(105)	*haḏī*	*s-siyyāra*	***māl-i***
	DEM.PROX.FSG	DEF-car.FSG	GEN-PRON.1SG

'This car is mine.' [S5]

(106)	*sannūr*	*uḫt-i*	***bunnī***
	cat.MSG	sister.FSG-PRON.1SG	brown

'My sister's cat is brown.' [S6]

(107)	*siyyārat-i*	***ḫarbāna***
	car.FSG-PRON.1SG	damaged.FSG

'My car is damaged.' [S7]

(108)	*haḏēlā*	*l-ḥarīm*	***min***	***ahl-i***
	DEM.PROX.FPL	DEF-woman.FPL	from	family-PRON.1SG

'These women are from my family.' [S9]

---

[48] In the following examples, the predicate phrase is highlighted in bold.

(109) *es-siyyāra* ***qiddām*** ***il-bwāb***

DEF-CAR.FSG in_front_of DEF-gate.MSG

'The car is in front of the gate.'[49] [S9]

When the predicate of a simple nominal clause is a noun phrase, it does not carry the definite article and it agrees with the predicand only in number and not in gender; in fact, "the predicate agrees with the predicand only insofar as the two nouns can logically refer to one and the same referent" (Watson 1993, 98). In (104), the predicate is the noun phrase *ʿamm-i* 'my uncle', consisting of a noun and a possessive suffixed pronoun. It is logically linked to the predicand, since they are both nouns denoting male entities.

When the predicate is an adjectival phrase, it is essentially indefinite, e.g., *ir-riggāl ṭawīl* 'the man is tall', *el-bint gamīla* 'the girl is beautiful'. In these cases, as far as agreement is concerned, the predicate follows the same rules that apply in the case of noun phrases: human plural predicands have strict agreement, whereas inanimate non-human plural predicands have deflected agreement, as in the examples below:

(110) *el-banāt* *mašġūlāt*

DEF-girls.FPL busy.PP.FPL

'The girls are busy.' [S3]

[49] A nominal clause consisting of a noun phrase and a prepositional phrase is also called 'locational clause', since it indicates a specific location in space: *al-wusāda fī-l-kurfāya* 'the pillow is on the bed'.

(111) *il-mustašfayāt ḥāṣṣa*

DEF-hospital.FPL private.FSG

'The hospitals are private.' [S1][50]

If the predicate is an adjective referring to a plural or dual predicand, it can be in its broken plural form (if it has one), as in:

(112) *in-naḫīl kibār*

DEF-palm.FPL old.PL

'The palms are old.' [S8]

(113) *ir-riggālīn ṭuwāl*

DEF-man.DL tall.PL

'The two men are tall.' [S14]

2.2. Simple Verbal Clause

A simple verbal clause includes a finite verb, e.g., *sawwēna* 'we built', and an optional explicit subject and other complements, e.g., *sawwēna bēt* 'we built a house'. It can also be modified by adverbs, prepositional phrases, or noun phrases used adverbially. These adverbials can express time, as in:

(114) *qabil ġurūb iš-šams yirūḥ il-wādī, masmūḥ*

before sunset.SG DEF-sun.FSG go.3MSG DEF-wadi allowed.PP.MSG

w-baʿad al-ġurūb mustahīl yirūḥ

CONJ-after DEF-sunset.SG impossible.PP.MSG go.3MSG

'Before the sunset, one goes to the wadi—it is allowed; but after the sunset it is impossible to go.' [S1]

[50] The reader can compare examples (110) and (111) with (4) and (6) respectively in the present chapter, §1.1.2.

(115) *bukra* *ṣ-ṣabāḥ* *yrūḥ* *ilā* *l-wādī*

tomorrow DEF-morning go.3MSG to DEF-wadi

'The morning after one goes to the wadi.' [S12]

(116) *baʿad* *ʿašar* *sanuwāt* *taqrīban* *ṭallaq-ha*

after ten.M year.FPL about divorced.3MSG-PRON.3FSG

'After about ten years he divorced her.' [S5]

or space, as in:

(117) *enām* *taḥt* *is-saṭḥ* *fi-l-kurfāya*

sleep.1SG below DEF-roof.SG in-DEF-bed.FSG

'I sleep on the bed under the roof.' [S8]

(118) *atīb* *qahwa* *hnā*

bring.1SG coffee here

'I bring coffee here.' [S15]

Before examining the structure of the simple verbal clause in further detail, it is worth discussing word order and agreement in verbal contexts as these appear in the primary data.

2.3. Word Order

In Arabic dialectological literature, the analysis of word order starts with the individuation of the three main sentence constituents: verb (V), subject (S), and object (O). Thus, the sentence typologies are SVO or VSO according to the order of the components in a given sentence. CA has been classified by Arabists as a VSO language, which means that the verb is in first position in the sentence, followed by the subject and then by complements. Modern Arabic dialects shows less strict ordering and both VSO and SVO systems may be found, sometimes varying according to the type of discourse, i.e., narration or dialogue.

In the primary data, both VSO and SVO sentence types are found: if the subject of a clause is definite, it precedes the verb (i.e., SVO), whereas if it is indefinite, it follows the verb (i.e., VSO), with the sole exception of the auxiliary *dār* 'start', which in the primary data always appear in first position in the sentence.

2.4. Some Remarks on the Agreement in Verbal Contexts

Consider the following examples of the VSO sentence-type:

(119) *kānat syūḥ*
was.3FSG empty_lot.PL
'There were empty lots of land.' [S2]

(120) *gyen madāris w-mustašfiyāt*
came.3FPL school.FPL CONJ-hospital.FPL
'Schools and hospitals arrived.' [S1]

(121) *kānat bint ṣaġīra*
was.3FSG girl.FSG small.FSG
'She was a young girl.' [S15]

(122) *kāno kill-hum ṣġār*
was.3MPL all-PRON.3MPL small.PL
'All of them were young.' [S14]

(123) *rabbit-he ḥobbōt-he*
took_care.3FSG-PRON.3FSG grandmother.FSG-PRON.3FSG
'Her grandmother took care of her.' [S1]

(124) *ydawrū-he* *il-gīrān*

look_for.3MPL-PRON.3FSG DEF-neighbour.MPL

'The neighbours looked for her.' [S14]

Examples (122), (123), and (124) are from narrative discourses, whereas all the others are from spontaneous speech recordings. When the head noun is singular, the verb agrees with it in gender and number: the verbs in (121) and (123) are in the feminine singular form according to their subjects.

All other examples show sound plural or broken plural heads, whose agreement patterns once again depend on their degree of animacy and individuation. So, in (120), the verb in first position is in the feminine plural and refers to two feminine inanimate head nouns coordinated. In (119), a broken inanimate plural, such as *syūḥ*, depends on the verb *kān* in its feminine singular form.[51]

Consider also these examples:

(125) اذا تحصل المفاتيح ترجعهن لي

iḏā *taḥsal* *el-mfātīḥ* *targiʿ-hin* *l-ī*

if find.3FSG DEF-key.FPL return.3FSG-PRON.3FPL to-PRON.1SG

'If she finds the keys, she'll give them back to me.' [S14]

[51] The verb *kān* 'be', when expressing past existential semantics, i.e., 'there was, there were', always appears in first position in the primary data, but its form may vary according to the head noun. Consider the following example: *kān ṯalāṯ madāris fī-ṣ-ṣulṭana* 'there were three schools in the Sultanate' [S1]—here the verb preceding a numeral is in its masculine singular form.

(126) الصغيرين يلعبو خارج

iṣ-ṣaġīrīn *yaʕlabo* *ḫārig*

DEF-small.MPL play.3MPL outside

'The kids are playing outside.' [S5]

(127) *el-banāt* *yitmarriḍen*

DEF-girl.FPL are_ill.3FPL

'The girls are ill.' [S12]

(128) *il-ḥarīm* *yištaġlen* *fī* *maṣnaʿ* *it-tumūr*

DEF-woman.FPL work.3FPL in factory.MSG DEF-date.PL

'The women work in a date factory.' [S2]

In (125) the object in the protasis is an inanimate broken plural, with which the suffixed object pronoun *-hin* in the apodosis agrees in its feminine plural form. In all other cases, i.e., (126), (127), (128), the subjects are human head nouns followed by the verb in second position and showing strict agreement.[52]

The case of *nās* 'people' is interesting when it comes to agreement rules. Brustad (2000, 54) considers *nās* a collective noun with a lack of 'individuation'. In the examples reported by Holes (2016, 333–34), *nās* shows both strict (masculine plural) and deflected agreement and this is due to a "difference in individuation," since "the likelihood of strict agreement is higher where the verb is s-stem and describes an actual event, lower when it is p-stem and describes habits or in unspecific terms what generally happens/used to happen" (Holes 2016, 334). In

[52] This is consistent with Bettega's (2017) findings regarding human plural controllers.

the primary data, *nās* appears to attract strict masculine plural agreement:

(129) *nās* *ʿind-hum* *fulūs*

people to-PRON.3MPL money.COLL

'People are rich (lit.: 'people they have money').' [S10]

(130) الناس بو عايشين طريقنا هنود

an-nās *bū* *ʿāyšīn* *ṭarīq-na* *hunūd*

DEF-people REL live.AP.MPL street.FSG-PRON.1PL Hindi.MPL

'The people who are living in our street are Indians.' [S5]

In (129), *nās* is an indefinite noun, indicating a non-individuated group of people, whereas in (130) the speaker is talking about specific people, i.e., the ones who live in her street. Despite this difference, in both cases *nās* attracts masculine plural agreement, i.e., in (129), the suffix pronoun *-hum*, and in (130), the AP عايشين.

Even in verbal contexts, *nās* still attracts strict agreement, with one exception: when the verb is in first position, and *nās* indicates a generic group of people, the verb has a masculine singular form. Consider the following examples from the primary data:

(131) *gē* *nās* *fī-l-bilād*

arrived.3MSG people in-DEF-country.FSG

'People arrived in the country.' [S14]

(132) *dār* *nās* *yištaglo*

started.3MSG people work.3MPL

'People started to work.' [S2]

In (132), the first verb (an auxiliary) is masculine singular, but the dependant verb, coming after the head noun, is conjugated as masculine plural. Both (131) and (132) have been extracted from narrative contexts.

According to Brustad (2000, 57), "viewing the grammatical feature of plural agreement as a continuum allows a principled account of the variation that occurs and reflects the speaker's control over this feature." Thus, "the choice of agreement depends on the features that influence individuation, especially specificity and agency." Based on this statement, *nās* can have various degrees of individuation and therefore attract either strict or deflected agreement. In the primary data, all the examples with *nās* take masculine plural agreement, and this can be explained by the fact that *nās*, meaning exclusively a group of 'humans', is grammatically treated like other human plurals, which usually take strict agreement (in this case, masculine).

2.5. Complex Clause

A complex clause is a clause that combines an independent clause (i.e., a nominal or verbal clause) with at least one dependant clause (i.e., adverbial, attributive, complement clause). In this subsection, the structure of complex clauses as they appear in the primary data is analysed, and they are divided into adverbial, conditional, and complement clauses.

2.5.1. Adverbial Clause

Adverbial clauses "modify a verb phrase or a whole clause" (Payne 1997, 316–17). In the linguistic literature, these clauses belong to the category of supplementation, which is to be distinguished from complementation. The former involves adding supplements to the clause (further investigated below, §2.5.2), while the latter involves providing constituents necessary to 'complete' a clause.

Adverbial clauses can modify a main clause in different ways. In this section I will analyse them following the distinction drawn by Payne (1997, 317–20) regarding adverbial clauses of time, location, manner, purpose, and reason.

Adverbial Clause of Time

Adverbial clauses of time address the question 'when?' and can be introduced by the conjunctions *lemme* / *yōm*[53] 'when'; by noun phrases used adverbially, e.g., *il-yōm* 'today', *iṣ-ṣabāḥ* 'this morning', *bukra ṣ-ṣabāḥ* 'tomorrow morning', *il-ʿām il-māḍī* 'last year'; prepositional phrases, e.g., *fī-ṣ-ṣabāḥ* 'in the morning', *fī l-lēl* 'in the night', etc.; and temporal adverbs, e.g., *bukra* 'tomorrow', *ems* 'yesterday', *taww* 'now', *taqrīban* 'about', *qabil* 'before', *lēn* 'until'.

---

[53] In Wādī Banī Kharūṣ, the noun *waqt* 'time' is also used to introduce a subordinate temporal clause. In the primary data, it occurs in a few examples from AS and OS: *waqt il-barad tnām fōq?* 'When it is cold/during cold season, do you sleep upstairs?' [S11].

(133) *ʿumr* *el-bint* *ṯalāṯ-ʿaš* *sana* ***lemme***

age.SG DEF-girl.FSG thirteen year.FSG when

tzawwag-he

married_off.3MSG-PRON.3FSG

'She was thirteen years old when he got her married off.' [S1]

(134) *mā* *ḥad* *kān* *yištġil* ***yōm*** *ṭwōfi*

NEG person was.3MSG work.3MSG when died.3MSG

abū-hum

father.MSG-PRON.3MPL

'None of them used to work when their father died.' [S1]

The conjunction *lemme* introduces an action that occurs simultaneously with another, as in (133), whereas *yōm* introduces a generic temporal clause, as in (134).

(135) *ḫt-ī* *mā* *ʿind-ha* *siyyāra* ***lēn*** *rāḥit*

sister.FSG-PRON.1SG NEG to-PRON.3FSG car.FSG until went.3FSG

masqaṭ

Muscat

'My sister did not have a car until she went to Muscat.' [S6]

(136) قبل عن اسافر باية اروح صلالة

qabil ʿan *asāfir* *bāya* *arūḥ* *ṣalāla*

before PREP leave.1SG want.AP.FSG go.1SG Salalah

'Before I leave, I want to visit Salalah.' [S5]

(137) الصفاري يحتاجن تغسيل قبل استخدامهن

iṣ-ṣafārī *yaḥtāgen* *tuġsīl* ***qabil*** ***ʿan***
DEF-pot.FPL need.3FPL wash.VN before PREP
yistiḫdām-hin
use.3MSG-PRON.3FPL
'Pots need a wash before using them.' [S7]

The temporal adverb *qabil* is followed by the particle *ʿan* when introducing an adverbial clause, as in (136) and (137). Otherwise, it simply precedes the noun phrase, e.g., *qabil il-maġrib* 'before the sunset'.

Adverbial Clause of Location

Adverbial clauses of location address the question 'where?' and are introduced by *ēn / wēn* 'where'; locative adverbs, e.g., *warā* 'behind', *fōq* 'up, above', *taḥt* 'under', *yasār* 'on the left', *yamīn* 'on the right', etc.; locative demonstratives, e.g., *hinā* 'here', *hināk* 'there'; or prepositional phrases, e.g., *min aš-šamāl* 'from the north', *min al-baʿīd* 'from far away', *fi-l-makān* 'in the place', *qiddām al-bāb* 'in front of the door', etc.

(138) *šūft* *el-makān* ***ēn*** *taskun*
saw.1SG DEF-place.MSG where live.2MSG
'I saw the place where you live.' [S12]

Adverbial Clause of Manner

Adverbial clauses of manner modify the main clause by describing the way in which the action expressed by the main verb is carried out. They are introduced by *kēf* 'how' or *kamā* 'as, like'.

(139) *yitṣarraf* **kamā** *iṣ-ṣaġīrīn* *yitṣarrafo*

behave.3MSG like DEF-small.MPL behave.3MPL

fī-l-madāris

in-DEF-school.FPL

'He behaves like kids behave in schools.' [S11]

(140) *mā* *ʿaraft* ***kēf*** *zōg*

NEG knew.1SG how husband.MSG

'I didn't know how a husband (was).' [S2]

Adverbial Clause of Purpose

Adverbial clauses of purpose express the resulting aim of the main clause. In the primary data, these clauses are introduced by the preposition *ʿašān* 'in order to'.

(141) *il-imām* *yaqrā* *ʿalī-ha* *min* *il-qurān*

DEF-imam.MSG read.3MSG to-PRON.3FSG from DEF-Quran

il-karīm ***ʿašān*** *yisgin-he*

holy.MSG in_order_to imprison.3MSG-PRON.3FSG

'The imam reads the Holy Quran in order to imprison her.' [S2]

(142) *qubbit* *šaʿar* *fī* *wsaṭ* *iṭ-ṭarīq*

made_a_dome.3FSG hair.COLL in middle DEF-street.FSG

ʿašān *tḫāf-o*

in_order_to scare.3FSG-PRON.3MSG

'She made a dome with her hair in the middle of the street in order to scare him.' [S2][54]

[54] Examples (141) and (142) are both from a story about *ginns* in Wādī Banī Kharūṣ.

Adverbial Clause of Reason

Adverbial clauses of reason address the question ‘why?’ and are introduced by *l-inn* ‘because’ and, in a few instances, by *ʿašān kḏāk* ‘so that’. The subordinating conjunction *l-inn* takes a suffix pronoun which agrees grammatically with the subject of the verb in the adverbial clause (if different from the one in the main clause).

(143) *ṭallaq-ha* *nafs* *eš-šey* ***l-inn**-he* *magnūna*

divorced.3MSG-PRON.3FSG same DEF-thing because-PRON.3FSG crazy.PP.FSG

‘He divorced her for the same reason, because she was crazy.’ [S1]

(144) *kān* *fīh* *ġamām* ***ʿašān kḏāk*** *sum-o* *masgid* *l-ġāma*

was.3MSG EXIST cloud.PL so that name-PRON.3MSG mosque DEF-cloud.SG

‘There were clouds, so its name is “mosque of the cloud.”’ [S2]

2.5.2. Circumstantial Clause

Circumstantial clauses are also known in the literature as *ḥāl*-clauses, and they “describe the manner [in] which one did something, the manner how something happened, one’s conditions when something happened, etc.” (Qafisheh 1977, 216). In terms of time reference, the circumstantial clause indicates an action or event simultaneous to the action or event expressed by the main verb. Consider the following example:

(145) رحت اتمشى اشوف النجوم

ruḥt	*itmašā*	*ašūf*	*an-nagūm*
went.1SG	walking.VN	see.1SG	DEF-star.FPL

'I went walking looking at the stars.' [S5]

In the example above, the main verb is expressed through an s-stem form, whilst the action of the circumstantial clause is expressed by means of a verbal noun. This is because the whole event happened in the past in relation to the time of the utterance. If, on the other hand, the event is happening in the present, both the main clause and the circumstantial clause can have a p-stem verb or an AP and a p-stem verb. Both structures express the idea of simultaneous action:

(146)

umm-i	*taqrā*	*kitāb*	*tišūf*
mother.FSG-PRON.1SG	read.3FSG	book.MSG	see.3FSG
iṣ-ṣaġīrīn			
DEF-small.MPL			

'Mum is reading a book (while) looking after the kids.' [S9]

(147)

wāṣal	*il-bēt*	*yaġnī*
arrive.AP.MSG	DEF-house.MSG	sing.3MSG

'He has arrived home singing.' [S7]

2.5.3. Conditional Clause

Conditional clauses are structured in terms of a protasis (i.e., the dependant clause expressing the condition) and an apodosis (i.e., the main clause expressing the consequence if the condition is not fulfilled). In the primary data, similar to Dhofari Arabic (Davey 2016, 207), the protasis can be introduced by the particles *law* and *iḏā* 'if'. Based on the examples in the primary data, the difference in their use seems to be that the former indicates a condition unlikely to be fulfilled, whereas the latter a condition more likely to happen.

Thus, the overall likelihood of the condition being fulfilled and the realis/irrealis contraposition in the conditional clause is mainly expressed through these particles. The verb forms vary according to the time reference of the conditional clause and according to the rules mentioned above.

Conditional clauses can be divided into three main types, according to the likelihood of the condition expressed happening.

The first type expresses a realis condition that is likely to be fulfilled. In this case, the primary data show both the protasis and the apodosis taking a p-stem verb, although the verb of the apodosis may also take the future/conditional verbal marker *bi-*:[55]

(148)	*iḏā*	*trīdi*	*malābis*	*gedīda*	*binrūḥ*	*w-ništrī*
	if	want.2FSG	cloth.MPL	new.FSG	FUT.go.1PL	CONG-buy.1PL

'If you want new clothes, we will go and buy (them).' [S12]

[55] In Dhofari Arabic, Davey (2016, 253) notes that the verbal prefix *bā-* is not obligatory with the verb of the apodosis when an outcome is achievable or likely to be fulfilled, but it occurs more often if the conditional clause is introduced by *iḏā*.

(149) *iḏā arūḥ taww batʿaššā maʿ-kum*
if go.1SG now FUT.have_dinner.1SG with-PRON.2FPL
'If I leave now, I will have dinner with you.' [S3]

The second type expresses a realis condition unlikely to be fulfilled. In this case, the protasis will show an s-stem verb (or a prepositional phrase), whereas the apodosis has a p-stem verb with no prefixes. These types of conditional clauses can be introduced by either *law* or *iḏā*:

(150) *law ʿind-i siyyāra, arūḥ rustāq*
if to-PRON.1SG car.FSG go.1SG Rustāq
'If I had a car, I would go to Rustaq.' [S6]

(151) *iḏā laqti šiḫḫa tqūli-he tursil-nī ʿaṭṭūr*
if met.2FSG Shiḫḫa tell.2FSG-PRON.3FSG send.3FSG-PRON.1SG medicine.SG
'If you meet Shiḫḫa, would you tell her to send me the medicine?' [S8]

In (151), the speaker is asking her niece to inform Shiḫḫa, his nurse, that he needs a new medicine. However, as Shiḫḫa was spending a few days in Muscat for work at the time, the likelihood of his niece meeting Shiḫḫa in al-ʿAwābī was low.

Finally, the third type expresses an irrealis condition, which is impossible to be fulfilled because it refers to a past event or a condition that cannot be changed anymore. In this case, the conditional clause is introduced by *law* and the protasis takes an s-stem verb (or a nominal, adjectival, or prepositional phrase), whereas the apodosis takes a p-stem verb.

(152) *law iṣ-ṣaġirīn mā marīḍīn, ašill-hum*

if DEF-small.MPL NEG sick.MPL take.1SG-PRON.3MPL

ilā l-falag

to DEF-falag

'If the kids weren't sick, I would have brought them to the falag.' [S10]

(153) *qāl law ʿind-i fulūs atzawwug*

said.3MSG if to-PRON.1SG money.COLL marry.1SG

ġēr-iš

other-PRON.2FSG

'He said, "If I had money, I would have married someone other than you."' [S14]

(154) لو ما كنت فقيرة واجد اعيش في بيت قصر

law mā kunt faqīra wāgid aʿyš fī bēt

if NEG was.1SG poor.FSG much live.1SG in house.MSG

qaṣr

mansion.MSG

'If I weren't so poor, I would have lived in a bigger house.' [S15]

All these examples show situations that cannot be changed at the moment of the utterance, either because of a physical state (i.e., the kids being sick) or because of a state like poverty that is very difficult to change.

2.5.4. Complement Clause

In the primary data, a complement clause can be introduced by the particle *inn-* 'that', or any other prepositional complement required by the verb.

The particle *inn-* can also take a suffixed pronoun in the event that the subject of the complement clause differs from the head noun or from the subject of the main clause:

(155) *manṣab-i* *mā* *yismaḥ* *inn-ī* *asawwi*
position-PRON.1SG NEG allow.3MSG that-PRON.1SG make.1SG
mašākil
problem.PL
'My position does not allow me to make trouble.' [S3]

In this case, the particle *inn-* carries the suffixed pronoun *-ī* for the first person singular since it is the subject of the subordinate clause. As in other Arabic dialects,[56] in the primary data, there is no specific category of verbs that takes the particle *inn-* before a complement clause.

Generally, verbs of 'saying' and 'thinking' carry the particle *inn-* to introduce a subordinate sentence:

(156) *aqūl-l-iš* *inn-iš* *rabša*
say.1SG-to-PRON.2FSG that-PRON.2FSG naughty.FSG
'I tell you that you are naughty.' [S12]

---

[56] Holes (2016, 374) notes that in Bahraini Arabic, noun clauses can lack the complementising particle *inn* "regardless of the type of verb which governs them if they are objects, or which is predicated of them if they are subjects," and generally follow the main verb directly.

(157) *eḍann* *inn* *haḏī* *l-gāmiʿa* *mumtaza*
think.1SG that DEM.PROX.FSG DEF-university.FSG excellent.FSG
'I think that this university is excellent.' [S5]

However, they can also be found without the introducing particle:

(158) *qāl* *l-ha* *mā* *trūḥi*
said.3MSG to-PRON.3FSG NEG go.2FSG
'He told her not to go.' [S4]

According to Holes (2016, 374), the sporadic use of the particle *inn-* with any category of verbs "may reflect the greater exposure of the user to varieties of Arabic which use a complementiser routinely (especially MSA)." This statement is consistent with the primary data presented in this study: most of the complement clauses introduced by the particle *inn-* have been recorded in al-ʿAwābī in YS and AS with an average to high level of education, whereas in Wādī Banī Kharūṣ, speakers tended not to use any particle between the main verb and the subordinate clause, as in example (158), regardless of their level of education. Hence, it is possible that people in the town are more exposed to different types of Arabic whether through education or greater freedom of movement.

Verbs of 'wanting' and 'ordering' do not take any complementiser in the primary data.

(159) *amar-ik* *trūḥ* *tinām*
order.1SG-PRON.2MSG go.2MSG sleep.2MSG
'I order you to go to sleep.' [S12]

(160) *bāya* *ašrab* *qahwa*

want.AP.FSG drink.1SG coffee

'I want to drink coffee.' [S5]

(161) *arīd-iš* *trūḫi* *maʕi* *ilā* *l-mustašfā*

want.1SG-PRON.2FSG go.2FSG with-PRON.1SG to DEF-hospital.FSG

'I want you to come with me to the hospital.' [S9]

(162) ابغاش تجيبي الصغيرين البيت

abġā-š *tigībi* *iṣ-ṣaġīrīn* *il-bēt*

want.1SG-PRON.2FSG bring.2FSG small.MPL DEF-house.MSG

'I want you to bring the children home.' [S10]

In (160), we see the AP form *bāya* introducing a complement clause. This is the most common way, according to the primary data, of expressing will and desire, although when the subject of the complement clause differs from the one of the main clause and, as already mentioned, a suffix pronoun is needed, the AP form *bāya* (or *bāġa*) cannot be used, and is replaced by the verbs *arīd* or *bġī*, as in example (161) and (162).

Verbs of 'liking' and 'loving' do not take any complementiser:

(163) *aḥibb* *al-iqrā*

love.1SG DEF-reading.VN

'I like reading.' [S3]

(164) *tḥibbi* *ṭ-ṭbaḫ?*

love.2FSG DEF-cooking.VN

'Do you like cooking?' [S7]

(165) يعجبك تشوف المباراة ؟

yiʿgib-ik *tišūf* *il-mubāra*

like.3SG-PRON.2MSG watch.2MSG DEF-match

'Do you like watching the football match?' [S5]

In examples (163) and (164), the main verb is followed by a verbal noun, which constitutes the usual construction in the primary data for the verb *ḥabb* 'love'. In (165), the main verb is followed by a p-stem verb, which agrees grammatically with the suffixed pronoun.

Two categories of verbs in the primary data that never take the complementiser to introduce the subordinate clause are modal verbs and auxiliaries. These categories are usually followed by the p-stem verb directly (as shown in the present chapter, §1.2.5).

A final category to be analysed in this section is that of complement clauses that function as indirect questions, also known as embedded questions. In the primary data, these clauses are introduced by *mū* or *šē* 'what', *lēš* / *amū* 'why', *kēf* 'how', *kam* 'how many', *min* 'who', *matā* 'when', and *ēn* / *wēn* / *hēn* 'where',[57] all of which directly govern the main verb.

(166) *mā* *aʿraf* ***mū*** *asawwi*

NEG know.1SG what do.1SG

'I don't know what to do.' [S12]

[57] For more details on interrogative pronouns in this vernacular, the reader is referred to ch. 3, §1.2.5.

(167) *mā afham* **lēš** *trūḥi ilā dubei maʕhum*

NEG understand.1SG why go.2FSG to Dubai with-PRON.3MPL

'I do not understand why you go to Dubai with them.' [S7]

(168) باية اعرف كم عدد المعازيم العرس

bāya aʕraf **kam** *ʕadad il-muʕāzīm*

want.AP.FSG know.1SG how_much number DEF-confirm.PP.MSG

il-ʕars

DEF-wedding.MSG

'I want to know how many are confirmed for the wedding.' [S5]

(169) *bāya aʕraf* **kēf** *umm-iš*

want.AP.FSG know.1SG how mother.FSG-PRON.2FSG

'I'd like to know how your mother is doing.' [S11]

(170) *bāġi yisāl* **min** *yisawwi šay kḏāk*

want.AP.MSG ask.3MSG who do.PRES.3MSG thing like_this

'He wants to ask who does (something) like this.' [S14]

(171) *ḫabbir-ni* **matā** *yikūn il-ʕars*

inform.IMP.2MSG-PRON.1SG when is.3MSG DEF-wedding.MSG

'Let me know when the wedding is.' [S9]

(172) *sāyla* **wēn** *aḫ-iš*

ask.AP.FSG where brother.MSG-PRON.2FSG

'I am asking where your brother is.' [S9]

3.0. Negation

The literature on negation in Arabic individuates two main isoglosses that divide the Arabic-speaking world: the western dialects (e.g., Moroccan, Egyptian, Tunisian), which combine some variants of /mā/ and /-š/, and eastern dialects (e.g., Syrian, Kuwaiti, Gulf), which use /mā/ and other particles (Brustad 2000, 277). In the Arabian Peninsula, there is a wide range of of negation strategies: in Ṣanʿānī Arabic, for example, we found *miš / maš, mā, mā...š* and *lā* (Watson 1993);[58] in Gulf Arabic, Holes (1990, 71–76) reports *mā* (usually adopted to negate perfective and imperfective verbs), *lā* (for imperatives), *lā...wila* (for coordinated clauses) and *mū* and its variants (adopted to negate a constituent of a sentence); in Najdi Arabic, Ingham (1994, 44) reports only the forms *mā* and *lā* to negate verbal sentences.

There are not many works on negation in Omani Arabic. In Dhofar, the main negation markers are *mā* (used to negate the lexical verb and existentials) and *lā* (used alongside *mā* to negate the imperative).[59] Holes (2008, 485) reports a few negation markers for Omani Arabic, such as *mā, māb* (in the Sharqiyyah region), *mu / muhu* (in Bedouin dialects of al-Batinah), and *lā* (especially for imperative).

3.1. Negation in the Data

In the primary data three main negation markers appear: *mā, lā,* and *ġēr.* In addition to these, the primary data also show the use of the older forms *šīši* and *-ši,* that will be briefly presented further in this section. I will divide the description of the negation

[58] In the Tihāma region of Yemen, alongside the *mūš / mīš*, also the discontinuous markers *mā...-ši* are attested (Simeone-Senelle 1996, 209).

[59] Davey (2016, 217).

system used by the informants in the al-ʿAwābī district in noun, verb, and prepositional phrases.

Negation of noun phrases is realised with the negative particle *mā* before the noun, the adjective, the demonstrative, or the participle it is meant to negate:

(173) *lākin hīya mā kabīra*
but PRON.3FSG NEG big.FSG
'But she isn't old.' [S1]

(174) *mā kḏāk*
NEG like_this
'Not like this.' [S7]

(175) *mā ḥad šūf-kum*
NEG person saw.3MSG-PRON.2MPL
'No one saw you.' [S11]

(176) *umm-he mā rāḍy<in>he*
mother.FSG-PRON.3FSG NEG accept.AP.FSG<in>PRON.3FSG
'Her mother did not accept her.' [S1][60]

---

[60] Brustad (2000, 290), in an analysis of negation of participles, reports a few remarks for dialects that show different negation markers for noun and verb phrases. In dialects where participles are treated as predicates (e.g., Egyptian, Syrian, Moroccan) they are negated by *miš*, *māši*, and *mū*; whereas when participles carry more verbal force, they tend to be treated as verbs and are negated by particle *mā* (e.g., Syrian, Kuwaiti). The primary data presented in this study do not distinguish between nominal and verbal negation; therefore, the participle is always negated by *mā*.

(177) *lā,* *mā* *qahwa,* *bāya* *šāy*

NEG NEG coffee want.AP.FSG tea

'No, not coffee. I want tea.' [S14]

(178) *hīya* *mā* *hnā*

PRON.3FSG NEG here

'She is not here.' [S12]

In example (173), only the adjective *kabīra* 'big, old' is negated by the negation marker, which is positioned just before the word, although a contrastive sense to the whole sentence is given by the initial *lākin* 'but'. In (175), *mā* followed by the indefinite pronoun results in the negative indefinite pronoun *mā ḥad* 'no one'.

In some cases, the adjective or a PP (as in the example below) can be negated by the noun *ġēr* 'other':

(179) *haḏā* *z-zōg* *riggāl* *ġēr*

DEM.PROX.MSG DEF-husband.MSG man.MSG other_than

maḍbūṭ

acceptable.MSG

'This husband is not an acceptable man.'[61] [S1]

As the examples above show, the negative marker in a noun phrase always precedes the lexical item it negates.

Verb phrases can be negated by either *mā* or *lā*, and both immediately precede the verb. More than depending on the morphological form of the VP (i.e., s-stem or p-stem), it seems that the negative markers are linked to the VP temporal and/or aspectual value. Therefore, *lā* tends to negate the past and *mā*

[61] According to Islamic rules (i.e., he would drink alcohol).

the non-past. This, however, is subject to a degree of variation: in (180), the speaker negates a past s-stem form in a narrative context with *mā*. This variation might be caused either by the influence of other Arabic dialects through television, for example, or by aspectual values inherent in the context of narration. By contrast, example (183) shows the negative marker *lā* negating a p-stem verb in a past narrative context.[62]

More insights are certainly needed. However, without trying to draw any final conclusion, it is worth mentioning that S2 in (180)—despite being an illiterate AS like S1 in (183)—was more exposed to the language of the media, since she was often found enjoying Egyptian soap operas.

(180) *il-imām* *mā* *ḫāf-he*

DEF-imam.MSG NEG feared.3MSG-PRON.3FSG

'The imam was not afraid of her.' [S2]

(181) مي ما تروم تطبح لان يدها متعورة

mm-ī *mā* *trūm* *taṭbaḥ* *l-inne*

mother.FSG-PRON.1SG NEG can.3FSG cook.3FSG because

yad-he *matʿūre*

hand.FSG-PRON.3FSG injured.PP.FSG

'My mother cannot cook because her hand is injured.' [S3]

(182) *hadī* *ṣaġīra,* *mā* *abġā-ha*

DEM.PROX.FSG small.FSG NEG want.1SG-PRON.3FSG

'This (girl) is young. I don't want her.' [S10]

[62] This is linked to the use of the p-stem verb in past contexts, which has been explained in the present chapter, §1.2.1.

(183) *hūwa* *lā* *yaʿṭi-he* *malābis* *w-fulūs*

PRON.3MSG NEG give.3MSG-PRON.3FSG cloth.MPL CONJ-money.COLL

'He doesn't give her clothes or cash.' [S1]

The negation marker *lā* is also used as a negator in prohibitive sentences:

(184) *lā* *taʿāl* *hinā*

NEG IMP.come.MSG here

'Do not come here!' [S12]

(185) *lā* *tūkli* *kḏāk*

NEG eat.2MSG like_this

'Do not eat like this!' [S9]

(186) *lā* *trūḥi!*

NEG go.2FSG

'Don't go!' [S6]

Finally, prepositional phrases are also negated by the particle *mā,* always positioned before the preposition:

(187) *mā* *fīh* *byūt,* *mā* *šey* *siyyāra*

NEG EXIST house.MPL NEG EXIST car.FSG

'There are no houses, there are no cars.' [S1]

(188) *mā* *ʿind-i* *fulūs*

NEG to-PRON.1SG money.COLL

'I do not have cash.' [S8]

(189) *mā* *ʿind-iš* *miftāḥ* *māl* *bēt*

NEG to-PRON.2FSG key.SG GEN house.MSG

'You do not have the house key.' [S9]

When two (or more) negated sentences are coordinated, the main verb (or noun) is negated by *mā* and the linkers are usually *wa* and *lā*, which negates the following verb (or noun):

(190) *mā fīh karhabā wa lā tilifūn wa lā*
NEG EXIST electricity.FSG CONJ NEG telephone.SG CONJ NEG
myā
water
'There is no electricity, nor telephone, nor water.' [S1]

(191) *ʿind-ha awlād ʿamm lākin mā ysālo*
to-PRON.3FSG child.MPL uncle.MSG but NEG ask.3MPL
ʿan-ha wa lā ʿarfū-he
about-PRON.3FSG CONJ NEG knew.3MPL-PRON.3FSG
'She had cousins, but they don't ask about her, nor did they know her.' [S14]

3.2. Remarks on Reinhardt's Negative Structure

As mentioned at the beginning of this section, there is a fourth negation linker used in the al-ʿAwābī district, i.e., the enclitic *-ši* and its emphatic form *šīši*. Reinhardt (1894, 282) states that the enclitic /-ši/ can be suffixed directly to the predicate it negates, e.g., *huwwa-ši sekrān* 'he is not a drunkard'. Consider these examples from his texts[63]:

(i) *u froḥ hest terāh baʿado mākil-ši šei*
'Denn er hatte noch nichts gegessen'
'Because he had not eaten yet' (Reinhardt 1894, 297)

[63] These are reported following Reinhardt's transcription and translation.

(ii) *lākin rām-ši*
'Konnte aber nicht'
'But he couldn't' (Reinhardt 1894, 299)

(iii) *u šiši emraḍ min mšaufit lʿado*
'Es giebt nichts Krankmachenderes als der Anblick des Feindes.'
'There is nothing more disastrous than the sight of the enemy.' (Reinhardt 1894, 301)

(iv) *ké hest-ši ʿaleykum*
'euch liegt wohl nicht viel daran'
'You don't care much about it' (Reinhardt 1894, 314)

As these examples show, the enclitic /-ši/ can be suffixed to any part of speech: a PP, as in (i); a s-stem verb, as in (ii); an adverb, as in (iv); and used as negative existential, as in (iii).

In his description of the negative clause, Reinhardt (1894, 281–82) reports various negative markers. In addition to the aforementioned *mā* and *lā*—"both negating the verb"—there are:

- the negative verb *laysa*, only used in the 3MSG form *lēs;*
- words like *ʿadem* 'absence' or *qille* 'small amount, little';
- The clitic *-ši,* "welche dem zu verneinenden worte angehängt wird" 'which is attached to the negated word'.

All these forms appear in the texts at the end of his study, albeit some more often than others. Diem (2014, 89) found that negations with the clitic *-ši* "considerably outnumber the negation with *mā/lā*" in the descriptive parts of Reinhardt's monograph, but in the texts he gives a different picture. In fact, the narrators of the stories reported use all means of negation, with the only exception of *ʿadem* and *qille*, which are still quite rare.

Lucas (2018, 2) reports a "purely postverbal negation of this kind" for (a) all of the sedentary dialects of historic Palestine, as well as those of northwestern Jordan, southwestern Syria and southern Lebanon; (b) marginally, Cairene Egyptian; (c) the Upper Egyptian dialect described by Khalafallah (1969); (d) Maltese, but only in prohibitives; (e) the Omani dialect described by Reinhardt; and (f) a small cluster of dialects spoken in the southern part of Yemeni Tihama.

Many modern Arabic dialects (e.g., Moroccan, Egyptian) use the negation complex *mā... -š* to negate both verbal and nonverbal predicates. Ouhalla (2008, 357) reports a few examples from Moroccan Arabic to show how the complex works: *mā* always appears before the s-stem or the p-stem verb, and *-ši* is suffixed to the verb negated, e.g., *mā ka-n-tkllam-ši maʿhum* 'I don't talk to them'. In the case of nominal predicates, the complex shows two main patterns: it can appear on the left edge of the predicate, e.g., *samīr maši hna* 'Samir is not here', or *-ši* appears as an enclitic whenever the predicate is a noun, an adjective, or an adverbial element, e.g., *samīr mā hnaši* 'Samir is not here'. It seems that in most of the dialects that show this negative complex, the use of the clitic *-ši* alone is not possible, even though there are a few dialects in between that allow it. Simeone-Senelle (1996, 213–14) reports the use of the suffixed marker *-š* alone, but always to negate verbs and not nouns; she also attests the use of a reinforced form *-šī*, clitic or not.

In the Omani dialects that have been documented so far there is no evidence of this negation complex nor of the only enclitic form /-ši/.

In none of Holes' works (1989; 1996; 1998; 2013) is the clitic *-ši* mentioned as a form of negation for Omani Arabic; neither is it in Kaplan's (2008) nor in Webster's (1991) work on Bahla in his description of the Āl Wahība of Oman.

Nevertheless, Brockett (1985) and Nakano (1994)—in their brief descriptions of Khabura and Zanzibar Arabic, respectively, provide some examples in favour of *-ši*. Brockett (1895, 140) says that *šīši* is "a Bedouin expression" according to one of his informants originating from the Jabal Akhdar region—hence, close to the district of al-ʿAwābī. Nakano, on the other hand, provides only one or two examples with *šīši* used as 'nothing' (cf. Diem 2014, 90). This is in accordance with Reinhardt (1894, 30), who reports *šyšy* and *māšay* as 'nothing'.

Having now compared the sources available, we can postulate—in accordance with Diem (2014)—that the clitic /-ši/ was probably the original negative construct used in the region, before being almost entirely replaced by *mā* under the influence of non-š-dialects as the ones spoken in the Arabian Peninsula.

Further evidence of this theory is given by the following extract, a traditional song of Jabal Akhdar performed by speaker 13:[64]

(192) *w-iḏa gīt w-int aġbār w-anā afrāḥ*
*w-ḥad-**ši** bēn^{i}-nā yislāḥ*
min šyuẖīn wa ʿorbān

[64] The text of the entire song is given in the Appendix.

*mā min šyuḫ ahel-**ši** d-dār*
w-eḍann mā egī aḫsār
w-agīb mṣarr min el-kbar
'If he goes and you are poor and I am happy
and no one is between us to mediate
among shaykhs and people,
which[65] of these shaykhs is not from the people (family) of the house
and I think I won't lose anything
I bring the biggest mṣarr (lit. 'a mṣarr among the biggest').' [S13]

In the song, the clitic *-ši* is used to negate two nominal predicates, i.e., *ḥad*, 'someone' and then *ahel* 'family, tribe', which is apparently a phenomenon that does not occur in any of the dialects cited above. The indefinite pronoun *ḥad-ši* 'no one' is reported by Reinhardt (1894, 29) as the most common form in his data, but in the speech of my informants it has become obsolete and almost completely replaced by the indefinite *mā ḥad*. Interestingly, the clitic *-ši* seems to interrupt the synthetic genitive construction in the song, which is not possible in any of the dialect cited above. Although it might also be due to poetic licence.

In general, *-ši* is not used as a negator in most of Oman today (Lucas 2018, 2), and the investigations conducted for this work in the al-ʿAwābī district confirmed this statement as far as my informants are concerned. This negative enclitic has not

[65] The use of *mā* as relative pronoun 'that which, what' is also reported by Johnstone (1967, 67) for Peninsular dialects, although in the primary data the form *mū* is more common.

been found in the primary data collected and it is definitely not in use in the everyday speech.

The emphatic *šīši*, on the other hand, is used by the OS in Wādī Banī Kharūṣ (i.e., speakers 4, 8, 13 and 15) as a negative existential 'there is/are not', instead of *mā šay / mā fīh*:[66]

(193) *šīši*	*šay*	*hnā*
NEG.EXIST	thing.MSG	here

'There is nothing here.' [S8]

(194) *mā*	*yrūm*	*yiṭlaʿ*	*l-inne*	*šīši*	*darag*
NEG	can.3MSG	come.3MSG	because	NEG.EXIST	stair.MSG

'He cannot go up because there are no stairs.' [S15]

[66] It is worth mentioning, however, that some of my informants told me that the negative existential *šīši* is normally used in the speech of OS in Rustaq.

CONCLUSION

This study had two main aims: providing a linguistic analysis of the Omani vernacular spoken in the al-ʿAwābī district (northern Oman) and assessing the diachronic variation this vernacular underwent by comparing the new data collected with the set provided by Carl Reinhardt in 1894. These aims sought to answer a few urgent questions such as: is Reinhardt's *Ein arabischer Dialekt gesprochen in 'Oman und Zanzibar* (1894) still a reliable account of the vernacular spoken in the same area in the present day by speakers originating from the same tribes? How much of his material is still valid? And finally, to what extent has the influence of more prestigious forms of Arabic or MSA used in broadcasting and education impacted the vernacular spoken nowadays?

To answer these questions, this work consists of four chapters and an Appendix, providing an account of the dialect spoken by the consultants in the al-ʿAwābī district.

The issue of the reliability of Reinhardt's (1894) work was addressed in different parts of this study: first, the examination of its strengths and weaknesses in ch. 1, §6.0, which provided the impetus for this research.

Second, in ch. 2 on Phonology, we saw how syncope is a much more widespread phenomenon in Reinhardt's account of this dialect than in the primary data, where syncope mainly depends on vowel quality (see ch. 2, §2.0). Monophthongisation seems to occur more frequently in the primary data than in Reinhardt's, who examines it only with regard to some specific

 https://doi.org/10.11647/OBP.0298.05

monosyllabic nouns (see ch. 2, §2.2). Admittedly, though, it is difficult to tell whether having access to more informants would have allowed the German scholar to sketch a different picture.

Third, in the section on nominal morphology, we saw how Reinhardt's set of data differs from the primary ones only in the field of numerals and pronouns. Particularly interesting in the light of diachronic variation is the neutralisation of the gender distinction in demonstrative prononuns which seems to be taking place in the district (or at least in my informants' speech). This neutralisation might easily be the result of the process of homogenisation, which is affecting the dialects of the Arabian Peninsula, since we have already seen it happening in other parts of the region.

In the section on verbal morphology, we found even more frequent differences: the realisation of the conjugation of the strong verb (see, for example, Table 3.37) and the formation of the future tense appear quite different (see for example the use of the *bi*-prefix in the primary data and the *ḥa*-prefix in Reinhardt's).

The chapter on syntax constitutes the real novelty of this study: the description of the syntax in Reinhardt (1894) is restricted to the analysis of very few sentence types, albeit providing numerous examples.

The discussion on the active participle is particularly interesting from a dialectological point of view. If, on the one hand, the morphological pattern of the AP remained unchanged, its syntax, conversely, seems to have a wider spectrum of functions when compared to Reinhardt. Indeed, the German author lacks an extensive analysis of the AP and the present study adds new elements to the literary debate, also demonstrating how the AP is a very productive feature in the informants' speech.

The major differences relative to Reinhardt's account of syntax can be seen in the use of the genitive markers and in the negation system. For example, we have demonstrated that *ḥāl* does not convey a genitive relation, but rather behaves as a preposition and that the clitic *-šī*, reported by Reinhardt as the main form of negation in the area, is found in the primary data only in a traditional song by one OS (i.e., S13), completely replaced by the mainstream *mā* in all the others.

We have also seen in the primary data some degree of retention of the VSO word order, and restricted use of the apophonic passive for specific I form verbs, e.g., *wilidt* 'I was born'. Interestingly, this vernacular seems to retain the characteristic feminine plural forms in nouns, adjectives, verbs, and pronouns. However, strong variation can be seen in the realisation of the demonstrative pronouns, where the gender differentiation for the distal and proximal plural forms is fading.

This is an example of the diachronic variation that this study seeks to document in the al-ʿAwābī district. Numerous instances show that some syntactic features are slowly becoming obsolete, being replaced by Gulf or MSA alternatives. Examples include the abundant use of the relative pronoun *illi* over *bū* and the widespread use of the negative marker *mā* in all sentence types. The latter phenomenon is especially noteworthy if we think about the negative system described by Reinhardt, which now appears highly obsolescent in YS and AS groups.

With regards to the criteria chosen for the recruitment of informants—i.e., age, provenance, and level of education—we have witnessed a remarkable homogeneity between al-ʿAwābī and Wādī Banī Kharūṣ, with the major differences found in the occurrence of *imāla* and use of archaisms in the lexicon—e.g., the cardinal points.

Level of education also seems to go hand in hand with age, since access to education was guaranteed to the Omani population only from the 1980s onwards. One big difference in terms of literacy of speakers is the use of the particle *inn-* to introduce complement clauses: according to the primary data, it is found in the speech of literate YS in the district, and never in the speech of the illiterate OS.

Oman's exit from isolationism certainly brought some extent of language variation—as also noticed by Leila Kaplan (2008) in regard to her informants in Bahla. This variation is especially visible if we consider the criterion of age. OS show a greater conformity to Reinhardt's material, compared to the other two groups: in terms of phonology, for example, the speech of OS shows no occurrence of *imāla* and a lower occurrence of monophthongisation. In terms of morphology, we have found frequent use of comparative forms of adverbs, e.g., *efwaq* < *fōq* 'up, above', in OS and sporadic use in that of YS and AS. Moreover, we saw how OS seem more inclined to use an impersonal form of the active verb to express passivity—although the primary data are not sufficient to postulate this for certain. By contrast, we have acknowledged that in the domain of syntax, *bū*—the relative pronoun also reported by Reinhardt (1894)—occurs more often in the speech of YS than in that of the OS, who tend to use the more mainstream *illi*. We have found traces of the use of the clitic *-šī* and its emphatic counterpart *šīši* in the speech of two old men in the district (i.e., S8 and S13) and in one old woman (i.e., S15).

Although gender was not one of the criteria used for recruiting participants, the primary data showed an interesting differentiation in this sense, that is the AP forms *bāġi* (only used by male speakers) and *bāya* (only used by female speakers).

One more conclusion we can draw from the argument explained in this study is the degree of influence of forms from neighboring dialects, the media and MSA. Evidence of a certain extent of influence can be found in the use of the relative pronoun *illi*—also found in Gulf, Ṣanʿānī, and Najdi Arabic—over *bū*; in the use of *bi-* as a prefix for future tense, whereas Reinhardt (1894) reported *ḥa-*; in the use of *mā* as negative marker for all sentence-types, except coordinated negative clauses and imperative mood, where *lā* is used instead. The latter is clear evidence of MSA influence—brought by education and broadcasting—since in the district we have found indications of other, older, forms of negation, which are also partly attested in neighbouring dialects. Finally, the use of the particle *inn-* in complement clauses—found predominantly in the speech of literate speakers—is another piece of evidence of MSA influence over this dialect.

Less influence from other Omani and neighbouring varieties seems to happen at a phonological level: we have seen how both Muscat and Dhofari Arabic show iambic stress, whereas the informants' speech in the al-ʿAwābī district maintain a trochaic stress.

The points made so far also support Holes' (2011b) thesis of a process of homogenisation which is happening in the Arabian Peninsula. The speed of diachronic change in this district of northern Oman—and in the region as a whole—is highly concerning and is demonstrated by the disappearance of certain lexical items and syntactic structures, which are progressively falling into oblivion through the generations. We have demonstrated how peculiar and rich the dialects of Oman can be: for example, the syntax of this vernacular showed a great number of archaisms, which at times relates this dialect to North Africa, e.g., the use of the auxiliary verb *dār/yidīr* 'to start' or the /-š/ negation.

These unique features, together with the knowledge of plant names, traditional medicine, natural environment, and arrays of orientation so treasured by local people, need to be protected and cherished both by urgently documenting the Arabic varieties spoken in Oman and the Peninsula and by creating awareness among the younger generation of traditional languages and cultural practices. It is hoped that this study might be a first step in this direction.

REFERENCES

Abu-Mansour, M. H. 1992. 'Closed Syllable Shortening and Morphological Levels'. *Perspective on Arabic Linguistics*. IV: 245–62 Amesterdam: John Benjamins.

Agius, D. 2002. *In the Wake of the Dhow: The Arabian Gulf and Oman*. London: Ithaca Press.

Agius, D. 2005. *Seafaring in the Arabian Gulf and Oman: The People of the Dhow*. London: Kegan Paul.

Beeston, A. F. L. 1982. *Sabaic Dictionary: English, French, Arabic*. Louvain-la-Neuve: Peeters and Beirut: Librarie du Liban.

Behnstedt, P., and M. Woidich. 2011. *Wortatlas der Arabischen Dialekte, Vol. I. Mensch, Natur, Flora und Fauna*. Leiden: Brill.

Bettega, S. 2017. 'Agreement with Plural Controllers in Omani Arabic'. In *Linguistics Studies in the Arabian Gulf (QuadRi - Quaderni di RiCOGNIZIONI)* 7: 153–74. Turin: University of Turin.

———. 2019a. *Tense, Modality and Aspect in Omani Arabic*. Naples: Università degli Studi di Napoli 'L'Orientale'.

———. 2019b. 'Genitive markers in Omani Arabic'. In *Romano-Arabica* 19: 223–37.

Biberstein-Kazimirski, A. 1860. *Dictionnaire Arabe-Français: Contenant Toutes les Raciness de la Langue Arabe, Leurs Dérivés, Tant dans L'Idiome Vulgaire que dans L'Idiome Littéral, ainsi que les Dialectes d'Alger et de Maroc*. Paris: Maisonneuve et cie.

Boersma, P., and D. Weenink. 2017. PRAAT: doing phonetics by computer [Computer program]. Version 6.0.24, retrieved 27 January 2017 from http://www.praat.org.

Brockett, A. A. 1985. *The Spoken Arabic of Khābūra on the Bāṭina of Oman*. Manchester: Manchester University Press.

Brustad, K. 2000. *The Syntax of Spoken Arabic: A Comparative Study of Moroccan, Egyptian, Syrian, and Kuwaiti Dialects*. Washington, D.C.: Georgetown University Press.

Cantineau, J. 1960. *Cours de Phonétique Arabe.* Paris: Libraire C. Klincksieck.

Caubet, D. 1991. 'The Active Participle as a Means to Renew the Aspectual System: A Comparative Study in Several Dialects of Arabic'. In *Semitic Studies in Honor of Wolf Leslau*, edited by Alan S. Kaye, 209–24. Wiesbaden: Harrassowitz.

Comrie, B. 1976. *Aspect.* Cambridge: Cambridge University Press.

———. 1985. *Tense*. Cambridge: Cambridge University Press.

Dahl, Ö. 1985. *Tense and Aspect Systems.* Oxford: Basil Blackwell.

Davey, J. R. 2016. *Coastal Dhofari Arabic: A Sketch Grammar.* Leiden: Brill.

Diem, W. 2014. *Negation in Arabic: A Study in Linguistic History.* Wiesbaden: Harrassowitz.

Eades, D. 2009. 'Retention of the Passive Verb in a Bedouin Dialect of Northern Oman'. *Zeitschrift für Angewandte Linguistik* 51: 5–21.

Eades, D., and M. Persson. 2013. 'Aktionsart, Word Form and Context: On the Use of the Active Participle in Gulf Arabic Dialects'. *Journal of Semitic Studies* 53/2: 343–67.

Eades, D., and J. C. E. Watson. 2013a. 'Tense and Aspect in Semitic: A Case Study Based on the Arabic of the Omani Šarqiyya and the Mehri of Dhofar'. In *Ingham of Arabia: A Collection of Articles Presented as a Tribute to the Career of Bruce Ingham*, edited by Clive Holes and Rudolph de Jong, 23–54. Leiden: Brill.

———. 2013b. 'Camel Culture and Camel Terminology Among the Omani Bedouins'. *Journal of Semitic Studies* 58: 169–219.

Eisele, J. C. 1993. 'Time Reference, Tense, and Formal Aspect in Cairene Arabic'. In *Perspective on Arabic Linguistics 5: Papers from the Fifth Annual Symposium on Arabic Linguistics*, edited by M. Eid and C. Holes, 173–212. Amsterdam: Benjamins.

———. 1999. *Arabic Verbs in Time: Tense and Aspect in Cairene Arabic*. Wiesbaden: Harrassowitz.

Eksell-Harning, K. 1980. 'The Analytic Genitive in the Modern Arabic Dialects'. PhD dissertation, Göteborg University.

ELAN (Version 5.6-FX)[Computer software]. 2018. Nijmegen: Max Planck Institute for Pshycholinguistics. Retrieved from http://tla.mpi.nl/tools/tla-tools/elan.

Ghazanfar, S. A. 1995. '*Wasm*: A Traditional Method of Healing by Cauterisation'. *Journal of Ethnopharmacology* 47: 125–28.

Ghubash, H. 2006. *Oman: The Islamic Democratic Tradition*. New York: Routledge

Glover, B. C. 1988. 'The Morphophonology of Muscat Arabic'. PhD dissertation, University of California, Los Angeles.

Haak, M. 2006. 'Auxiliary'. In *Encyclopedia of Arabic Language and Linguistics*, edited by K. Versteegh et al., I: 216–21. Leiden: Brill

el-Hassan, S. 2008. 'Mood (Arabic Dialects)'. In *Encyclopedia of Arabic Language and Linguistics*, edited by K. Versteegh et al., III: 262–69. Leiden: Brill.

Hayes, B. 1995. *Metrical Stress Theory*. Chicago: The University of Chicago Press.

Hoffman-Ruf, M. 2013. 'Aspects of the Relationship Between Oman and Germany in the Late 19th and Early 20th Century'. In *Oman and Overseas*, edited by M. Hoffmann-Ruf and A. Al Salimi, 449–61. New York: Georg Olms.

Holes, C. 1989. 'Towards a Dialect Geography of Oman'. *Bulletin of the School of African and Oriental Studies* 52/3: 446–62.

———. 1990. *Gulf Arabic*. Croom Helm Descriptive Grammars Series. London: Routledge.

———. 1995. *Modern Arabic: Structures, Functions and Varieties*. Harlow, Essex: Longman.

———. 1996. 'The Arabic Dialects of South Eastern Arabia in a Socio-Historical Perspective. *Zeitschrift für Arabische Linguistik* 31: 34–56.

———. 1998. 'Retention and Loss of the Passive Verb in the Arabic Dialects of Northern Oman and Eastern Arabia. *Journal of Semitic Studies* 43/2: 347–62.

———. 2004a. 'Quadriliteral Verbs in the Arabic Dialects of Eastern Arabia'. In *Approaches to Arabic Dialects: A Collection of Articles Presented to Manfred Woidich on the Occasion of his Sixtieth Birthday*, edited by M. Haak, R. de Jong, and K. Versteegh, 97–115. Leiden: Brill

———. 2004b. *Modern Arabic: Structures, Functions and Varieties.* Washington, D.C.: Georgetown University Press.

———. 2006. 'The Arabic Dialects of Arabia'. In *Proceedings of the Seminar for Arabian Studies, Archeopress* 36: 25–34.

———. 2008. 'Omani Arabic'. In *Encyclopedia of Arabic Language and Linguistics*, edited by K. Versteegh et al., III: 478–91. Leiden: Brill.

———. 2011a. 'A Participial Infix in the Eastern Arabian Dialects, an Ancient Pre-conquest Feature?' *Jerusalem Studies in Arabic and Islam* 38: 75–97.

———. 2011b. 'Language and Identity in the Arabian Gulf'. *Journal of Arabian Studies* 1/2: 129–45.

———. 2013. 'An Arabic Text from Ṣūr'. In *Ingham of Arabia: A Collection of Articles Presented as a Tribute to the Career of Bruche Ingham*, edited by C. Holes and R de Jong, 88–107. Leiden: Brill.

———. 2016. *Dialect, Culture, & Society in Eastern Arabia, Part 3: Phonology, Morphology, Syntax, Style.* Handbook of Oriental Studies 51. Leiden: Brill.

———. 2017. 'The Omani Arabic Dialects in their Regional Context'. In *Süd-Arabien/South Arabia: A Great 'Lost Corridor' of Mankind—A Collection of Papers Dedicated to the Re-*

establishment of South Arabian Studies in Austria, edited by R. Stiegner I: 287–95. Münster: Ugarit-Verlag.

——— (ed.). 2018. *Arabic Historical Dialectology: Linguistic and Sociolinguistic Approached.* Oxford: Oxford University Press.

Horesh, U. 2009. 'Tense'. In *Encyclopedia of Arabic Language and Linguistics*, edited by K. Versteegh et al., IV: 454–57. Leiden: Brill.

Ingham, B. 1994. *Najdi Arabic: Central Arabian.* Amsterdam: John Benjamins.

Iványi, T. 2006. 'Diphthongs'. In *Encyclopedia of Arabic Language and Linguistics*, edited by K. Versteegh et al., I: 640–43. Leiden: Brill.

Jastrow, O. 1980. *Handbuch der arabischen Dialekte.* Edited by W. Fisher. Wiesbaden: Harrassowitz

Jayakar, A. S. 1889. 'The O'manee Dialect of Arabic: Parts I–II'. *Journal of the Royal Asiatic Society* 21: 649–87; 811–80.

———. 1900. 'Omani Proverbs'. *Journal of the Bombay Branch of the Royal Asiatic Society* 21. Cambridge: The Oleander Press (reprint 1987).

Johnstone, T. M. 1967. *Eastern Arabian Dialects Studies.* Oxford: Oxford University Press.

Joyce, M. 1995. *The Sultanate of Oman: A Twentieth Century History.* Westport, CT: Praeger.

Kaplan, L. 2008. 'Remarks on the Bahla Dialect (Oman)'. In *Between the Atlantic and Indian Ocean: Studies on Contemporary Arabic Dialects*, edited by S. Prochazka and V. Ritt-Benmimoun, 265–78. Vienna: Lies Münster.

Kayapinar, M. A. 2008. 'Ibn Khaldun's Concept of *Assabiyya*: An Alternative Tool for Understanding Long-term Politics'. *Asian Journal of Social Science* 36: 375–407.

Ibn Khaldun. 1980. *The Muqaddimah: An Introduction to History*. 3 vols. Translated from the Arabic by Franz Rosenthal. Princeton, NJ: Princeton University Press.

King, G. R. D. 2012. 'Al-Rubʿ al-Khālī'. In *Encyclopaedia of Islam,* edited by P. Bearman, Th. Bianquis, C. E. Bosworth, E. van Donzel, W. P. Heinrichs. 2nd edition, accessed 25 November 2018. http://dx.doi.org/10.1163/1573-3912_islam_SIM_6318

Landen, R. G. 1967. *Oman since 1856: Disruptive Modernization in a Traditional Arab Society*. Princeton, NJ: Princeton University Press.

Levin, A. 1998. *Arabic Linguistic Thought and Dialectology*. The Max Schloessinger Memorial Series. Jerusalem: The Hebrew University of Jerusalem.

Lucas, C. 2018. 'On Wilmsen on the Development of Postverbal Negation in Dialectal Arabic. *Zeitschrift für Arabische Linguistik* 67: 44–71.

al-Maamiry, A. H. 1988. *Omani Sultans in Zanzibar (1832–1964)*. New Delhi: Lancers Publishers.

McCarthy, J. J. 1979. 'On Stress and Syllabification'. *Linguistic Inquiry* 10/3: 443–65.

Morano, R. 2020. 'Functions and Uses of Active and Passive Participial Forms in al-ʿAwābī District Vernacular of Northern Oman'. *Al-ʿArabiyya: The Journal of the American Association of Teachers of Arabic* 53: 109–28.

———. 2022. 'The Expression of Possession in the al-ˁAwābī District (Northern Oman)'. In *Semitic Dialects and Dialectology: Fieldwork, Community, Change*, edited by M. Klimiuk, 31–43. Heidelberg: Heidelberg University Publishing. Available open-access at https://heiup.uni-heidelberg.de/reader/download/859/859-69-99051-1-10-20220628.pdf

Nakano, A. 1994. *A Basic Vocabulary of Zanzibar Arabic*. Tokyo: Institute for the Study of Languages and Cultures of Asia and Africa.

Nash, H., and A. Agius Dionisius. 2011. 'The Use of Starts in Agriculture in Oman'. *Journal of Semitic Studies* 56/1: 167–82.

Noeldeke, T. 1895. 'Über einen arabischen Dialekt'. *Wiener Zeitschrift für die Kunde des Morgenlandes* 9: 1–25.

Ouhalla, J. 2008. 'Negation'. In *Encyclopedia of Arabic Language and Linguistics*, edited by Versteegh et al., III: 355–60. Leiden: Brill

Owens, J. 2008. 'Participle'. In *Encyclopedia of Arabic Language and Linguistics*, edited by Versteegh et al., III: 541–46. Leiden: Brill

———. 2018. 'Dialects (Speech Communities), the Apparent Past, and Grammaticalization: Towards an Understanding of the History of Arabic'. In *Arabic Historical Dialectology: Linguistic and Sociolinguistic Approaches*, edited by C. Holes, 206–56. Oxford: Oxford University Press.

Owtram, F. 2004. *A Modern History of Oman: Formation of the State since 1920*. London: I. B. Tauris.

Payne, T. E. 1997. *Describing Morphosyntax: A Guide for Field Linguists.* Cambridge: Cambridge University Press.

Peterson, J .E. 2004. 'Oman's Diverse Society: Northern Oman'. *The Middle East Journal* 58: 32–51. Washington, D.C.: Middle East Institute

Persson, M. 2008. 'The Role of the *b*-prefix in Gulf Arabic Dialects as a Marker of Future, Intent and/or Irrealis. *Journal of Arabic and Islamic Studies* 8: 26–52.

———. 2015. 'Verb Form Switch as a Marker of a Clausal Hierarchies in Urban Gulf Arabic Dialects. In *Arabic and Semitic Linguistics Contextualized: A Festschrift for Jan Retsö*, edited by Lutz Edzard, 227–59. Wiesbaden: Harrassowitz.

Prochazka, T. 1988. *Saudi Arabian Dialects.* Leiden: Brill.

Prochazka, S. 2004. 'Unmarked Feminine Nouns in Modern Arabic Dialects'. In *Approaches to Arabic Dialects: A Collection of Articles Presented to Manfred Woidich on the Occasion of his Sixtieth Birthday*, edited by M. Haak, R. de Jong, and K Versteegh, 237–62. Leiden: Brill.

———. 2008. 'Prepositions'. In *Encyclopedia of Arabic Language and Linguistics*, edited by Versteegh et al., III: 699–709. Leiden: Brill.

Qafisheh, A. H. 1977. *A Short Reference Grammar of Gulf Arabic.* Tucson, AZ: The University of Arizona Press.

Rhodokanakis, N. 1908. *Der vulgärarabische Dialekt im Dhofār (Ẓfār), Bd. I: Prosaische und poetische Texte, Uebersetzung und Indices.* SAE 8. Vienna: Hölder.

———. 1911. *Der vulgärarabische Dialekt im Dhofār (Ẓfār), Bd. II: Einleitung, Glossar und Grammatik.* SAE 10. Vienna: Hölder.

Reinhardt, C. 1894. *Ein arabischer Dialekt gesprochen in ‘Oman und Zanzibar*. Lehrbücher des Seminars für Orientalische Sprachen zu Berlin. 13. Stuttgart-Berlin: W. Spemann.

Rentz, G. 2012. ‘Banū Kharūṣ’. In *Encyclopaedia of Islam,* edited by P. Bearman, Th. Bianquis, C. E. Bosworth, E. van Donzel, W. P. Heinrichs, 2nd edition, accessed 25 November 2018. http://dx.doi.org/10.1163/1573-3912_islam_SIM_4218

Retsö, J. 1983. *The Finite Passive Voice in Modern Arabic Dialects*. Göteborg: Acta Universitatis Gothoburgensis

———. 2014. ‘b-imperfect’. In *Encyclopedia of Arabic Language and Linguistics*, Online, accessed 16 February 2022. http://dx.doi.org/10.1163/1570-699_Encyclopedia of Arabic Language and Linguistics_SIM_001004

Riphenburgh, J. Carol. 1998. *Oman: Political Development in a Changing World*. London: Praeger.

Al Salimi, A. and E. Staples. 2019. *A Maritime Lexicon: Arabic Nautical Terminology in the Indian Ocean*. Studies on Ibadism and Oman 11. Hildesheim: Georg Olms Verlag.

Simeone-Senelle, M. 1996. ‘Negation in Some Arabic Dialects of the Tihaamah of the Yemen’. *Perspective on Arabic Linguistics* 9: 207–21. Philadelphia: John Benjamins Publishing.

Taine-Cheikh, C. 2008. ‘Numerals’. In *Encyclopedia of Arabic Language and Linguistics*, edited by Versteegh et al., III: 447–52. Leiden: Brill

Thesiger, W. (1959) 2007. *Arabian Sands*. London: Penguin Classics.

Valeri, M. 2017. *Oman: Politics and Society in the Qaboos State.* London: Hurst & Company.

Versteegh, C. H. M. 1997. *The Arabic Linguistic Tradition.* London, New York: Routledge

———. 2010. 'Contact and the Development of Arabic'. In: *Handbook of Language Contact*, edited by R. Hickey, 634–51. Chichester: Wiley-Blackwell.

Vollers, K. 1895. 'Ein arabischer Dialekt gesprochen in Omān und Zanzibar, nach praktischen Gesichtspunkten für das Seminar für Orientalische Sprachen in Berlin bearbeitet von Dr. Carl Reinhardt, K. Dragoman'. *Zeitschrift der Deutschen Morgenländischen Gesellschaft* 49: 484–515.

Watson, J. C. E. 1993. *A Syntax of Ṣanʿānī Arabic*. Göttingen: Harrassowitz.

———. 2002. *The Phonology and Morphology of Arabic*. Oxford: Oxford University Press

———. 2006. 'Arabic Moprphology: Diminutive Verbs and Diminutive Nouns in San'ani Arabic'. *Morphology* 16: 189–204.

———. 2011a. 'Arabic Dialects (General Article)'. In *The Semitic Languages: An International Handbook*, edited by S. Weninger et al., 851–96. Boston: De Gruyter Mouton.

———. 2011b. 'Word Stress in Arabic'. In *The Blackwell Companion to Phonology*, edited by M. V. Oostendorp, C. Ewen, E. Hume, and K. Rice, V: 79–121. Oxford: Wiley Blackwell.

Wilkinson, J. C. 1987. *The Imamate Tradition of Oman.* Cambridge: Cambridge University Press

Wilmsen, D. 2015. 'Perfect Modality: Auxiliary Verbs and Finite Subordinates in Levantine (and Other) Arabics'. *Al-ʿArabiyya* 48: 157–74.

Youssef, I. 2013. 'Place Assimilation in Arabic: Contrasts, Features, and Constraints'. PhD dissertation, University of Tromsø.

el-Zarka, D. 2009. 'Reduplication'. In *Encyclopedia of Arabic Language and Linguistics*, edited by Versteegh et al., IV: 50–53. Leiden: Brill.

APPENDIX

This Appendix includes two sample texts, i.e., a monologue and a dialogue. They illustrate some interesting syntactic and morphological features pertaining to one or the other type, as discussed in the book.

Following the sample texts, the reader can enjoy some proverbs collected first-hand in the district and the full text of the traditional song mentioned in ch. 4, §3.2.

Sample Text 1

Duktūr māl wasm (Stāl, WBK–20/3/2017)

This text was recorded in Stāl with Maryam, a famous traditional healer in Wādī Banī Kharūs. Maryam is renowned in the district for her ability to heal people by *wasm* 'cauterisation' without leaving visible scars.[1] This practice is used only for specific types of diseases and when modern medicine has failed. In this sample text, the reader will find some interesting terms identifying the diseases cured by cauterisation.

For the transcription and translation of this text I was helped by S11. The text is a monologue, sometimes interrupted by S11's questions (reported in bold).

(1) *anā yōm ašūf bāġīn wasm w-awsum-hum*

[1] This traditional healing method is slowly disappearing in Oman. For more details about this practice, its history, and its applications, the interested reader is referred to Ghazanfar (1995).

 https://doi.org/10.11647/OBP.0298.06

(2) *yumkin ṣdr-o, yumkin ar-rīḥ, yumkin šey ġēr*

(3) *matā an-nās ygyo?*

(4) *yōm yikūn baʿad fi-l-bidāya*

(5) *mū maraḍ?*

(6) *haḏā… ism-o il-muʿalda*

(7) *ašūf il-qafaṣ aṣ-ṣadri yiḍġaṭ ʿali-hum*

(8) *w-baʿadīn lāzim al-wams awsum taḥt aṣ-ṣadr martīn, fī l-yasār wa-l-yamīn*

(9) *w-baʿadīn aftaḥ šweyya*

(10) *yumkin wāḥid isbūʿ aw yawmīn yikūn ġēr*

(11) *w-baʿadīn ʿan ar-rīḥ awsum il-maʿida martin aw fī-ṣ-ṣboʿ al-wāḥde*

(12) *baʿadīn ʿan il-ḥabbe*

(13) *yōm yikūn il-ḥabbe fī ṭm-o… waram dāḫil dāḫil*

(14) *w-yistwi il-waram mā yiqdar yigraʿ*

(15) *lāzim awsam fi-l-qafed*

(16) *yōm yistwi waram dāḫil il-gism… il-wasm fi-l-qafed*

(17) *wa ʿan el-ʿurq… haḏā l-maraḍ yikūn bēn il-ʿoyūn wa-l-uḏūn wa-l-asnān*

(18) *iḏā l-wigaʿ fī haḏā l-ʿurq būsum fi-l-qafed wa fōq ar-rās*

(19) *baʿadīn wāḥid isbūʿ inšāllah tikūn murṭayba*

(20) *mū ġēr tūsmi nōbe?*

(21) *awsum ʿan el-ġašya, lūʿān wa-l-ḥmūḍa nōbe*

(22) *ʿan yizūʿ awsum fi-l-baṭin*

(23) *wa ʿan wigaʿ ar-rās, yaʿni aš-šaqīqa?*

(24) *maraḍ aš-šaqīqa ygī awgaʿ ʿind il-maġrib w-ʿind šuruq aš-šams*

(25) *awsum warā il-uḏūn*

(26) *baʿadīn ʿan il-ẖabīṯ namūntīn, nuʿīn*

(27) *wāḥid ẖabīṯ ruṭub wa wāḥid ẖabīṯ yābis*

(28) *inn-o il-ishāl il-ḥādd wa-l-imsāk*

(29) *awsum fōq as-surra aw taḥt as-surra*

(30) *ʿan wigaʿ fi-l-ʿurq an-nisā il-wasm taḥt baʿad rābaʿa aṣ-ṣabeʿ*

(1) When I check, they want the cauterisation, then I cauterise them

(2) it might be his chest, maybe a hernia, maybe something else

(3) when do people come?

(4) when it's just after the beginning (i.e., when the problem or the disease is in its initial stages)

(5) what disease?

(6) This... its name is *muʿalda* (i.e., asthma affecting children between birth and 3 years old)

(7) I check the rib cage (if) it presses on them

(8) then if the cauterisation is necessary, I cauterise them under the chest two times, one on the left and one on the right

(9) and then I open it a little

(10) it may be a week or a couple of days, it is different

(11) then, the hernia… I cauterise on the stomach two times or on the first finger

(12) then, about the swelling

(13) when the swelling is in the mouth… the bulge is deep into the mouth

(14) and the bulge prevents you from swallowing

(15) then I cauterise on the nape

(16) when the bulge is inside the body… the cauterisation is on the nape

(17) then, about the vein… this disease is between the eyes, the ears, and the teeth

(18) if the pain is in this vein, I cauterise on the nape and above the head

(19) and maybe after a week, she is healed *inshallah*

(20) what else do you cauterise for?

(21) I also cauterise for gastritis, nausea, and heartburn

(22) like… one vomits, I cauterise on the belly

(23) and what about headache, migraine?

(24) migraine gets worse at sunset and at the sunrise

(25) I cauterise behind the ears

(26) and then, about two types of virulent (diseases)

(27) one is virulent wet, and one is virulent dry

(28) that is strong diarrhoea and constipation

(29) I cauterise above the navel or under the navel

(30) for the pain in the sciatic nerve... I cauterise under the fourth finger

Sample Text 2

ʿayš māl gebel (al-ʿAlya, WBK–22/2/2017)

This text is a dialogue between S15 and, S11 and S8. It is set in the *mazraʿ* 'palm garden' of S8.

S11 is S8's nurse and S15's niece. She has spent the previous couple of weeks working in Muscat and passed by to say hello and see how they were doing. She invited me to go with her to listen to S8's stories. This section of the dialogue illustrates numerous features discussed in this book, such as the use in WBK of *gins* 'sex' instead of *ḥāl* in the formula *kēf ḥāl?* 'how are you?', the common use of APs, some examples of agreement with collective nouns, and one instance of apophonic passive i.e., *yinšad* 'to be asked'.

(S15) *Qarbo! Qarbo!*

(S11) *kēf ḥāl-iš ḫālt-i? mū ḫbār-iš?*

(S15) *bi-ḫēr wa-l-ʿafya, alḥamdillah, mū gins-kom?*

(S11) *kull-na aṭyāb, šukran ḫālt-i*

(S8) *ʿayni tūgaʿni, sāyir martin lī-l-mustašfi lākin qalat-he iḏā laqti šiḫḫa tqūli-he tursilni ʿaṭṭūr*

(S11) *nzēn aba, mā muškila, anā hnā taww, agib-l-ek*

(S15) *qarbi min al-bāb ilā dāḫil*

(S11) *a-ah ḫālti, iḥna mistaʿgilīn*

(S15) *atīb qahwa hnā*

(S8) *marra wāḥid surt ʿind awlād-i fi rustāq, šarraft il-makān wa-rigaʿt*

(S15) *dār yōm haḏāk yitmarraḍ w-yiglis arbaʿa ayyām aw ḫamse iyyām, awlād-o bāġīn bi-alfīn ryāl, qālo yalla sawwi biʿna il-hōš bi-alfīn lākin qāl-hum mā bāġī abīʿ-hin*

(S8) *aqul-l-iš yōm ar-rasūl yinšad ʿan al-ḥarām qāl tinšid ʿan al-ḥalāl, lā tinšid ʿann-o, il-ḥalāl yidḫal min bāb wa yiḫrag min sabaʿ. mū l-ḥarām?*

(S11) *subḥānallah… gīb kill šey ʿind-ik, bāya tismaʿ kill šey min ʿind-ik. ḫabbir-ha ʿan ʿyšt-ik māl gebel*

(S8) *ʿyšt-i māl gebel? kān asawwi ʿarīš. wa-l-ʿarīš wa-qafā ʿali-he sabaʿīn ryāl, min fōq tšinko wa blēwit w-min taḥt w-dōr dāyor saḥāf, dʿūn. usammar dōr dāyor bi-msāmīr*

(S11) *waqt il-barad tnām fōq saṭḥ?*

(S8) *a-ah, lā, waqt il-harr enām fi-s-saṭḥ*

(S15) *mā yrūm yiṭlaʿ l-inne šīši darag*

(S8) *a-ah, taḥt fi-l-kurfāya. yōm yikūn šittā enām dāḫil, asawwi qahwa wāḥd-i wa-l-ʿayš yiṭal-ni, w-marra leben w-marra ṣalūna*

(S11) *kam sanāt ʿyšt fi-l-gebel?*

(S8) *wāgid*

(S15) Come! Come!

(S11) How are you auntie? What news do you have?

(S15) I am fine and in good health, praise to Allah, how are you?

(S11) All of us are fine, thanks auntie.

(S8) My eye is bothering me, I have already been twice to the hospital, but I told her "If you meet Shiḫḫa, would you tell her to send me the medicine?"

(S11) That's fine, *aba*, no problem. I'll bring it to you.

(S15) Come inside! (lit. 'Come from the door into the inside')

(S11) No, auntie, we are in a hurry.

(S15) I'll bring coffee here.

(S8) Once I went to my children in Rustaq, I visited the place and I came back.

(S15) That day he fell sick and stayed like this for four or five days, his children wanted 2,000 ryals, they said "Let's sell the goats," but he said to them "No, I don't want to sell them."

(S8) Listen (lit. 'I tell you'), when the Prophet was asked about what is prohibited he said "Question about what is legitimate, do not question about that, what is legitimate enters from one door and exits from seven." What is prohibited?

(S11) Glory be to God!... Give (us) everything you have, she wants to hear everything you have (to say). Tell her about your life in the mountains.

(S8) My life in the mountains? I used to make an *ʿarīš* (i.e., an open hut made of palm-tree branches) and it was worth about 70 ryals, above there were zinc plates and all around palm leaves... I hammered with nails all around.

(S11) When it is cold do you sleep under the roof?

(S8) No, no, when it is hot I sleep on the roof.

(S15) He cannot climb up because there are no stairs.

(S8) No, (when it is cold) I sleep down(stairs) on the bed. When it is winter I sleep inside, I make myself a coffee and (somebody) brings me (lit. 'it comes to me') rice, sometimes *leben* (i.e., type of milk), sometimes *ṣalūna* (i.e., fish soup with rice).

(S11) How many years did you live in the mountains?

(S8) Many.

Proverbs

The proverbs presented in this Appendix were collected in Stāl and al-ʿAwābī with the help of speakers 7, 2, 12, and 15. For each expression a transcription and the equivalent English proverb are given; if not available, the translation and a brief explanation of the contexts of use are given.

Although the collection of proverbs was not one of the aims of this study, the core presented here traces a continuity with Reinhardt's (1894) work, especially since two of these proverbs were also reported by the German author. Admittedly, I did not check the whole list of proverbs in Reinhardt (1894, 396–418) with the informants, but rather they spontaneously provided me with some of them. Thus, there might be different ones which will correspond entirely to Reinhardt's with an in-depth analysis and collection—which, however, needs to be postponed to a future study.

متى طلعت القصر قال امس عصر

matā ṭalʿat el-qaṣr qāl ems ʿaṣar

'After seeing the castle, he says yesterday is old.'

Meaning: something that was the normality before turns to be outdated after seeing someone else's fortune.

ابليس ما يكسر وعيانه

iblīs mā yikassar wa ʿayyāna

'The Devil does not break his kitchen stuff.'

Meaning: nothing good can happen if the Devil is supporting you or is on your side, e.g., he helps you not to get caught if you behave badly.

كسير وعوير و ابليس ما فيه خير

ksīr wa ʿawīr wa iblīs mā fīh ḫēr

'There is no good in defeat, blindness and Iblis.'

Meaning: often used for people who have bad luck.

يوم خلص العرس جا الشايب يرقص

yōm ḫallaṣ el-ʿurs gē eš-šāyb yarqaṣ

'When the wedding is over, the elders start to dance.'

Meaning: often used in busy situations when only one group of people is working hard, while others are sitting doing nothing and suddenly become active again when everything is over.

لا تسرف و لو من البحر تغرف

lā tisruf w-law min el-baḥr taġraf

'Do not desire more, even if your source is the sea.'

English: 'Desire has no rest'.

يعيبوعلى الناس والعيب فيهم

yaʿyyibo ʿalā n-nās wa l-ʿayb fi-hum

'He who criticises people—the shame is in them.'

English: 'One does the blame, another bears the shame.'

Meaning: you only embarrass yourself by criticising someone.

البيدار ما له خص يوم الهنقري راضي

el-bīdār mā la-hu ḫaṣṣ yōm el-hanqrī rāḍī[2]

'Nothing belongs to the farmer when the rich (one) is satisfied'.

Meaning: while the landowner is making his fortune, the farmer is suffering and does not enjoy any of that fortune. Equally, some people build their fortune on the hard work of others.

المستعجل ماكل شوبه ني

al-mustaʿgil mākil šōbe nay

'The person in a hurry eats the ripe things'.

English: 'Grasp all, lose all'.

الفار يوم ما ينطال اللحم يقول خايس

al-fār yōm mā yinṭāl el-laḥm yaqūl ḫāys

'When the mouse cannot jump to the meat, it says it's rotten'.

English: 'Sour grapes.'

حد في همة و سيفوه يغلي الكمة

ḥad fī humma wa sēfū-hu yaġlī el-kumma

'Someone is very busy and Sayf is playing with his kumma.'

Meaning: often used to address people who are sitting doing nothing, while someone else is busy working.

---

[2] Also reported by Reinhardt (1894, 400).

جرة ولقيت غطاها

garra w-laqīt ġiṭā-he

'Every pot has its own lid.'

English: 'One size does not fit all.'

تولف العد والحربي

tūllef el-ʿid wa-l-ḥarbī

'Il-ʿid and il-ḥarbī combined.'

Meaning: *al-ʿid* and *al-ḥarbī* are two smaller streams in Wādī Banī Kharūṣ that originate in al-ʿAlya. They are very dangerous when their flood combines during the rainy season. The proverb is used for people who are usually quiet, but suddenly erupt in anger.

بو يتكل على غيره واقل خيره

bū yatkall ʿalā ġēr-o w-qallal ḫēr-o

'Who relies on someone else loses his right.'

Meaning: never emulate anyone, always be yourself.

الشيفة شيفة والمعاني ضعيفة

aš-šīfa šīfe wa-l-maʿānī ḍaʿīfe[3]

'The appearing is shown, and the meaning is weak.'

English: 'The cowl does not make the monk.'

[3] Also reported by Reinhardt (1894, 401).

A Traditional Song

The traditional song presented here has been recorded with speaker 13, a man from Stāl in Wādī Banī Kharūṣ.

mṣarr al-ʿōd mā tāynno
who is bringing him the big mṣarr
min smāhil šārāynno
he is buying it from Smāhil
w-fōq ar-rās dāynno
and is putting it on the head
wa ʿan eš-šams taḥmanī
because the sun is burning
waʿan il-ḥumma tūgaʿni
unless the fever hurts me
w-iḏa gīt w-int aġbār w-anā afrāḥ
If he goes and you are poor and I am happy
w-ḥad-ši bēnⁱnā yislāḥ
and no one is between us to mediate
min šyuẖīn wa ʿorbān
among shaykhs and people
mā min šyuẖ ahel-ši d-dār
which of these shaykhs is not from this tribe (family)
(lit. 'from the family of the house')
w-eḍann mā egī aẖsār
and I think I won't lose anything
w-agīb mṣarr min el-ekbar
I bring the biggest mṣarr (lit. 'a mṣarr among the biggest')
w-atbāhā bi-l-bilād

I will show off in the village
w-qalūlī l-boẖal ḍayyil (= wāgid)
They told me I am very stingy
w-ḍammūnī ḥuwāni
Brothers, give me a hug
w-ḍammūnī banī slīma
Give me a hug, Banī Slīma (i.e., name of tribe)
šillo ʿan-nī al-qima
They took my dignity from me

INDEX

adjective, 7, 70, 81, 82, 86, 88, 97, 101, 112–16, 122, 124, 143, 145, 148–49, 156, 163, 165, 169, 172, 175, 192, 221, 243–44, 249, 255

adverb, 35, 81–82, 113, 116, 124–26, 148, 161, 187, 218, 221, 227, 228, 230, 232, 248–49, 256

degree, 124, 126

manner, 124–25

spatial, 124–25

temporal, 113, 124, 191, 193, 200, 217, 228, 230

adverbial clauses, 161, 218, 227–28, 230–32

of location, 230

of manner, 230

of purpose, 231

of reason, 232

agreement, 20, 35, 97, 116, 119, 122, 160–62, 164, 165, 166–69, 192, 214, 220, 222, 224–27, 275; strict, 165–66, 192, 220, 225–27; deflected, 165–66, 220, 225, 227; *see also* phrase, clause

al-ʿAwābī district, i, 2–5, 8, 14, 32, 33, 40, 44–45, 47–52, 55, 57, 60, 65, 68–69, 71, 74–75, 81, 84, 107, 111, 116–117, 125, 135, 152, 154, 157, 159–60, 171, 181, 183, 187, 190, 204–5, 208–11, 235, 238, 243, 247, 250–51, 253, 255–56, 258, 265, 279

apophonic (passive), 150–53, 156, 158, 255, 275

Arabian Peninsula, i, 1, 4, 6, 11–14, 23–24, 28–30, 147, 198, 203, 242, 250, 254, 258

aspect, 39, 127, 146, 157, 160, 185–86, 188, 191, 193–97, 207–8, 244

auxiliaries, 143–44, 161, 207–9, 211, 213–15, 223, 227, 240, 258

Banū Kharūṣ, 15, 35, 43, 45–46, 55, 59, 63, 72, 76, 81–83, 113, 152, 159, 201, 268

clause, 5, 42, 54–55, 160–62, 176, 181–82, 184–86, 200–2, 207, 216, 218–23, 227–

35, 237–40, 242, 248, 256–57; adverbial, 161, 218, 227–28, 230–32; attributive, 160, 162, 181, 184; circumstantial, 232–33; complement, 218, 227, 237–40, 256–57, 261; complex, 54, 161, 218, 227; conditional, 161, 201–2, 233–35; existential, 216; nominal, 161, 176, 218–20; possessive, 216, 218; verbal, 42, 218–19, 221–22, 227
colour, 113, 115, 136; *see also* adjectives
comparative, 52, 56, 70, 86, 115–17, 170, 173, 256; *see also* adjectives
consonants, 32, 59–62, 67, 73–75, 86, 129, 135–36
copula, 82, 143, 207; *see also* verbs
definiteness, 81–82, 163–65, 169
diminutive, 101–2, 113, 117, 126; *see also* adjectives
diphthong, 59, 65, 68–71; *see also* vowels
existential, 144, 161, 216–17, 224, 242, 248, 252
future, i, 2, 15, 56–57, 82, 142, 186, 189, 191–93, 198–202, 217, 234, 254, 257, 279
gender, 7, 32, 48, 81–82, 90, 96–97, 100, 102, 113–14, 116–19, 121, 126, 128, 146–47, 149, 162, 164, 166, 169, 173–74, 177, 181, 184, 195, 203, 207, 210–11, 214, 220, 224, 254, 255, 257
genitive, 44, 54–55, 91, 112, 160, 162, 170–77, 179–80, 251, 255; analytic, 162, 170, 172–73, 177, 181; synthetic, 91, 170–73, 175, 177, 180–81, 251
Ibadism, 46, 268
imāla, 64–68, 71, 87, 89, 153, 208, 256
imperative, 82, 144–45, 197, 242, 257
indefiniteness, 82, 112, 118
modifier, 5, 82, 113, 160, 162–64, 170–72, 174–75, 178, 180–81; *see also* adjective, quantifiers
mood, 39, 82, 127, 144–45, 197–200, 213, 257

negation, 5, 17, 54–55, 77, 161, 183, 190, 216, 241–44, 246–52, 255, 257–58
noun, 5, 7, 9, 42, 64, 66–67, 70–71, 81–84, 86, 88, 93–94, 96–102, 110–116, 118–127, 143, 146, 149–51, 160, 162–77, 181–82, 184, 191, 194, 211, 216–21, 224–28, 230, 233, 237, 240, 243–44, 247, 249, 254–55, 275; basic, 81–84, 86, 88, 100; derived, 81–82, 86; *see also* phrase
number, 3, 7–8, 22, 26, 42, 56, 69, 81–82, 84, 90, 100, 114, 116, 118, 120–121, 123, 128, 142, 146–47, 149, 162–64, 171, 173–74, 176, 182, 194–95, 210–11, 214, 220, 224, 241, 258; broken plural, 70, 86, 103, 105, 110, 114, 166, 221, 224–25; sound plural, 100–2, 114, 120, 224
numerals, 81–82, 100–1, 113, 162–63, 254; cardinal, 118, 120–21, 125, 163; ordinal, 118, 121–22
Oman, i, 1–4, 11–25, 27–44, 46–47, 49–51, 56–57, 59, 62, 66, 68, 73, 76, 78–79, 90–91, 97, 99, 102, 109, 112, 117, 126, 136, 142, 147, 151–52, 157, 159, 161, 165, 169, 172–73, 183, 185, 191–94, 199, 201–4, 213, 242, 249–51, 253, 256, 258–69, 271
participle, 5–6, 8, 31, 70, 82, 87, 101, 145, 151, 175, 194, 207, 243, 254; active, 31, 52, 82, 87, 145–46, 151, 254; passive, 70, 82, 87, 145, 149–51
passive, 5, 32, 70, 82, 138, 140, 145, 150–53, 155–56, 158, 255, 275
phrase, 5, 42, 112, 122, 124, 126–27, 160–63, 165, 168, 170–71, 174–77, 181, 185, 215–21, 227–28, 230, 235, 243–44, 246; noun, 42, 124, 127, 160, 162–65, 168, 176, 181, 217–21, 228, 230, 243–44; propositional, 161–62, 215–16, 218–21, 228, 230, 235, 243, 246; verb, 160, 162, 185, 227, 243–44
possession, 92, 161, 170–73, 175, 177, 180, 215, 218

preposition, 127, 160–62, 174, 177, 179, 215–16, 218–21, 228, 230–31, 235, 237, 243, 246, 255
pronoun, 5, 7, 76–77, 81–82, 89–95, 125, 165, 172, 181, 183, 240, 254–55; demonstrative, 7, 90–91, 163, 169, 171, 230, 243, 254–55; indefinite, 93–94, 244, 251; interrogative, 95, 240; personal, 89; possessive, 7, 67, 77, 92, 162, 178, 220; reflexive, 95,
p-stem, 128–35, 137–44, 146, 151, 153, 155, 186, 188–91, 194–96, 199–201, 203, 205–14, 225, 233–35, 240, 244–45, 249; *see also* phrase
plural, *see* number
quantifiers, 82, 122–24, 163
Reinhardt, i, 1–5, 9, 28, 35, 39–44, 47, 49, 51, 54, 56, 59, 61–66, 69–70, 73, 76–77, 81, 83–84, 88–90, 92, 94–111, 113–18, 120–21, 126–28, 130, 132, 141–42, 145, 152–53, 156, 159–61, 166–69, 173–74, 179, 183, 185–86, 191, 196, 201, 211, 214, 247–51, 253–57, 268–69, 279, 281–82
relative, 41–42, 51, 84, 88, 95, 101, 174, 178–79, 181–83, 251, 255, 257; *see also* attributive clause
s-stem, 128–35, 137–41, 143, 151, 153, 186–90, 193, 203, 206, 208–9, 212, 225, 233, 235, 244, 248–49; *see also* phrase
stress, 7, 59, 66, 74, 76–79, 258
Sultan Qaboos, 18, 21–26, 37, 49, 188, 213–14
superlative, 117
tense, 7–8, 39, 82, 127, 151, 160, 18–86, 190–91, 207–8, 254, 257
tribe, 11, 15, 19, 24–5, 38, 45–48, 50, 52–53, 57, 62, 88, 102, 151, 205, 251, 253, 283–284
verb, 5, 31–32, 36, 42, 55, 64, 66, 68, 70, 73, 75, 81–84, 86–87, 96, 101, 124, 127–46, 149–53, 155–57, 160–62, 165, 185–87, 190–201, 203–18, 221–27, 230, 232–35, 237–40, 242–45, 247–49, 254–56, 258; strong, 66,

82, 128, 131, 136–37, 139, 141, 149, 254; geminate, 68–70, 129, 136, 141, 150; hamzated, 68, 82, 130, 141; weak, 68, 82, 131, 136, 141, 150; quadriliteral, 36, 82, 134–35; derived forms, 82, 86, 96, 136–41, 146, 148, 150–51; *see also* phrase
verbal prefix, 161, 197–98, 201, 234
vowels, 7, 33, 59, 64–69, 73–76, 78–79, 83, 86–87, 92–93, 103, 112, 114–15, 117, 129–31, 135–37, 143, 146, 148, 151, 153, 176, 253
Wādī Banī Kharūṣ, 6, 9, 20, 40, 45–46, 50, 62, 68, 72, 85, 116, 125, 127, 154, 181, 184, 187, 202, 205, 208, 213, 228, 231, 238, 252, 256, 282, 283
word order, 160–61, 222, 255

Cambridge Semitic Languages and Cultures

General Editor Geoffrey Khan

OPEN ACCESS

About the series

This series is published by Open Book Publishers in collaboration with the Faculty of Asian and Middle Eastern Studies of the University of Cambridge. The aim of the series is to publish in open-access form monographs in the field of Semitic languages and the cultures associated with speakers of Semitic languages. It is hoped that this will help disseminate research in this field to academic researchers around the world and also open up this research to the communities whose languages and cultures the volumes concern. This series includes philological and linguistic studies of Semitic languages, editions of Semitic texts, and studies of Semitic cultures. Titles in the series will cover all periods, traditions and methodological approaches to the field.

This is the first Open Access book series in the field; it combines the high peer-review and editorial standards with the fair Open Access model offered by OBP. Open Access (that is, making texts free to read and reuse) helps spread research results and other educational materials to everyone everywhere, not just to those who can afford it or have access to well-endowed university libraries.

Copyrights stay where they belong, with the authors. Authors are encouraged to secure funding to offset the publication costs and thereby sustain the publishing model, but if no institutional funding is available, authors are not charged for publication. Any grant secured covers the actual costs of publishing and is not taken as profit. In short: we support publishing that respects the authors and serves the public interest.

UNIVERSITY OF CAMBRIDGE
Faculty of Asian and Middle Eastern Studies

You can find more information about this serie at:
http://www.openbookpublishers.com/section/107/1

Other titles in the series

Sefer ha-Pardes by Jedaiah ha-Penini
A Critical Edition with English Translation

David Torollo

https://doi.org/10.11647/OBP.0299

Neo-Aramaic and Kurdish Folklore from Northern Iraq
A Comparative Anthology with a Sample of Glossed Texts, Volume 1

Geoffrey Khan, Masoud Mohammadirad, Dorota Molin & Paul M. Noorlander

https://doi.org/10.11647/OBP.0306

Neo-Aramaic and Kurdish Folklore from Northern Iraq
A Comparative Anthology with a Sample of Glossed Texts, Volume 2

Geoffrey Khan, Masoud Mohammadirad, Dorota Molin & Paul M. Noorlander

https://doi.org/10.11647/OBP.0307

The Neo-Aramaic Oral Heritage of the Jews of Zakho

Oz Aloni

https://doi.org/10.11647/OBP.0272

Points of Contact
The Shared Intellectual History of Vocalisation in Syriac, Arabic, and Hebrew

Nick Posegay

ȣ *Winner of the British and Irish Association of Jewish Studies (BIAJS) Annual Book Prize*

https://https://doi.org/10.11647/OBP.0271

A Handbook and Reader of Ottoman Arabic

Esther-Miriam Wagner (ed.)

https://doi.org/10.11647/OBP.0208

Diversity and Rabbinization
Jewish Texts and Societies between 400 and 1000 CE

Gavin McDowell, Ron Naiweld, Daniel Stökl Ben Ezra (eds)

https://doi.org/10.11647/OBP.0219

New Perspectives in Biblical and Rabbinic Hebrew

Aaron D. Hornkohl and Geoffrey Khan (eds)

https://doi.org/10.11647/OBP.0250

The Marvels Found in the Great Cities and in the Seas and on the Islands

A Representative of 'Aǧā'ib Literature in Syriac

Sergey Minov

https://doi.org/10.11647/OBP.0237

Studies in the Grammar and Lexicon of Neo-Aramaic

Geoffrey Khan and Paul M. Noorlander (eds)

https://doi.org/10.11647/OBP.0209

Jewish-Muslim Intellectual History Entangled

Textual Materials from the Firkovitch Collection, Saint Petersburg

Camilla Adang, Bruno Chiesa, Omar Hamdan, Wilferd Madelung, Sabine Schmidtke and Jan Thiele (eds)

https://doi.org/10.11647/OBP.0214

Studies in Semitic Vocalisation and Reading Traditions

Aaron Hornkohl and Geoffrey Khan (eds)

https://doi.org/10.11647/OBP.0207

Studies in Rabbinic Hebrew

Shai Heijmans (ed.)

https://doi.org/10.11647/OBP.0164

The Tiberian Pronunciation Tradition of Biblical Hebrew

Volume 1

Geoffrey Khan

Winner of the 2021 Frank Moore Cross Book Award for best book related to the history and/or religion of the ancient Near East and Eastern Mediterranean

https://doi.org/10.11647/OBP.0163

The Tiberian Pronunciation Tradition of Biblical Hebrew
Volume 2

Geoffrey Khan

ȣ *Winner of the 2021 Frank Moore Cross Book Award for best book related to the history and/or religion of the ancient Near East and Eastern Mediterranean*

https://doi.org/10.11647/OBP.0194

www.ingramcontent.com/pod-product-compliance
Lightning Source LLC
Chambersburg PA
CBHW050208240426
43671CB00013B/2258